THE
PACKAGE DESIGN
BOOK
2

pentawards

THE
PACKAGE DESIGN
BOOK
2

TASCHEN

body

Essay by
Brian Houck
Henkel Consumer Goods

234

luxury

Essay by Joe Wang
& Yuan Zonglei
Shanghai Jahwa

282

other markets

Essay by
Daniel Dittmar
BIC USA Inc.

364

FOREWORD

Jean Jacques & Brigitte Evrard
Founders of Pentawards

In only a few short years, the Pentawards have come to set the international benchmark for packaging design. Such success is not only because of competition itself, but also the sheer quality of the creations competing in this annual event.

Half the members of the multinational Pentawards jury are well-known names in packaging design, while the rest are marketing specialists representing major brands: Danone Waters (France), Suntory (Japan), Bic (USA), Procter & Gamble (Europe), Jahwa (China), Henkel Dial (USA), Aekyung (South Korea). Each year, more than 1,000 entries from all four corners of the Earth are assessed for creativity, innovation and marketing relevance. The most outstanding receive Bronze, Silver, Gold or Platinum Pentawards. The single entry that most impresses the judges and gets the most votes receives the prestigious Diamond Pentaward.

This book brings together all the prizewinning entries for 2011 and 2012. It showcases the very best in present-day worldwide packaging design, while serving as a benchmark and source of inspiration for everyone who is passionate about packaging — people such as students, manufacturers, designers, packaging engineers, brand managers or consumers.

Apart from awarding prizes, Pentawards aims to promote packaging design to commerce and industry, the press, financial and political authorities, and the general public around the world.

We hope you will enjoy looking through this reference book and that it will give you a completely new take on products you buy every day, enabling you to see them from a completely different angle — the angle of creativity, quality, and innovation, which are the driving forces behind our modern civilisation.

Bon voyage to the world of packaging!

VORWORT

Jean Jacques & Brigitte Evrard
Gründer von Pentawards

In nur wenigen Jahren sind die Pentawards zum internationalen Maßstab für das Verpackungsdesign geworden. Ein solcher Erfolg wurzelt nicht nur im Wettbewerb und der Konkurrenz selbst, sondern rein auch in der Qualität der Kreationen, die bei diesem jährlichen Event gegeneinander antreten.

Eine Hälfte der multinationalen Pentawards-Jury sind wohlbekannte Namen aus dem Verpackungsdesign, und die andere gehört als Marketingspezialisten zu großen Marken: Danone Waters (Frankreich), Suntory (Japan), Bic (USA), Procter & Gamble (Europa), Jahwa (China), Henkel Dial (USA), Aekyung (Südkorea). Jedes Jahr werden über eintausend Werke aus allen Gegenden der Welt eingereicht und dann auf Kreativität, Innovation und Marketingrelevanz geprüft. Die Preisträger erhalten ihre Pentawards in Bronze, Silber, Gold oder Platin. Jenem Einzelwerk, von dem die Juroren am stärksten beeindruckt sind und das die meisten Stimmen auf sich vereinen kann, wird der prestigeträchtige Pentaward Diamond verliehen.

Dieses Buch vereint alle Preisträger der Jahre 2011 und 2012. Es zeigt das Beste vom Besten des heutigen weltweiten Verpackungsdesigns und dient als Maßstab und Inspirationsquelle für alle, die sich leidenschaftlich für Verpackung interessieren: Studierende, Hersteller, Designer, Verpackungsingenieure, Markenmanager oder Verbraucher.

Über die Preisverleihung hinaus haben die Pentawards zum Ziel, das Verpackungsdesign in einer Welt von Kommerz und Industrie, Presse, finanziellen und politischen Behörden sowie der allgemeinen Öffentlichkeit überall in der Welt zu bewerben und zu fördern.

Wir hoffen, dass Sie viel Freude beim Durchsehen dieses Referenzwerks haben und so einen völlig neuen Blick auf die Produkte gewinnen, die Sie alltäglich kaufen. Die können Sie nun wohl unter einem ganz anderen Aspekt betrachten: aus der Perspektive von Kreativität, Qualität und Innovation — jenen Antriebskräften hinter unserer modernen Zivilisation.

Bon voyage in die Welt der Verpackung!

PRÉFACE

Jean Jacques & Brigitte Evrard
Fondateurs des Pentawards

En quelques années seulement, les Pentawards sont devenus la référence mondiale parmi les professionnels du packaging design. Ce succès n'est pas seulement dû à la compétition elle-même, mais surtout à la qualité remarquable des créations qui y sont présentées chaque année.

Le jury international des Pentawards est composé pour moitié de noms réputés du packaging design et, d'autre part, de responsables design de grandes marques Danone Waters (France), Suntory (Japon), Bic (USA), Procter & Gamble (Europe), Jahwa (Chine), Henkel Dial (USA), Aekyung (Corée du Sud). Chaque année, plus d'un millier d'emballages, provenant des quatre coins du monde, sont jugés pour leur créativité, leur innovation, leur pertinence marketing, et les plus remarquables sont récompensés de Bronze, Silver, Gold et Platinum Pentawards. L'emballage qui a su séduire l'ensemble du jury et qui a remporté le plus de suffrages reçoit l'unique et prestigieux Diamond Pentaward.

Ce livre regroupe toutes les créations récompensées en 2011 et 2012. Il s'agit donc de ce qui se fait de mieux dans le domaine du packaging design aujourd'hui dans le monde, une référence et source d'inspiration pour tous les passionnés d'emballages, étudiants, designers, fabricants, ingénieurs, responsables de marques, consommateurs...

Outre la remise de récompenses, Pentawards a pour mission la promotion de packaging design auprès des sociétés, de la presse, des autorités économiques et politiques et du grand public en général, partout dans le monde.

Nous vous souhaitons beaucoup de plaisir à parcourir ce livre référence et espérons qu'il vous fera découvrir les produits que vous achetez quotidiennement sous un autre angle, celui de la créativité, de la qualité et de l'innovation, qui sont les moteurs de notre civilisation.

Bon voyage au pays des emballages !

THE SECRETS OF PENTAWARDS

Gérard Caron
Founder of Carré Noir
Designer of the website www.admirabledesign.com
Chair of the Pentawards jury since 2007

The marketing director of a large group in the food-processing industry recently told me that every year he and his team make a close analysis of Pentaward winners. "My product managers and I study them carefully. We stop and look at the most innovative and discuss whether such and such a product or such and such a packaging might have a chance of success in our market."

Brigitte and Jean Jacques Evrard, founders of these international awards, probably hold one of the keys to the staggering success of the Pentawards. Not only does the event promote packaging design, a sphere of creativity often overshadowed by those sectors that attract more media coverage (such as fashion, interior design and furniture), but it has also become a useful means of analysis and forecasting.

What can we learn about creativity from the most recent vintage of Pentawards displayed in this book, which brings together the list of award winners for the last two years? Which major trends happen simultaneously to cross the minds of designers in fifty-odd countries? What kind of customer expectations do they reflect?

In an attempt to answer these questions, I have focused not just on the prizewinners but also on all the thousand competitors, classifying all the creations from around the globe according to their most striking characteristic. Having completed this task, I found ten revealing key trends in worldwide design. Some of these have been around for a long time, while others appear in specific market sectors but with a local twist.

1 — Single idea packaging

This is the kind of packaging designed to communicate one single idea. These forms of packaging, also known as "one-shot" packaging, aim to communicate product content with no attempt to develop complex ideas or provide additional information. This form of packaging is a favourite with marketing executives who want to say everything in one go.

2 — The return of the drawing

To tell the truth, packaging design has never really stopped using drawings but they have to an extent been rejected in favour of photographs. Today, the drawing seems to have returned to its legitimate place without challenging the supremacy of the photographic reproduction. It is an ideal means of using humour or caricature, or can simply be employed as decoration, or to create a certain ambience.

3 — Packaging can be "tuned"

These days anyone can tune their car and fit it out with additional accessories to match their own taste, so making the car more "personal". Of course, when it comes to packaging, tuning is a little more subtle. For example, we might find a key stuck on to a bottle, some string arranged to create a banana shape, and even a shoe-shop carrier bag made from real shoelaces. Anything goes if it gets the product noticed!

4 — Newspaper style

They say print media is dying. Packaging is ready to take up the baton. We now see so much packaging with newspaper-like mastheads and acres of print and little or nothing in the way of visuals. Consumers at the point of sale are eager for more and more information about the products they buy and this is a good way of speaking straight to the customer. After all, aren't we forever being told that packaging is a medium in itself?

5 — Focusing on the human story

The earliest eco-friendly and biodegradable packaging was basic, somewhat sad, and even a little crude, with colours to match the earth and sky. As time went on, this kind of packaging began to toe the line and became as appealing and colourful as the rest. Consumers had realised what was meant by bio packaging. We still have some way to go with fair trade, where we have to justify, explain and demonstrate why it is a good thing to pay a bit more for a packet of coffee to benefit a small community of producers in Guatemala. That explains the number of visuals showing real people and descriptions of the type of products originating from around the world, from Taiwan to Canada by way of the Netherlands. The day will come when committed consumers will no longer need all these justifications; they will still appear on the Internet, but will be less conspicuous on packaging.

6 — Looks come first

Design can do a lot to promote aesthetic values. Beautiful design can brighten all our lives and some packaging is designed to do no more than this. Maybe the product is well known and the market is saturated. Maybe consumers can't tell one product from another. This is where appearance is the best means of attracting consumers and encouraging them to buy. There are some fine examples of this in this book, especially in the world of wine.

7 — Signs that say "stop and look"

The whole purpose of packaging is to get the consumer to stop and look. It's what our craft is all about and is the designer's main objective. So, for example, we have logos with double meanings, graphics worthy of a road sign, and striped packaging. You can't miss them!

8 — The brand and only the brand

What more can you say when you are a world-famous, well-loved brand? Maybe "Here I am. Yes, it's me. Don't forget me!" No need for persuasion, no need to proclaim the product's advantages — there aren't any! Reputation is the best selling point. So someone must start building one...

9 — A tale to tell

There are a number of examples in the most recent crop of Pentaward candidates that tell a little story in words or pictures. Some resemble a page from a magazine with photos, drawings and text. Everyone knows about reading breakfast cereal packets, but the trend seems to be growing. Maybe it's a by-product of using the Internet, which encourages dialogue between brand and consumer?

10 — *Trompe-l'œil* packaging

This is the most puzzling section of the book and probably the most innovative. It features packaging that bears no resemblance whatever to what it really is! The complete opposite of what they teach at schools of design, namely that the packaging is an extension of the product and should tell the consumer something about it, etc. Here we have a cigarette packet that looks like an audio-cassette, taken from a carton that resembles a tuner. And baby socks packed in what looks like a bento box from a sushi bar! Very funny and absolutely spot on in a world of products where habit has killed stone dead people's curiosity about brand names.

These are some of the main features of this new and extraordinarily accomplished edition. As I said before, packaging design is the most creative of all forms of design. It is the one that comes closest to people's lives and the most surprising of all of them. And this latest edition of Pentawards is not about to prove me wrong.

DIE GEHEIMNISSE DER PENTAWARDS

Gérard Caron
Gründer von Carré Noir
Designer der Website www.admirabledesign.com
Seit 2007 Vorsitzender der Pentawards-Jury

Der Marketingleiter einer großen Gruppe in der Lebensmittelbranche berichtete mir kürzlich, dass er jedes Jahr zusammen mit seinem Team die Pentawards-Gewinner genau unter die Lupe nimmt. „Meine Produktmanager und ich studieren sie sehr sorgfältig. Wir nehmen uns viel Zeit, um die innovativsten Beispiele anzusehen und zu diskutieren, ob dieses oder jenes Produkt bzw. diese oder jene Verpackung auf unserem Markt Erfolgschancen hätte."

Brigitte und Jean Jacques Evrard, die Begründer der internationalen Auszeichnung „Pentawards", halten wahrscheinlich einen der Schlüssel für ihren atemberaubenden Erfolg in Händen. Dieses Event wirbt nicht nur für das Design von Verpackungen (diese Sphäre der Kreativität wird oft von Bereichen wie Mode, Innenarchitektur oder Möbel überschattet, denen ein größeres Medienecho sicher ist), sondern wurde überdies zu einem sehr praktischen Instrument für Analyse und Prognose.

Was können wir von dieser neuesten Auslese von Pentawards — das Buch stellt die aktuelle Liste von Preisträgern vor — über Kreativität lernen? Welche großen Trends geschehen simultan und tauchen unabhängig im Geiste der Designer aus über 50 Ländern auf? Welche Art von Kundenerwartung spiegeln sie wider?

Bei meinem Versuch, diese Fragen zu beantworten, habe ich mich nicht nur auf Preisträger konzentriert, sondern auch auf die Tausenden anderen Mitbewerber. Ich habe alle Kreationen rund um den Globus entsprechend ihrer auffälligsten Kennzeichen klassifiziert. Am Ende kristallisierten sich für mich zehn aussagekräftige Schlüsseltrends im weltweiten Design heraus. Manche Entwicklungen gibt es schon länger, andere treten in speziellen Marktsektoren auf und zeigen eine besondere lokale Prägung.

1 — Verpackung mit einer einzigen Idee

Dies ist die Art Verpackung, deren Gestaltung eine einzige Idee oder ein Konzept vermitteln soll. Auch bekannt als „One Shot Packaging", zielt sie darauf ab, den Produktinhalt zu kommunizieren, ohne dabei komplexe Ideen zu entwickeln oder zusätzliche Informationen anzubieten. Dies ist der Favorit bei Marketingleitern, die in einem Rutsch alle Aussagen über ihr Produkt vermitteln wollen.

2 — Die Rückkehr der Zeichnung

Ehrlich gesagt, hat man beim Verpackungsdesign nie aufgehört, mit Zeichnungen und Grafiken zu arbeiten, aber sie sind in gewisser Weise zugunsten von Fotos ins Hintertreffen geraten. Heute scheinen Zeichnungen auf ihren legitimen Platz zurückzukehren, ohne die Überlegenheit der fotografischen Reproduktion herausfordern oder infrage stellen zu wollen. Zeichnungen sind ein ideales Mittel für Humor oder Karikaturen, können auch gut dekorativ eingesetzt werden oder um bestimmte Stimmungen zu vermitteln.

3 — Verpackung kann „getunt" werden

Heutzutage tunen alle ihre Autos und statten sie nach ihrem Geschmack mit zusätzlichen Accessoires aus, um sie „persönlicher" zu gestalten. Wenn es um Verpackungen geht, wird ein Tuning natürlich subtiler. Da finden wir beispielsweise einen Schlüssel an einer Flasche angebracht, mit einer Schnur wird eine Bananenform geschaffen, und Tragetaschen aus einem Schuhladen können sogar aus echten Schnürsenkeln bestehen. Anything goes — wenn das Produkt bloß wahrgenommen wird!

4 — Zeitungsstil

Überall sagt man, Druckmedien seien im Aussterben begriffen. Hier steht die Verpackung in den Startlöchern, um den Staffelstab zu übernehmen. Wir finden heutzutage viele Verpackungen mit zeitungsähnlichen Aufmachern und regelrechten Bleiwüsten, aber wenig oder gar nichts in Richtung optischem Blickfang. Die Konsumenten vor den Regalen gieren nach immer mehr Informationen über die Produkte, und dies ist ein guter Weg für direkte Kundenansprache. Immerhin werden wir ständig darauf aufmerksam gemacht, dass die Verpackung selbst schon ein Medium ist.

5 — Konzentration auf den Faktor Mensch

Die ersten umweltfreundlichen und biologisch abbaubaren Verpackungen waren schlicht, irgendwie auch traurig, ein wenig grob und mit zu Himmel und Erde passenden Farben gestaltet. Im Laufe der Zeit haben sich solche Verpackungen immer mehr angepasst, und sie wurden so ansprechend und farbenfroh wie alle anderen. Die Verbraucher hatten kapiert, was mit Bioverpackung gemeint war. Mit Blick auf den fairen Handel gibt es für uns noch einiges zu tun: Wir müssen begründen, erklären und zeigen, warum es eine gute Sache ist, etwas mehr für ein Paket Kaffee zu bezahlen, um eine kleine Herstellergemeinschaft in Guatemala zu unterstützen. Das erklärt die zahlreichen Bilder auf den Packungen, die reale Menschen zeigen und die Produkte beschreiben, die über die Niederlande aus der ganzen Welt von Taiwan bis Kanada zu uns kommen. Der Tag wird kommen, an dem all diese Rechtfertigungen für engagierte Verbraucher nicht mehr nötig sind. Im Internet wird es das weiterhin geben, aber auf Verpackungen weniger ins Auge fallen.

6 — Aussehen steht im Vordergrund

Design kann eine Menge dafür tun, ästhetische Werte zu vermitteln. Ein schönes Design erhellt unser aller Leben, und manche Verpackung dient in ihrer Gestaltung allein diesem Zweck. Vielleicht ist das Produkt wohlbekannt und der Markt gesättigt. Vielleicht können Verbraucher die Produkte nicht mehr voneinander unterscheiden. Hier wird Aussehen das beste Mittel, um Verbraucher anzusprechen und sie zum Kaufen zu ermutigen. Es gibt ein paar sehr schöne Beispiele dafür in diesem Buch, vor allem aus der Welt der Weine.

7 — Zeichen, die sagen: „Halt, schau mich an!"

Hauptabsicht von Verpackungen ist es eigentlich, den Verbraucher auszubremsen, damit er sich etwas genauer ansieht. Darum geht es in unserer Branche, und das ist Hauptziel des Designers. Also haben wir z. B. Logos mit hintergründigen Bedeutungen, Grafiken so nachdrücklich wie ein Verkehrsschild und Packungen mit Streifen. Das kann man einfach nicht übersehen!

8 — Einzig und allein die Marke

Was bleibt einem noch zu sagen, wenn man bereits eine weltberühmte und beliebte Marke ist? Vielleicht noch etwas wie „Hier bin ich. Genau, ich bin's! Vergessen Sie mich nicht!" Nicht mehr nötig, sich fürs Überzeugen anzustrengen oder die Vorteile des Produkts zu proklamieren ... alles bekannt! Der eigene Ruf wird zum besten Verkaufsargument. Also sollte man anfangen, so etwas aufzubauen ...

9 — Eine Geschichte wird erzählt

In dieser neuesten Auslese der Pentawards-Kandidaten gibt es zahlreiche Beispiele, die mit Worten oder Bildern kleine Geschichten erzählen. Manche erinnern mit ihren Fotos, Zeichnungen und Texten an Magazinseiten. Alle wissen, dass die Packung des Frühstücksmüslis gelesen wird, doch dieser Trend scheint weiter zuzunehmen. Vielleicht gar ein Nebenprodukt der Internetnutzung, das zum Dialog zwischen Marke und Konsument ermutigt?

10 — Trompe-l'Œil-Verpackungen

Dieser Teil des Buches ist besonders verblüffend und wahrscheinlich auch der innovativste. Hier werden Verpackungen vorgestellt, die in keinster Weise darauf schließen lassen, was sich darin verbirgt! Sie sind das komplette Gegenteil dessen, was an Designschulen gelehrt wird, dass nämlich Verpackung eine Erweiterung des Produkts ist und dem Konsumenten etwas darüber verraten soll etc. Hier gibt es Zigarettenpackungen, die wie Audiokassetten aussehen und aus einem Karton kommen, der an einen Tuner erinnert. Und Babysocken verpackt in etwas, das wie die Bentobox aus einer Sushi-Bar aussieht. Sehr lustig und absolut treffend in einer Welt von Produkten, in der die menschliche Neugier von Gewohnheiten völlig abgetötet worden ist.

Dies sind einige der wichtigsten Merkmale dieser neuen und außergewöhnlich zusammengestellten Edition. Wie schon gesagt, ist Verpackungsdesign die kreativste Form des Designs überhaupt. Sie kommt dem Alltag der Menschen am nächsten und birgt von allen die meisten Überraschungen. Und diese neueste Ausgabe der Pentawards enthält nichts, was das widerlegen könnte.

LES SECRETS DES PENTAWARDS

Gérard Caron
Fondateur de Carré Noir
Editeur de www.admirabledesign.com
President du jury Pentawards depuis 2007

Le directeur du marketing d'un grand groupe du secteur de la transformation alimentaire m'a récemment dit que chaque année, lui et son équipe procèdent à une analyse détaillée des lauréats des Pentawards. « Mes chefs de produit et moi les étudions avec beaucoup d'intérêt. Nous examinons les plus novateurs et nous essayons de déterminer si tel ou tel produit ou tel ou tel emballage pourrait avoir une chance sur notre marché. »

Brigitte et Jean Jacques Evrard, les fondateurs de ces récompenses internationales, détiennent probablement l'une des clés du succès stupéfiant des Pentawards. Cet événement non seulement promeut la conception d'emballage, une sphère créative souvent éclipsée par les secteurs qui attirent davantage l'attention des médias, comme la mode, la décoration intérieure ou les meubles, mais est également devenu un instrument très utile pour analyser et prévoir les tendances.

Que pouvons-nous apprendre sur la créativité à partir du dernier millésime de Pentawards présenté dans ce livre, qui rassemble les lauréats les plus récents ? Quelles grandes tendances ont émergé simultanément comme par magie dans les esprits de créatifs de cinquante et quelques pays ? Reflètent-elles des attentes particulières de la part des clients ?

Pour tenter de répondre à ces questions, j'ai étudié non seulement les lauréats, mais aussi les mille concurrents. J'ai classé toutes les créations de tous les pays en fonction de leur caractéristique la plus frappante. Une fois cette tâche effectuée, j'ai trouvé dix grandes tendances révélatrices dans le design mondial. Certaines d'entre elles sont loin d'être nouvelles, tandis que d'autres apparaissent sur un marché spécifique, mais avec une touche locale.

1 — L'emballage centré sur une idée unique

C'est le type d'emballage qui est conçu pour communiquer une seule idée. Ces emballages, aussi appelés emballages « one-shot », visent à communiquer le contenu du produit sans essayer de développer des idées complexes ou de fournir des informations supplémentaires. Ce genre d'emballage est très apprécié des responsables marketing qui veulent tout dire en une fois.

2 — Le retour du dessin

À dire vrai, le dessin n'a jamais vraiment disparu des emballages, mais il a été remplacé dans une certaine mesure par la photographie. Aujourd'hui, le dessin semble avoir retrouvé sa place légitime sans pour autant menacer la suprématie de la reproduction photographique. C'est un véhicule idéal pour l'humour ou la caricature, mais il peut aussi être employé tout simplement pour décorer, ou pour créer une certaine atmosphère.

3 — L'emballage peut être « tuné »

Aujourd'hui, n'importe qui peut tuner sa voiture et l'équiper d'accessoires qui correspondent à ses goûts pour la personnaliser. Bien sûr, en ce qui concerne les emballages, le tuning est un peu plus subtil. Par exemple, on peut trouver une clé collée sur une bouteille, une ficelle disposée de façon à dessiner la forme d'une banane, ou même un sac de boutique de chaussures dont les anses sont de vrais lacets. Tout est envisageable, du moment que le produit se fait remarquer !

4 — Le style journal

Il paraît que la presse écrite est mourante. L'emballage est prêt à prendre la relève. Aujourd'hui, on voit des quantités d'emballages qui arborent des titres de journaux et des kilomètres d'encre, sans illustration ou presque. Sur le lieu de vente, les consommateurs sont de plus en plus en demande d'information sur les produits qu'ils achètent, et ce type d'emballage est un bon moyen de s'adresser directement au consommateur. Après tout, n'entend-on pas dire sans relâche que l'emballage est un support de communication en soi ?

5 — L'histoire humaine au centre

Les premiers emballages écologiques et biodégradables étaient basiques, plutôt tristes et même un peu rudimentaires, avec des couleurs rappelant la terre et le ciel. Au fil du temps, ce type d'emballage a commencé à rattraper son retard, et est devenu aussi attrayant et coloré que les emballages traditionnels. Les consommateurs ont compris ce que l'emballage bio signifie réellement. Il y a encore du chemin à faire dans le secteur du commerce équitable, où il faut justifier, expliquer et démontrer pourquoi cela vaut la peine de payer le paquet de café un peu plus cher pour aider une petite communauté de producteurs au Guatemala. Cela explique le nombre de visuels montrant des personnes réelles et de descriptions de produits issus des quatre coins du monde, de Taïwan au Canada, en passant par les Pays-Bas. Le jour viendra où les consommateurs engagés n'auront plus besoin de toutes ces justifications. Elles seront toujours disponibles sur Internet, mais prendront moins de place sur l'emballage.

6 — L'esthétique avant tout

Le design peut faire beaucoup pour promouvoir les valeurs esthétiques. Un beau design peut égayer nos vies, et certains emballages ne sont conçus que dans cet unique but. Le produit peut être connu, mais sur un marché saturé. Les consommateurs peuvent ne pas faire la différence entre ce produit et un autre. C'est dans ce genre de cas que l'apparence est le meilleur moyen d'attirer les consommateurs et de les encourager à acheter. Ce livre en présente d'excellents exemples, particulièrement dans le monde du vin.

7 — Des panneaux qui disent « arrêtez-vous et regardez »

La mission de l'emballage est de faire en sorte que le consommateur s'arrête pour regarder. C'est toute la raison d'être de notre métier, et c'est le principal objectif du designer. C'est ainsi que, par exemple, nous avons des logos à double signification, des graphismes dignes de panneaux indicateurs, et des emballages à rayures. Vous ne pouvez pas les manquer !

8 — La marque et seulement la marque

Lorsqu'on est une marque connue et aimée dans le monde entier, qu'y a-t-il de plus à dire ? Peut-être « Je suis là, oui, c'est moi, ne m'oubliez pas ! » Nul besoin de convaincre ou de clamer les avantages du produit — il n'y en a pas ! La renommée est le meilleur argument de vente. Alors il faut commencer à en bâtir une ...

9 — Une histoire à raconter

Dans la dernière moisson de candidats aux Pentawards, il y a de nombreux exemples qui racontent une petite histoire à l'aide de mots ou d'images. Certaines ressemblent à une page de magazine, avec des photos, des dessins et du texte. Tout le monde a déjà lu un paquet de céréales au petit-déjeuner, mais la tendance semble prendre de l'ampleur. Peut-être est-ce un effet secondaire d'Internet, qui encourage le dialogue entre la marque et le consommateur ?

10 — L'emballage en trompe-l'œil

C'est le chapitre le plus surprenant du livre, et probablement le plus riche d'innovation. Il présente des emballages qui ne ressemblent en rien à ce qu'ils sont vraiment ! C'est exactement le contraire de ce qui est enseigné dans les écoles de design, c'est-à-dire que l'emballage est une extension du produit et doit dire au consommateur quelque chose sur ce produit, etc. Ici, nous avons un paquet de cigarettes qui ressemble à une cassette audio, et que l'on extrait d'une cartouche qui ressemble à un auto-radio. Et des chaussettes pour bébé emballées dans ce qui ressemble à une boîte bento de restaurant japonais ! Très drôle et absolument parfait dans un monde de produits où l'habitude a réduit à néant la curiosité des gens pour les noms de marque.

Voici donc un aperçu de ce que vous trouverez dans cette nouvelle édition extraordinairement réussie. Comme je l'ai déjà dit, la conception d'emballage est la forme de design la plus créative de toutes. C'est celle qui se rapproche le plus de la vie des gens, et c'est aussi la plus surprenante. Et la toute dernière édition des Pentawards est là pour me donner raison.

diamond

Best of the show

PENTAWARD'S DIAMOND

By its very nature, an international jury composed of packaging design specialists and marketing chiefs from prestigious worldwide brands represents the foremost cultures of the industrialised world. The Pentawards jury brings together ten nationalities and hence ten cultures.

Of course, the deep cultural roots of the Japanese are very different from those of the French, the Argentines and even the Koreans. The same goes for the cultural differences between citizens of the UK and the USA.

While marketing processes and the techniques of production and distribution comply with international norms, it is culture, in its literal sense, which characterises different civilisations. At the same time it gives each of us our own individual way of looking at the world, based on our education and the cultural milieu in which we move.

In this beautiful book you will find packaging that is uniquely Japanese, totally British, or 100% American. While you are sure to be inspired and amazed by such fabulous and creative examples, many of them were not really intended to be marketed worldwide. But the same doesn't apply to some of the others.

Every year members of the international, intercultural Pentawards jury reach a unanimous decision as to which packagings will have genuinely universal appeal. Whatever their nationality, these creations are intended to be used throughout the world. No one can say where and in which cultural setting they were designed. These are global packagings, inspired by a mélange of all the cultures of humankind and achieving classic status from the day they were first conceived. And just one among them is named the most outstanding.

The 2008 Diamond Pentaward went to an upside-down champagne bottle and the following year to triangular Kleenex boxes designed to look like slices of fruit. Then in 2010 it was the turn of a range of Japanese hair-care products in organically-shaped bottles — these can be found in the "Diamond" chapter in the first *Package Design Book*. In 2011, mineral water bottles won the Diamond Pentaward and in 2012 it was the simplest thing of all, a Diet Coke can.

Such treasures are rare but, as the song says, "Diamonds are Forever".

Naturgemäß repräsentiert eine internationale Jury, die sich aus Spezialisten des Package Designs und Marketingchefs prestigeträchtiger Weltmarken zusammensetzt, die wesentlichen Kulturkreise der industrialisierten Welt. Die Pentawards-Jury bringt zehn Nationalitäten und somit auch zehn Kulturen zusammen.

Selbstverständlich liegen die kulturellen Wurzeln von Japanern ganz woanders als die der Franzosen, der Argentinier oder auch der Koreaner. Das Gleiche gilt für die kulturellen Unterschiede zwischen den Bürgern des Vereinigten Königreichs und der USA.

Marketingabläufe, Produktionstechnik und Logistik halten sich an internationale Normen, doch ist es hingegen die Kultur im Wortsinne, die die unterschiedlichen Zivilisationen kennzeichnet. Zugleich entwickelt sich aus ihr heraus jedes individuelle Weltbild — basierend auf unserer Bildung und dem kulturellen Milieu, in dem wir uns bewegen.

In diesem wunderschönen Buch finden Sie Verpackungen, die eindeutig japanisch, vollkommen britisch oder hundertprozentig amerikanisch sind. Sie werden sich gewiss davon inspirieren lassen und erstaunt sein über diese fabelhaften und kreativen Beispiele, viele davon waren jedoch eigentlich nicht für eine weltweite Vermarktung konzipiert. Aber für manche gilt das eben auch nicht.

Jedes Jahr gelangen die Mitglieder der internationalen und interkulturellen Pentawards-Jury zu einer einmütigen Entscheidung, welche Verpackungen eine wirklich echte und universelle Ausstrahlung zeigen. Egal, welcher nationalen Herkunft, sind diese Kreationen für eine weltweite Nutzung gedacht. Niemand kann sagen, wo und in welchem kulturellen Ambiente sie gestaltet wurden. Hier handelt es sich um globale Verpackungen, inspiriert von einer Melange aller menschlichen Kulturen. Sie erringen ab jenem Tag, seit dem sie als Idee existieren, den Status eines Klassikers. Und genau einer von ihnen wird dann schließlich als herausragend beurteilt.

Der Diamond Pentaward ging im Jahr 2008 an eine umgedrehte Champagnerflasche und im folgenden Jahr an die dreieckigen Kleenex-Kartons, die aussahen, als wären es Fruchtschnitten. Dann kamen 2010 japanische Haarpflegeprodukte an die Reihe, die in organisch geformte Fläschchen gefüllt waren — diese finden Sie im Kapitel Diamond des ersten *Package Design Book*. 2011 gewannen Mineralwasserflaschen den Diamond Pentaward, und 2012 ging der Preis an eine simple Dose Diet Coke.

Solche Schätze sind wirklich rar, aber wie schon das Lied sagt: „Diamonds are Forever".

PENTAWARD'S DIAMOND

Un jury international composé de spécialistes de la conception d'emballage et de directeurs du marketing de grandes marques mondiales représente forcément les cultures les plus avancées du monde industrialisé. Le jury des Pentawards rassemble dix nationalités, et donc dix cultures.

Bien sûr, les racines culturelles profondes des Japonais sont très différentes de celles des Français, des Argentins ou même des Coréens. Il en va de même pour les différences culturelles entre les habitants de la Grande-Bretagne et des États-Unis.

Les processus du marketing et les techniques de production et de distribution se conforment aux normes internationales, mais c'est la culture, dans son sens le plus littéral, qui caractérise les civilisations. Dans le même temps, c'est en elle que nous puisons notre façon individuelle de regarder le monde, en fonction de notre éducation et du milieu culturel dans lequel nous évoluons.

Dans ce superbe ouvrage, vous découvrirez des emballages qui sont typiquement japonais, totalement britanniques ou 100 % américains. Vous ne manquerez pas de trouver surprise et inspiration dans ces exemples fabuleusement créatifs, mais bon nombre d'entre eux n'ont pas vraiment été conçus pour une commercialisation internationale. Cependant, certains sont à part.

Chaque année, les membres du jury international et multiculturel des Pentawards prennent une décision unanime sur les emballages qui ont un attrait véritablement universel. Quelle que soit leur nationalité, ces créations sont pensées pour être utilisées partout dans le monde. Personne ne peut dire où ni dans quel milieu culturel elles ont été conçues. Il s'agit d'emballages sans frontières, inspirés par un mélange de toutes les cultures de l'humanité, et qui accèdent au statut de classique dès leur naissance. Et il faut décider lequel d'entre eux est le plus exceptionnel.

Le Diamond Pentaward 2008 a été décerné à une bouteille de champagne tête en bas, et celui de l'année suivante à des boîtes de mouchoirs triangulaires qui ressemblent à des tranches de fruits. Puis en 2010, c'est une gamme de produits japonais pour les cheveux dans des bouteilles aux formes organiques qui a pris la relève — vous la trouverez dans le chapitre Diamond du premier tome de *Package Design Book*. En 2011, des bouteilles d'eau minérale ont remporté le Diamond Pentaward, et en 2012 c'était le sommet de la simplicité, une cannette de Coca-Cola Diet.

De tels trésors sont rares, mais, comme le dit la chanson, « les diamants sont éternels ».

Ramlösa is a table-water from an accredited natural mineral source in Sweden and has been a widely recognised brand in the country since the well was discovered in 1707. Being sold in exclusive restaurants, venues and night-clubs a premium packaging was needed to distinguish it from the standard PET bottle sold in stores. The new premium bottle in PET, a plastic not associated with exclusivity by the target group, gained plaudits for its aesthetics as well as the environmentally positive effects compared with glass. Form and shape were modelled on old crystal glasses, the creative work being made harder because carbonated water makes plastic materials expand.

Ramlösa ist ein Tafelwasser aus einer zertifizierten schwedischen Quelle, 1707 entdeckt. Die Marke ist seither landesweit bekannt. Weil sie nun auch in exklusiven Restaurants, Tagungsorten und Nightclubs angeboten wird, war eine Premium-Verpackung nötig, um sich von der PET-Standardflasche im Einzelhandel abzuheben. Die neue Premium-Flasche aus PET (einem Kunststoff, den die Zielgruppe nicht mit Exklusivität verbindet) erhielt für ihre Ästhetik ebenso Beifall wie für die ähnlich dem Glas positiven Umwelteffekte. Form und Prägung wurden von alten Kristallgläsern abmodelliert. Die kreative Ausarbeitung wurde dadurch erschwert, dass sich Kunststoffe durch die Kohlensäure im Wasser ausdehnen.

Ramlösa est une eau de table qui provient d'une source minérale naturelle certifiée en Suède. C'est une marque très connue dans ce pays depuis que la source a été découverte en 1707. Elle est vendue dans des restaurants, boîtes de nuit et autres lieux exclusifs, il lui fallait donc une bouteille de qualité supérieure pour la distinguer des bouteilles standard en PET vendues dans les magasins. Cette nouvelle bouteille haut de gamme en PET, un plastique que le groupe cible n'associe pas à l'exclusivité, a été applaudie pour son esthétique ainsi que pour ses effets positifs sur l'environnement par rapport au verre. Sa forme a été modelée sur des verres en cristal anciens. Le travail créatif a été compliqué par le fait que l'eau gazeuse cause une dilatation du plastique.

RAMLÖSA

Client Service Direction: Lotta Onajin
Creative Direction: Isabelle Dahlborg Lidström
Industrial Design: Åsa Johnsson,
Sofia Berg (No Picnic)
Graphic Design: Björn Studt, Jonas Torvestig
Account Management: Pia Lundström
Company: Nine
Country: Sweden

DIAMOND PENTAWARD 2011
ESKO PRIZE

DIET COKE CROP PACKAGING

Creative Direction: David Turner,
Bruce Duckworth, Sarah Moffat
Design: Rebecca Williams, Josh Michels
Design Direction: Pio Schunker, Hazel Van Buren
(The Coca-Cola Company)
Company: Turner Duckworth,
London & San Francisco
Country: UK

DIAMOND PENTAWARD 2012
ESKO PRIZE

With the nationwide release of new **Diet Coke** packaging a fresh look was created for the fall season in the US. As the country's number-2 sparkling beverage brand, Diet Coke was already well known to consumers, and the Coca-Cola Company North America set the challenge of extending that confidence in the brand to packaging. The resulting design delivered a bold perspective by focusing on the union of the "D" and "K" as the key recognisable elements of the logo. The unique crop of the main logo is at the centre of a visual identity, which appears at point of sale and in advertising for the drink.

Mit dieser Version einer neuen **Diet Coke**-Verpackung wurde ein frischer neuer Look für die Herbstsaison in den USA geschaffen. Den Verbrauchern war Diet Coke als Nummer zwei der prickelnden Getränkemarken bereits wohlbekannt, und Coca-Cola North America stellte sich der Herausforderung, dieses Vertrauen in die Marke auch auf die Verpackung auszuweiten. Das Design zeugt von einer mutigen Perspektive: Es konzentriert sich auf die Zusammenführung von „D" und „K" als Elemente des Logos mit zentralem Wiedererkennungswert. Der unverwechselbare Anschnitt des Hauptlogos steht im Zentrum der visuellen Identität, die sowohl am Point of Sale als auch in der Werbung für dieses Getränk besticht.

Un look novateur a été créé pour la mise sur le marché américain d'un nouvel emballage de **Diet Coke** à l'automne. En tant que marque numéro 2 de boisson pétillante dans le pays, Diet Coke était déjà bien connue des consommateurs, et la Coca-Cola Company d'Amérique du Nord a décidé de traduire sur l'emballage cette confiance dans la marque. Le graphisme qui en résulte offre une perspective audacieuse en faisant du « D » et du « K » les éléments clés du logo. Le cadrage original du logo principal est au cœur de l'identité visuelle, qui apparaît sur le point de vente et dans les publicités.

Milk*

*pinot noir

A milk bottle?
Yes, we know that you have
never received this kind of gift.
That's why we've packed our
finest Pinot Noir in this
bottle of milk.
Enjoy it!

ampro design

beverages

Essay by

MICHAEL AIDAN

Evian Global Brand Director at Danone Waters
Member of the Pentawards Jury 2009–2011

Storytelling in a shoebox, what else is packaging design? No room for "once upon a time", no time for "that's all folks". When advertising has the luxury of 30 seconds and repeat views, not to mention "share" and "post", packaging design has to tell more with less.

Why more? Because only packaging has to communicate and inform and be functional and convenient and safe to use and recyclable... so many constraints, so little space.

I remember from my first marketing class on the subject of design at ESCP that packaging design only had functional aims, 5 of them to be specific — impact, information, category coding, positioning, functionality... 5 functions but no emotions required... time has changed.

Since it has now been widely agreed that marketing has little to do with science and a lot more in common with the art of storytelling, it is clear that the first role of any packaging is to tell its share of the brand story and, in doing so, convey emotions. Some brands, like Monoprix, the well-known French private-label chain, have even taken this literally and pushed it to the max, turning private labels — that a "brand lover" like me would never have put in his shopping basket — into daily talking companions that lighten my day with their witty lines.

So when it comes to bottled water, what part of the brand story do we want to tell? And more importantly, what part of the brand story do you want to hear? What will trigger the right emotions and make you love the product and the brand?

According to the hundreds of cases that I saw in my 3 years on the judging panel of the Pentawards, it seems that the most emotionally compelling story a bottle on your table can tell is that of its untouched purity, its natural origin and its slow filtration through thousands of years of rock strata. An Evian bottle, in the end, should be nothing but a slice of the French Alps on your table. Protected nature in a bottle.

This is what led us to the Pure bottle in 2008 (designed by Grand Angle). The subsequent version in 2010 became even clearer, with an embossed "Pure".

Who knows what the next one might look like. Purity needs few signs, transparency speaks for itself. I wish one day we could go further and find a container that requires no cap and no label and makes you feel as if you were taking water direct from the source... as if the Alps were in your hands. Many a brand has this ambition. Few have got close. One day maybe.

But is this the end of it or might a bottle of water tell another story?

At the end of 1999, a drop-shaped bottle with a funny blue cap was introduced... complicated to produce, difficult to fill, a nightmare to pour from... it was a real success. Purity? Maybe, but more importantly a story of happiness and celebration for a festive season.

Since then fashion designers have added their spin to tell their own different parts of the brand story whilst reinterpreting Alpine purity. The crazy and colourful stripes of Sir Paul Smith, the flowery happiness of Issey Miyake or the snowy embroidery of Christian Lacroix all add a flavour of joy to the pure taste of the Alps for special occasions. A design interpretation of the Live Young brand theme.

An American design student armed with Photoshop recently launched a UFO on the web which created waves all the way to Lucasfilm Studios: mocked-up and discontinued Evian bottles had been turned into a *Star Wars* character. Inspiring. Storytelling at its peak, when purity meets the Force. Delivery? TBD. Could be water or more.

Packaging design has elevated itself from being just about the product to communication and storytelling. Many great beverage brands and Pentawards winners are inspiring examples of that. A lot can fit in a shoebox.

Was könnte Verpackungsdesign anderes sein als Geschichtenerzählen im Kleinstformat? Da gibt es keinen Platz für „Es war einmal ..." oder „Das war's schon, Freunde ...". Wenn Werbung den Luxus von 30 Sekunden Dauer hat und man sie wiederholt betrachten kann, ganz zu schweigen von der Weiterleitung an Freunde und dem „Posten" für andere, dann bekommt das Verpackungsdesign den Job, mit weniger mehr erzählen zu können.

Warum mehr? Weil nur Verpackungen kommunizieren und informieren müssen, gleichzeitig funktional und praktisch zu sein haben, einfach zu verwenden und wiederverwertbar sein sollen ... so viele Anforderungen und nur so wenig Platz.

Wie in meinem ersten Marketingseminar bei der ESCP beim Thema Design gesagt wurde, Verpackungsdesign habe nur fünf funktionale Ziele: Wirkung, Information, Kategorienkodierung, Positionierung, Funktionalität ... fünf Funktionen, aber Emotionen unnötig ... wie die Zeiten sich geändert haben!

Weil nun allgemein akzeptiert ist, dass Marketing weniger mit Wissenschaft als vielmehr etwas mit der Kunst des Erzählens von Geschichten gemein hat, muss jede Verpackung in erster Linie ihren Teil der Markenstory transportieren und dabei auch Emotionen vermitteln. Viele Anbieter, wie auch die bekannte französische Handelskette Monoprix, haben das wörtlich genommen und optimal ausgereizt, indem sie Eigenmarken (die sich ein Markenliebhaber wie ich niemals in den Einkaufswagen legen würde) in Gesprächspartner des Alltags verwandeln, die mit ihren geistreichen Anmerkungen den Tag aufhellen.

Wenn es nun also um in Flaschen abgefülltes Wasser geht, welchen Teil der Markenstory wollen wir erzählen? Und was noch bedeutsamer ist: Welchen Teil der Markenstory wollen Sie hören? Was löst die richtigen Emotionen aus und veranlasst Sie, das Produkt und die Marke zu lieben?

Eingedenk der vielen Hunderten von Einreichungen, die ich in meinen drei Jahren in der Pentawards-Jury gesehen habe, ist die wohl emotional am stärksten überzeugende Story, die eine Flasche auf Ihrem Tisch erzählen kann, jene von ihrer unberührten Reinheit, von ihrem natürlichen Ursprung und der jahrtausendelangen Filterung durch Gesteinsschichten. Eine Flasche Evian sollte am Ende nichts weniger sein als ein Teil französischer Alpen auf Ihrem Tisch. Geschützte Natur in einer Flasche.

Das führte uns 2008 zu der Flasche *Pure* (designt von Grand Angle). 2010 wurde deren Nachfolgerin noch klarer und deutlicher und bekam ein „Pure" eingeprägt. Wer weiß, wie die Nächste aussieht? Reinheit braucht wenig Zeichen, Transparenz spricht für sich. Ich wünschte, wir könnten eines Tages noch weiter gehen und einen Behälter finden, der weder Deckel noch Etikett benötigt und Ihnen das Gefühl vermittelt, Wasser direkt aus der Quelle zu trinken ... als hielten Sie die Alpen in Ihren Händen. Nicht wenige Marken haben solche Ambitionen. Kaum eine ist dem näher gekommen. Eines Tages vielleicht.

Aber ist dies das Ende der Geschichte, oder könnte eine Flasche Wasser noch andere Geschichten erzählen?

Ende 1999 wurde eine tropfenförmige Flasche mit einem eigenartigen blauen Deckel vorgestellt ... kompliziert zu produzieren, schwierig zu befüllen, ein Drama, daraus einzuschenken ... doch ein wahrer Erfolg. Reinheit? Vielleicht ja, aber wichtiger noch ist hier die Geschichte des Glücks und der Feierlichkeit zu festlichen Anlässen.

Dem haben seitdem Modedesigner ihren ureigenen Stempel aufgedrückt, um selbst weitere Teile der Markengeschichte zu erzählen und die alpine Reinheit darin neu zu interpretieren. Die verrückten und farbenprächtigen Streifen von Sir Paul Smith, die blumige Fröhlichkeit von Issey Miyake oder Christian Lacroix' schneegleiche Verzierungen ergänzen das reine Aroma der Alpen für besondere Gelegenheiten um den ihrigen Geschmack der Freude. Die Interpretation des Evian-Themas *Live Young* als Design.

Ein amerikanischer Designstudent startete kürzlich, bewaffnet mit Photoshop, ein UFO im Internet und schlug damit Wellen bis in die Lucasfilm-Studios: Nachgemachte und ausrangierte Evian-Flaschen verwandeln sich in Figuren aus den *Star-Wars*-Filmen. Sehr inspirierend! Welch Höhepunkt des Geschichtenerzählens: Hier trifft Reinheit auf die Macht. Was soll dadurch verkauft werden? Muss noch entwickelt werden. Könnte um Wasser gehen oder auch um anderes.

Das Verpackungsdesign hat sich weiterentwickelt — es geht nicht mehr nur einfach um das Produkt, sondern um Kommunikation und das Geschichtenerzählen. Viele große Getränkemarken und Pentawards-Preisträger sind inspirierende Beispiele dafür. Da geht eine Menge in solch einem kleinen Format.

Qu'est-ce qu'un emballage, sinon une boîte à chaussures qui raconte une histoire ? Il n'y a pas de place pour « il était une fois » ni pour « et ils vécurent heureux ». La publicité a le luxe de disposer de 30 secondes et de visionnages multiples, sans parler des boutons « partager » et « publier », mais l'emballage doit en dire plus avec moins.

Pourquoi plus ? Parce que seul l'emballage doit communiquer et informer, être fonctionnel, pratique, sans danger et recyclable ... tant de contraintes, si peu d'espace.

Lors de ma première classe de marketing sur le design à l'ESCP, j'ai appris que la conception d'emballage avait des objectifs exclusivement fonctionnels. Cinq, pour être plus précis : impact, information, codage catégorie, positionnement, fonctionnalité ... Cinq fonctions, mais aucune émotion. Les temps ont changé.

Aujourd'hui, tout le monde s'accorde à penser que le marketing a peu à voir avec la science, et beaucoup plus de choses en commun avec l'art de la narration. Il ne fait aucun doute que le rôle principal de tout emballage est de raconter sa part de l'histoire de la marque et, ce faisant, de véhiculer des émotions. Certaines marques, comme Monoprix, la célèbre chaîne de distribution française, ont même pris cette idée au sens littéral et l'ont poussée à son paroxysme, en transformant les marques de distributeur, qu'un « fana de marques » tel que moi-même n'aurait jamais mis dans son panier, en compagnes quotidiennes douées de parole qui égaient ma journée avec leurs remarques pleines d'esprit.

Alors quand il s'agit d'eau en bouteille, quelle partie de l'histoire de la marque devons-nous raconter ? Et surtout, quelle partie de l'histoire de la marque voulez-vous entendre ? Comment déclencher les émotions voulues et vous faire aimer le produit et la marque ?

D'après les centaines de cas que j'ai pu voir au cours de mes trois années dans le jury des Pentawards, il semble que l'histoire la plus convaincante du point de vue émotionnel qu'une bouteille puisse vous raconter concerne sa pureté absolue, son origine naturelle et sa filtration naturelle à travers des milliers d'années de strates rocheuses. En fin de compte, une bouteille d'Evian ne devrait être rien d'autre qu'une tranche des Alpes françaises posée sur votre table. De la nature protégée dans une bouteille.

C'est ce qui nous a menés à la bouteille Pure en 2008 (conçue par Grand Angle). La version suivante en 2010 était encore plus transparente, avec le mot « Pure » en relief. Qui sait comment sera la prochaine. La pureté n'a pas besoin de beaucoup de signes extérieurs, la transparence parle d'elle-même. J'espère qu'un jour nous pourrons aller plus loin et trouver un récipient qui ne requiert ni bouchon ni étiquette, et qui vous donne l'impression de prendre l'eau directement à la source... comme si vous teniez les Alpes au creux de vos mains. De nombreuses marques ont cette ambition. Peu s'en sont approchées. Un jour, peut-être.

Mais est-ce la fin, ou y a-t-il une autre histoire qu'une bouteille d'eau pourrait raconter ?

À la fin de l'année 1999, une bouteille en forme de goutte avec un drôle de bouchon bleu a été lancée sur le marché... compliquée à produire, difficile à remplir, un cauchemar pour servir l'eau... Elle a rencontré un vrai succès. Pureté ? Peut-être, mais aussi et surtout, une histoire de bonheur et de célébration pour la saison des fêtes.

Depuis lors, des créateurs de mode ont raconté leurs propres chapitres de l'histoire de la marque dans leur style personnel, tout en réinterprétant la pureté alpine. Les rayures folles et colorées de Sir Paul Smith, la joie fleurie d'Issey Miyake ou la broderie neigeuse de Christian Lacroix ajoutent toutes une saveur de gaieté au goût pur des Alpes pour les occasions spéciales. C'est une interprétation par le design du thème Live Young de la marque.

Un étudiant de design américain armé de Photoshop a récemment lancé sur le web un OVNI qui a créé des remous jusqu'aux studios Lucasfilms : d'anciennes bouteilles d'Evian avaient été transformées en personnage de *La Guerre des Étoiles*. Superbe. La narration au meilleur de sa forme, lorsque la pureté rencontre la Force. Qu'est-ce que cela pourrait vendre ? On ne sait pas encore. Cela pourrait être de l'eau, ou quelque chose d'autre.

La conception d'emballage va maintenant au-delà du produit, il s'agit de communiquer et de raconter une histoire. De nombreuses grandes marques de boisson et lauréats des Pentawards en sont des exemples édifiants. On peut faire entrer beaucoup de choses dans une boîte à chaussures.

To catch the eye of an elite night-club clientele, the new STR bottle from **Heineken** really does light up the night. The special spot-UV ink is 100% invisible in daylight, but in a dark setting under UV the ink suddenly flares up on the bottle's surface revealing a brightly glowing design: a sky filled with shooting stars that makes club connoisseurs the star of the evening. With the smart, minimalist design on the aluminium bottle emphasising Heineken's broad appeal, the STR has been launched successfully in 40 markets around the world and featured widely in the press.

Als Blickfang für Gäste in elitären Nightclubs bringt die neue STR-Flasche von **Heineken** die Nacht zum Leuchten. Der Spezialaufdruck aus Spot-UV-Tinte ist bei Tageslicht unsichtbar, aber in dunkler Umgebung unter UV-Licht zeigt sich auf der Flaschenoberfläche ein strahlendes Design: Ein Himmel voller Sternschnuppen macht die Nightclubgäste zu Stars des Abends. Das clevere, minimalistische Design auf der Aluflasche betont die große Ausstrahlung von Heineken. Die STR-Flasche wurde erfolgreich auf 40 Märkten weltweit gelauncht und sorgte für breites Medienecho.

Pour attirer l'attention de la clientèle d'élite des boîtes de nuit, la nouvelle bouteille STR de **Heineken** brille dans le noir. Son encre UV spéciale est 100 % invisible à la lumière du jour, mais dans les ambiances sombres et sous lumière UV elle s'illumine soudainement à la surface de la bouteille et révèle des motifs éclatants : un ciel rempli d'étoiles filantes qui convertit les noctambules avertis en astres de la soirée. Le graphisme élégant et minimaliste de la bouteille en aluminium souligne l'attrait de Heineken. La STR a été lancée avec succès sur 40 marchés dans le monde entier et a beaucoup fait parler d'elle dans la presse.

HEINEKEN
STR BOTTLE

Design: Ramses Dingenouts, Stéphane Castets (dBOD),
Pascal Duval (Iris Amsterdam)
Company: dBOD
Country: Netherlands
Category: Best of the category beverages

PLATINUM PENTAWARD 2011

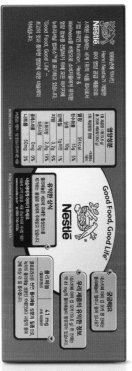

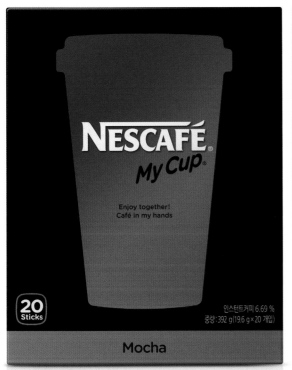

NESCAFÉ
MY CUP

Design: Yoon Jung Lee, Eun Young Lee,
Eun Hye Park, Hanna Jung
Company: Phoenixcom
Country: South Korea
Category: Best of the category beverages

PLATINUM PENTAWARD 2012

SERYAB

Creative Direction: Andrei Petrov
Design: Viktor Ryabov
Company: R2H (UK) Ltd.
Country: Russia
Category: Water

GOLD PENTAWARD 2011

Seryab, a mineral water from Russia launched in summer 2010, takes its name from the Russian word for "silver", used in the filtration of artesian spring sources. To enhance its appeal a packaging design was developed to showcase the simple natural beauty of water, offset with the luxury of decanters and silverware. A new amphora-shaped container was found to be more pleasing to hold, and advantageously more material-efficient, whilst labels were dispensed with, the barcode and other information being printed on a heat-shrunk sleeve covering the cap. The curving design on the bottle's surface makes the water refract light and shine like crystal, additionally reinforcing the structure and so also saving material. A full size-range of PET bottles resulted, called Ice Amphoras — part bottles, part sculpture.

Das russische Mineralwasser **Seryab** startete im Sommer 2010. Der Name stammt vom russischen Wort für „Silber", das bei der Filterung artesischer Brunnen verwendet wurde. Die neue Verpackung stellt die natürliche Schönheit des Wassers heraus, verbunden mit dem Luxus von Dekantern und Silberbesteck. Die Form einer Amphore liegt deutlich angenehmer in der Hand und punktet besonders mit Materialeffizienz: Auf Etiketten wird verzichtet, der Strichcode und weitere Informationen finden mittels Wärmeschrumpffolie auf dem Deckel Platz. Die gekrümmte Oberfläche der Flasche bricht das Licht im Wasser und sorgt für kristallenes Funkeln. Zugleich verstärkt sie die Struktur und spart Material. Eine vollständige Palette verschieden großer PET-„Ice Amphoras" entstand — teils Flasche, teils Skulptur.

Seryab, une eau minérale russe lancée durant l'été 2010, tient son nom du mot russe signifiant « argent », matériau utilisé pour le filtrage des puits artésiens. Pour la rendre plus séduisante, sa bouteille a été conçue de façon à mettre en valeur la beauté naturelle de l'eau, neutralisée par le luxe des carafes et de l'argenterie. La forme de l'amphore a été choisie parce qu'elle est plus agréable à prendre en main et qu'elle est plus efficiente du point de vue du matériau. Les étiquettes ont été éliminées ; le code-barres et les autres informations sont imprimés sur un manchon thermorétractable qui recouvre le bouchon. Les motifs en relief sur la bouteille réfléchissent la lumière et font briller l'eau comme du cristal, tout en renforçant la structure et en économisant de la matière. Une gamme complète de bouteilles en PET a vu le jour, intitulée Ice Amphoras, bouteilles et sculptures à la fois.

BADOIT

Design: Christophe Pradère, Aurélia Jacques,
Juliette Damoiselle, Adrien Vicariot
Company: BETC Design
Country: France
Category: Water

GOLD PENTAWARD 2012

MAGMA DE CABREIROÁ

Design: Seisgrados
Company: Hijos de Rivera S.A.
Country: Spain
Category: Water

SILVER PENTAWARD 2011

A WAT'ART

Creative Direction/Bottle Shape: Juris Dzenis
3D Design/Visualisation: Dmitry Volovik
Brand Design: Girts Libeks
Company: Octagon Branding
Country: Latvia
Category: Water

SILVER PENTAWARD 2011

BRU

Design: Jérôme Lecabellec
Company: CB'a
Country: France
Category: Water

BRONZE PENTAWARD 2011

the water
that has never
seen sunlight

de Cabreiroá

agua de aguja
de origen magmático

SPA
BOTTLE & GLASS SET

Design: Olof ten Hoorn (Brandnew Design),
Stephan Rein, Iris van der Heide (Flex/The Innovation Lab)
Company: Brandnew
Country: Netherlands
Category: Water

SILVER PENTAWARD 2012

EVIAN

Design: Christophe Pradère, Adrien Vicario (BETC Design)
Marketing: Michael Aidan, Florence Bossard (Danone Waters)
Company: Danone Waters
Country: France
Category: Water

BRONZE PENTAWARD 2012

GUMUS

Product Design Direction:
Yesim Bakirkure (Ypsilon Tasarim)
Product Design: Yesim Bakirkure, Serpil Erden
Graphic Design Direction: Bulent Erkmen (Bek Tasarim)
Graphic Design: Haluk Tuncay, Baris Akkurt
Photography: Serdar Tanyeli
Company: Ypsilon Tasarim
Country: Turkey
Category: Water

SILVER PENTAWARD 2012

WATERHOUSE
EIRA

Creative Direction/Design: Bjørn Rybakken
Managing Direction: Line Støtvig
Account Management: Bente Hauge
Production Lead: Klaus Dalseth
Marketing Management: Reidar Høidal (Waterhouse)
Managing Direction: Torvald M. Jørstad (Waterhouse)
Company: Tangram Design
Country: Norway
Category: Water

BRONZE PENTAWARD 2012

AQUA
REFLECTIONS

Creative Direction: Sofan Man
Graphic Design: Sebastian Gunawan
Bottle Design/3D: Christophe Blin
Production Artist: Dicky Fong
Company: Brandimage – Desgrippes & Laga
Country: China
Category: Water

BRONZE PENTAWARD 2011

ACQUA PANNA
S. PELLEGRINO

Design: Paolo Rossetti
Company: Rossetti Design
Country: Italy
Category: Water

BRONZE PENTAWARD 2011

AQUA MONACO

Design: Timo Thurner
Art Direction: Timo Thurner, Jan Alt
Company: Timo Thurner
Country: Germany
Category: Water

BRONZE PENTAWARD 2012

Since 1955, fruit expert Piet **Hoogesteger** has supplied his local, seasonal juice to hotels and restaurants. To reflect his uncompromising approach to producing the purest juices it was important that the packaging represented the range as an honest and straightforward brand. Bottles with clean, simple lines and a label signed "by Hoogesteger" achieved these aims. To convey the idea that the juice is "just picked and pressed" the design illustrates fruit morphing into juice and allows the ingredients to speak for themselves.

Seit 1955 liefert Fruchtexperte Piet **Hoogesteger** seine lokal und saisonal produzierten Säfte an Hotels und Restaurants. Die Produktpalette präsentiert sich als ehrlich und geradlinig, sie demonstriert den kompromisslosen Ansatz, dass nur reinste Säfte produziert werden. Die Flaschen zeigen klare, einfache Linien und ein mit „by Hoogesteger" signiertes Etikett. Früchte, die sich gerade in Saft verwandeln, vermitteln ein Gefühl von Frisch-gepflückt-und-gepresst: So kann der Inhalt für sich selbst sprechen.

L'expert en fruits, Piet **Hoogesteger** fournit les hôtels et restaurants en jus locaux et de saison depuis 1955. Pour refléter sa démarche sans compromis dans la production des jus les plus purs, il était important que l'emballage de la gamme représente l'idée d'une marque honnête et sans détours. Les bouteilles affichent donc des lignes pures et simples, et l'étiquette est signée « by Hoogesteger ». Pour transmettre l'idée que le jus est « tout simplement pressé dès la cueillette », le graphisme évoque des fruits qui se transforment en jus et laisse les ingrédients parler d'eux-mêmes.

HOOGESTEGER

Creative Direction: Claire Parker
Design Direction: Denise Faraco
Design: Luke Morreau
Direction: Melinda Szentpetery
Company: Design Bridge
Country: UK
Category: Soft drinks, juices

GOLD PENTAWARD 2011

SUNNIVA
VÅR FRUKTMOST

Bottle Design: Johan Verde
Label Design: Gerd Ismar Gulbrandsen
(Design House Lund & Partners AS)
Company: FellesJuice AS
Country: Norway
Category: Soft drinks, juices

BRONZE PENTAWARD 2012

SCHWEPPES

Creative Direction: Fred & Farid
Art Direction: Amélie Pichon
Agency Supervision: Thomas Bacharzyna,
Hélène Camus, Olivia Courbon
Advertising Supervision: Hugues Pietrini,
Stanislas de Parcevaux, Émilie de Fautereau
Packaging Production: Ball
Company: Fred & Farid, Paris
Country: France
Category: Soft drinks, juices

SILVER PENTAWARD 2012

COCA-COLA
ARCTIC HOME

Creative Direction: Sarah Moffat,
David Turner, Bruce Duckworth
Design: Butler Looney
Illustration: Darren Whittington
Design Direction: Pio Schunker,
Frederic Kahn (The Coca-Cola Company)
Company: Turner Duckworth,
London & San Francisco
Country: UK
Category: Soft drinks, juices

GOLD PENTAWARD 2012

Coca-Cola and the World Wildlife Fund (WWF) joined forces in a bold new campaign to help protect the polar bear's Arctic home. For the first time ever, **Coca-Cola** turned its familiar red cans white in honour of this endangered animal and committed some $3 million to its conservation through the WWF. The can's distinctive red background was replaced with an all-white panorama, highlighted by the Coca-Cola script printed in red. The eye-catching design included the image of a mother bear and her two cubs making their way across the Arctic. A complementary red can was also released as part of this holiday season initiative.

Coca-Cola und der World Wildlife Fund (WWF) setzen sich mit vereinten Kräften in einer neuen Kampagne das Ziel, die Arktis als Heimat des Polarbären zu schützen. Zum ersten Mal überhaupt wählte **Coca-Cola** zu Ehren dieses vom Aussterben bedrohten Tieres anstatt seiner vertrauten roten Dosen die Farbe Weiß und spendete zu dessen Rettung etwa 3 Millionen Dollar an den WWF. Der typisch rote Hintergrund der Dose wurde durch ein klares weißes Panorama ersetzt, von dem sich der rote Coca-Cola-Schriftzug gut abhebt. Zum auffälligen Design gehört das Bild einer Bärenmutter und ihrer beiden Jungen, die sich durch die Arktis kämpfen. Als Teil dieser für die Urlaubszeit geplanten Aktion erschien auch eine entsprechende rote Dose.

Coca-Cola et le World Wildlife Fund (WWF) font équipe dans une nouvelle campagne audacieuse pour contribuer à la protection de l'habitat arctique de l'ours polaire. Pour la toute première fois, **Coca-Cola** a revêtu de blanc ses canettes traditionnellement rouges en l'honneur de cet animal en voie de disparition, et s'est engagé à verser quelque 3 millions de dollars au WWF pour sa protection. Le fond rouge caractéristique de la canette a été remplacé par un panorama tout blanc, rehaussé par les lettres de Coca-Cola imprimées en rouge. Ce graphisme accrocheur comprend l'image d'une ourse et de ses deux petits déambulant sur la glace. En complément, une canette rouge a également été éditée pour les fêtes.

SCHULP
SAPTAP

Design: Jon Sonneveld, Teun de Kort
Company: PROUDdesign
Country: Netherlands
Category: Soft drinks, juices

SILVER PENTAWARD 2011

TUMULT

Creative Direction: Spencer Buck
Design: Casey Sampson
Illustration: Sam Hadley
Visualisation: James Gilmore
Typography: Rob Clarke
Company: Taxi Studio
Country: UK
Category: Soft drinks, juices

BRONZE PENTAWARD 2012

FROOSH

Creative Direction: Natalie Chung
Design: Sarah Pidgeon
Copy Text: Sylvie Saunders
Strategy: Georgia Levison
Client Service Direction: Matt Small
Company: Pearlfisher
Country: UK
Category: Soft drinks, juices

SILVER PENTAWARD 2011

GOKURI
PEACH

Creative Direction: Yoji Minakuchi,
Hiroyuki Ishiura (Suntory)
Art Direction: Kiyono Morita (Suntory)
Design: Kotobuki Seihan Printing Co., Ltd.
Illustration: Masahiro Ooka
Company: Suntory, Kotobuki Seihan Printing Co., Ltd.
Country: Japan
Category: Soft drinks, juices

SILVER PENTAWARD 2012

HONEYDROP

Design: Lisa Simpson, Rochelle Martyn
Company: Monday Collective
Country: USA
Category: Soft drinks, juices

BRONZE PENTAWARD 2011

SAFT
TRUE FRUITS JUICE

Design: Inga Koster, Marco Knauf,
Nicolas Lecloux, Matthias Zimmer
Company: True Fruits
Country: Germany
Category: Soft drinks, juices
BRONZE PENTAWARD 2012

ROOSVICEE
FRUIT & ROZENBOTTEL

Design: Jon Sonneveld
Company: Mountain Design
Country: Netherlands
Category: Soft drinks, juices
BRONZE PENTAWARD 2011

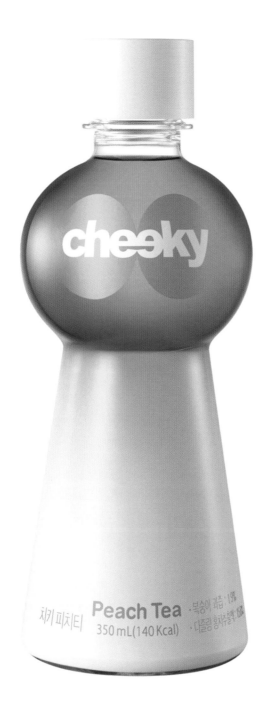

**PARIS BAGUETTE
CHEEKY**

Design: Karim Rashid
Company: Karim Rashid Inc.
Country: USA
Category: Coffee & tea (ready-to-drink)

GOLD PENTAWARD 2011

For Paris Baguette's Cheeky Tea, bursting with fresh peach flavour, a novel packaging was developed to represent its fruitiness. The container is designed to feel both organic and sensual, with the graphics intentionally a little provocative. The bulbous peach-like shape and clear plastic at the top hint at the flavour and source of the beverage within. The smooth curved base of the bottle makes it comfortable to carry and hold, whilst being shaped like a white pedestal it draws the eye up the bottle. The logo is as playful as the form, with **Cheeky** suggesting the shape of a peach, the human body and of the bottle itself, as well as the *chic* quality of the actual product, the tea.

Cheeky Tea von Paris Baguette platzt beinahe vor frischem Pfirsichgeschmack. Eine neuartige Verpackung sollte diese Fruchtigkeit verdeutlichen. Der Behälter fühlt sich gleichermaßen organisch und sinnlich an, wobei die grafische Gestaltung gewollt etwas anzüglich wirkt. Die bauchige, pfirsichförmige Flasche und der durchsichtige obere Bereich deuten Geschmack und Ursprung des Getränks darin an. Durch die glatte, gebogene Basis liegt die Flasche angenehm in der Hand, ihre Säulenform zieht Blicke auf sich. Das Logo ist verspielt wie die Form: **Cheeky** lässt an einen Pfirsich denken, an den menschlichen Körper und die Flasche selbst, aber auch an die elegante Qualität des eigentlichen Produkts: Tee.

Une bouteille originale a été mise au point pour représenter le goût fruité du Cheeky Tea de Paris Baguette, qui regorge de pêche fraîche. Elle est conçue pour évoquer des notions de naturel et de sensualité, et son graphisme est délibérément provocateur. En haut, la forme renflée comme une pêche en plastique transparent fait référence au goût et à l'origine de la boisson. La base lisse et ronde de la bouteille la rend agréable à prendre en main, mais c'est aussi un piédestal blanc qui guide le regard vers le haut. Le logo est aussi ludique que la forme. **Cheeky** (« effronté ») évoque la forme d'une pêche, du corps humain et de la bouteille elle-même, ainsi que le raffinement du produit, du thé.

SOKENBICHA

Design: Glenn Geisendorfer, Gabe Goldman
Company: Platform, Inc.
Country: USA
Category: Coffee & tea (ready-to-drink)

SILVER PENTAWARD 2011

NONG FU ORIENTAL LEAF

Creative Direction: Natalie Chung
Creative Partner: Jonathan Ford
Design: Sarah Pidgeon
Strategy: Tess Wicksteed
Copy: Sylvie Saunders
Illustration: Daisy Fletcher
Company: Pearlfisher
Country: UK
Category: Coffee & tea (ready-to-drink)

SILVER PENTAWARD 2012

TINE ISKAFFE

Creative Direction/Design: Bjørn Rybakken
Design: Kiki Plesner
Production Lead: Mette Nerhagen
Managing Direction: Line Støtvig
Account Management: Stine Wergeland
Marketing Management: Malin Valdal Corneliussen
Brand Management: Anette Tvenge
Company: Tangram Design
Country: Norway
Category: Coffee & tea (ready-to-drink)

GOLD PENTAWARD 2012

IYEMON CHA
HOJICHA OF AUTUMN 2010

Creative Direction: Yoji Minakuchi
Art Direction: Akiko Kirimoto
Design: Yoshiko Fujita
Company: Suntory
Country: Japan
Category: Coffee & tea (ready-to-drink)

SILVER PENTAWARD 2011

DYDO DRINCO
SAMURAI-ESPRESSO

Design: Tomohiro Okugawa,
Kanako Matsuyama, Yoshihiko Miyagi
Company: Rengo Co., Ltd.
Country: Japan
Category: Coffee & tea (ready-to-drink)

SILVER PENTAWARD 2011

GEORGIA
URESHII AMASANO
MILD CAFÉ AU LAIT

Design: Bravis creative team
Company: Bravis International
Country: Japan
Category: Coffee & tea (ready-to-drink)

BRONZE PENTAWARD 2011

FUZE TEA
THE COCA-COLA COMPANY

Creative Direction: Gerard Rizzo (Anthem Worldwide)
Design: Elisabetta Rametta (Anthem Worldwide)
Group Direction/Global Design:
Todd Brooks (The Coca-Cola Company)
Design Management/Global Design:
Gillian Mauldin (The Coca-Cola Company)
Design Management/Integrated Marketing
Communications Brazil: Cristiana Grether
(The Coca-Cola Company)
Company: Anthem Worldwide
Country: USA
Category: Coffee & tea (ready-to-drink)

SILVER PENTAWARD 2012

**IYEMON CHA
GREEN ESPRESSO**

Creative Direction: Yoji Minakuchi
Art Direction/Design: Keiko Genkaku
Design: IFF Company Inc.
Company: Suntory
Country: Japan
Category: Coffee & tea (ready-to-drink)

BRONZE PENTAWARD 2012

GEORGIA
EUROPEAN KOKU NO BLACK

Group Management: Tsuyoshi Imaizumi
(Coca-Cola Japan Co., Ltd.)
Design: Bravis International
Company: Coca-Cola Japan Co., Ltd.
Country: Japan
Category: Coffee & tea (ready-to-drink)

BRONZE PENTAWARD 2011

BABA COFFEE
CARAMEL AFFOGATO
& SKINNY CAFFELATTE

Design: Choi Jin-kyu, Lee Sang-hee,
Heo In-sung, Lee you-na, Back Shin-young
Company: Woongjin Foods
Country: South Korea
Category: Coffee & tea (ready-to-drink)

BRONZE PENTAWARD 2012

Founded in 1997, **Level Ground Trading** works fairly and directly with small-scale producers in developing countries to market their products in North America, offering customers ethical choices. This close relationship with suppliers became the brand identity's core as the company grew, and brings a human touch to the packaging design itself, making the producer the real hero. Photographs of smiling local farmers grace authentic kraft bags, with labels that declare Level Ground's deep knowledge of the origins and taste profiles of each variety of coffee. Zip-locks ensure re-sealable freshness, while back labels feature stories about individual growers and initiatives to give substance to how the company interacts with its trading-partner communities.

Seit 1997 arbeitet **Level Ground Trading** fair und direkt mit Kleinproduzenten in Entwicklungsländern zusammen und vermarktet deren Produkte in Nordamerika. Die Marke ermöglicht Konsumenten ethische Entscheidungen. Die enge Beziehung zu den Produzenten wurde Kern der Markenidentität, sobald das Unternehmen zu wachsen begann. Das Verpackungsdesign selbst zeigt die menschliche Note, der Hersteller wird zur eigentlichen Hauptperson. Fotos von lächelnden Bauern zieren authentische Taschen aus Kraftpapier. Die Beschriftung bezeugt die umfassenden Kenntnisse von Level Ground über Ursprung und Geschmacksprofil aller Kaffeesorten. Der Reißverschluss sichert die Frische des Produkts. Die Rückseite berichtet von einzelnen Pflanzern und Initiativen — als Zeugnis für den regen Austausch mit den Partnergemeinschaften.

Fondée en 1997, **Level Ground Trading** travaille équitablement et directement avec de petits producteurs de pays en voie de développement pour commercialiser leurs produits en Amérique du Nord, en proposant aux clients des choix éthiques. Au cours de la croissance de l'entreprise, cette relation étroite avec les fournisseurs est devenue le cœur de l'identité de la marque et apporte une touche d'humanité à l'emballage lui-même en donnant au producteur le rôle de protagoniste. Des photographies de fermiers souriants ornent les sachets en papier kraft authentique, et les étiquettes témoignent de la connaissance approfondie de Level Ground des origines de chaque variété de café ainsi que son profil gustatif. Les fermetures zip-lock garantissent la fraîcheur du produit, tandis que les étiquettes du dos présentent des histoires de chaque producteur et les initiatives afin de rendre vivante l'interaction entre l'entreprise et les communautés partenaires.

LEVEL GROUND TRADING

Creative Direction: Roy White, Matthew Clark
Design: Matthew Clark, Roy White
Copy Text: Derek Perkins, Matthew Clark
Illustration: Matthew Clark
Photography: Hugo Ciro (Farmers)
Company: Subplot Design
Country: Canada
Category: Coffee & tea (dry and capsules)

GOLD PENTAWARD 2011

DIRECT FAIR TRADE
TANZANIA
ORGANIC COFFEE / CAFÉ BIOLOGIQUE

A deep, wild, full-flavoured cup with pleasant earthiness, juicy acidity and a fearless dark chocolate finish.

WHOLE BEAN
DARK ROAST

Agvesi
Mbozi,
Tanzania

300g (10.5oz)

DIRECT FAIR TRADE
PERU
ORGANIC COFFEE / CAFÉ BIOLOGIQUE

A sweet, crisp coffee with a bright, citrus-hinted entry, delicate cocoa notes and a clean fruity finish.

WHOLE BEAN
MEDIUM ROAST

Enrique
Fungos,
Peru

300g (10.5oz)

Jaime Marín
Jardin,
Colombia

DIRECT FAIR TRADE
COLOMBIA
SINGLE-ORIGIN COFFEE / CAFÉ D'ORIGINE UNIQUE

This classic, bold, full-bodied Colombian coffee boasts a full-flavoured entry with hints of cocoa, and a rich, spicy finish.

WHOLE BEAN
DARK ROAST

300g (10.5oz)

DIRECT FAIR TRADE
DECAF Colombia
SINGLE-ORIGIN COFFEE / CAFÉ D'ORIGINE UNIQUE

This coffee is natural-water decaffeinated and presents a clean, full-bodied taste with hints of cocoa and black currants.

WHOLE BEAN
DARK ROAST

Chepe
Andes,
Colombia

300g (10.5oz)

DIRECT FAIR TRADE
COLOMBIA
SINGLE-ORIGIN COFFEE / CAFÉ D'ORIGINE UNIQUE

Luscious acidity, lively citrus notes and a savory bouquet deliver a fresh perspective on a classic Colombian coffee.

WHOLE BEAN
LIGHT ROAST

Jaime Vargas
Jardin,
Colombia

300g (10.5oz)

Doña Nicasia
Los Yungas,
Bolivia

DIRECT FAIR TRADE
BOLIVIA
ORGANIC COFFEE / CAFÉ BIOLOGIQUE

In this rich, well balanced coffee, citrus and floral blossom into caramel and finish delicately with lingering hints of milk chocolate.

WHOLE BEAN
MEDIUM ROAST

300g (10.5oz)

DIRECT FAIR TRADE
ESPRESSO
ORGANIC COFFEE / CAFÉ BIOLOGIQUE

This organic blend of African and South American coffee has a lively entry, rich crema and tremendous character with a cocoa finish.

WHOLE BEAN
MED-DARK ROAST

Sara Jemsi
Mbozi,
Tanzania

300g (10.5oz)

DIRECT FAIR TRADE
FRENCH ROAST
SINGLE-ORIGIN COFFEE / CAFÉ D'ORIGINE UNIQUE

Unapologetically sweet and smoky, this dark and full-flavored roast lingers with cinnamon notes and undertones of nutmeg.

WHOLE BEAN
DARK ROAST

Ever Antonio
Belanica,
Colombia

300g (10.5oz)

DIRECT FAIR TRADE
ETHIOPIA
ORGANIC COFFEE / CAFÉ BIOLOGIQUE

Berries and honey provide a bright, playful entry, with smooth centre notes, and a lingering cocoa finish.

WHOLE BEAN
MEDIUM ROAST

Yrgalem
Sidama, Ethiopia

300g (10.5oz)

338 is a new premium coffee and a blend of the best coffee beans from the 338 districts in Peru where coffee grows. The quality of Peruvian coffee is now recognised internationally and in presenting this brand the idea was to reflect the product's origins, to express respect for the environment and at the same time to project a modern and sophisticated design. This was done by incorporating a well-known local legend about La Pachamama, that is to say Mother Earth, who guards and protects natural resources and oversees a coexistence between humans and nature that is based on respect.

338 ist ein neuer Premiumkaffee, verschnitten aus den besten Kaffeebohnen der 338 peruanischen Bezirke, in denen Kaffee wächst. Die Qualität des peruanischen Kaffees ist nun international anerkannt. Der Präsentation dieser Marke lag die Idee zugrunde, die Herkunft des Produkts widerzuspiegeln und den Respekt gegenüber der Umwelt auszudrücken. Gleichzeitig wird ein modernes und geistreiches Design vermittelt. Dafür griff man die national bekannte Legende von La Pachamama auf. Sie steht für Mutter Erde, diese bewacht und beschützt die natürlichen Ressourcen. Darum wacht sie auch über die Koexistenz von Mensch und Natur, die auf Respekt beruht.

338 est un nouveau café haut de gamme et un mélange des meilleurs grains des 338 districts du Pérou où pousse le café. La qualité du café péruvien est maintenant reconnue dans le monde entier et, pour présenter cette marque, l'idée était de refléter les origines du produit, et d'exprimer le respect de l'environnement tout en projetant une image moderne et sophistiquée. Pour ce faire, l'emballage reprend une légende traditionnelle locale sur la Pachamama, c'est-à-dire la Terre-Mère, gardienne des ressources naturelles et de la cohabitation respectueuse entre les humains et la nature.

338

Account Direction: Claudia Boggio
Creative Direction: Alfredo Burga
Design: Jenny Casachahua
Company: Infinito
Country: Peru
Category: Coffee & tea (dry and capsules)

GOLD PENTAWARD 2012

PEEZE

Design: Sogood creative team
Company: Sogood
Country: Netherlands
Category: Coffee & tea (dry and capsules)

SILVER PENTAWARD 2011

GUANGDONG YAWEI
A WISP OF TEA

Design: Lin Shaobin
Company: Lin Shaobin Design
Country: China
Category: Coffee & tea (dry and capsules)

SILVER PENTAWARD 2011

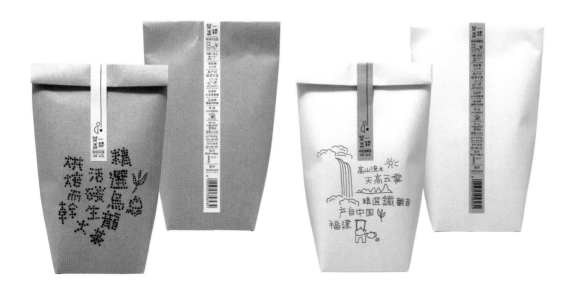

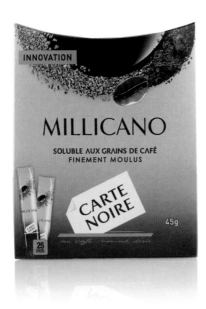

CARTE NOIRE
MILLICANO

Creative Direction/Consumer Branding: Angélique Lecussan
Art Direction/Consumer Branding: Morgan Franck de Préaumont
Project Management: Clarisse Brun
Company: Dragon Rouge
Country: France
Category: Coffee & tea (dry and capsules)

BRONZE PENTAWARD 2012

RUBRA
SILKEN PYRAMID TEA BAG PACKS

Design: Geoff Bickford, Esther Lee
Company: Dessein
Country: Australia
Category: Coffee & tea (dry and capsules)

BRONZE PENTAWARD 2011

LAUGHING MAN WORLDWIDE
COFFEE & TEA

Executive Creative Direction: Sam O'Donahue
Design/Creative Direction: Pierre Jeand'heur
Company: Established
Country: USA
Category: Coffee & tea (dry and capsules)

SILVER PENTAWARD 2012

DOUTOR

Art Direction/Design: Goro Shibata
Photography: Akira Kitaoka
Production: Reishi Kakishima
Company: Light Publicity Co., Ltd.
Country: Japan
Category: Coffee & tea (dry and capsules)

BRONZE PENTAWARD 2011

CIELITO QUERIDO CAFÉ

Design: Ignacio Cadena Rubio,
Hector Esrawe, Rocío Serna, Joaquin Ceballos
Company: Cadena + Asociados Branding
Country: Mexico
Category: Coffee & tea (dry and capsules)

SILVER PENTAWARD 2012

TEA BAR

Design: Joep Janssen, Steven de Cleen
Company: PROUDdesign
Country: Netherlands
Category: Coffee & tea (dry and capsules)

BRONZE PENTAWARD 2012

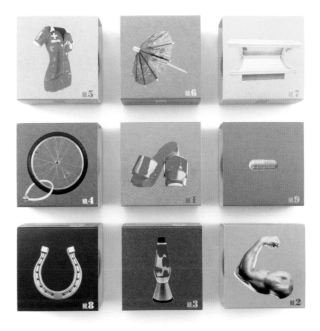

MAKE MINE A BUILDERS

Brand Management: Jonathan Chiu
Design Direction: Martyn Hayes
Artwork: Ryan Ruschiensky
Account Management: Miles McDermott
Company: Elmwood
Country: UK
Category: Coffee & tea (dry and capsules)

BRONZE PENTAWARD 2011

NECTAR FUEL
THE ULTIMATE SPORTS FUEL

Design: Jeremy Martin, Alex Brooks, Stuart Jeffreys, Gavin Blake
Company: My Goodness Ltd.
Country: UK
Category: Functional beverages

GOLD PENTAWARD 2012

SO

Design: Bravis International design team
Company: Bravis International
Country: Japan
Category: Functional beverages

SILVER PENTAWARD 2012

GIZE+

Art Direction: Achim Bach
Creative Direction: Reiner Rempis
Copy Text: Frank Jöricke
Design: Werbeagentur Zweipunktnull GmbH
Company: C.M.W. Canadian Mineral Water
Development S.A.
Country: Luxembourg
Category: Functional beverages

GOLD PENTAWARD 2011

GATORADE
G SERIES FIT

Creative Direction: Stanley Hainsworth
Art Direction: Matt Schmunk
Design: Brian Piper, Daniel Petrzelka, Lizzy Showman
Industrial Design: Jay Ostby
Company: Tether Inc.
Country: USA
Category: Functional beverages

SILVER PENTAWARD 2011

MYSMOOTHIE

Design: Jonas Lundin
Company: LA+B, Love for Art and Business
Country: Sweden
Category: Functional beverages

SILVER PENTAWARD 2012

BENECOL DRINKS

Creative Direction: David Turner, Bruce Duckworth
Design Direction: Clem Halpin
Design: Gavin Hurrell
Photography: Andy Grimshaw
Retouching: Peter Ruane
Artwork: James Norris
Creative Partnership: Johnson & Johnson Global
Strategic Design Office
Company: Turner Duckworth, London & San Francisco
Country: UK
Category: Functional beverages

BRONZE PENTAWARD 2012

CEETHREE'S IO

Creation/Lead Design: Jonas Lundin
Original Artwork: Martin Ring
Art Direction: Magdalena Adaktusson
Project Management: Elin Trogen, Frida Guldstrand
Company: LA+B, Love for Art and Business
Country: Sweden
Category: Functional beverages

BRONZE PENTAWARD 2011

I ABOVE
AEROTONIC FLIGHT BEVERAGE

Design: Mike Tisdall, Simon Cairns, Jamie McLellan,
Mark di Somma, Ben Reid, Tristan O'Shannessy
Client: Roger Boyd
Company: Insight Creative Ltd.
Country: New Zealand
Category: Functional beverages

BRONZE PENTAWARD 2011

Monteith's Single Source is a lager beer from New Zealand that respects tradition — true to the land and its people and batch-brewed with handpicked ingredients. The black bottle helps to keep the contents fresh by blocking sunlight, but also enables it to stand out from other beers whilst providing a striking counterpoint to the labelling. The signature silhouette was retained to ensure its identification with the Monteith's family of beers. For the launch a special box was designed as a gift presentation for the first 100 bottles produced, all hand-signed and numbered by the brewer and closed with a wax seal.

Das Lagerbier Monteith's Single Source aus Neuseeland respektiert die Tradition — dem Land und seinen Menschen treu, aus handverlesenen Zutaten gebraut. Die schwarze Flasche schützt vor Sonnenlicht und hält den Inhalt länger frisch. Zugleich hebt sie sich so von anderen Biersorten ab und setzt einen spannenden Kontrast zum Etikett. Die charakteristische Silhouette blieb, um die Identifikation mit den Bieren der Monteith-Familie sicherzustellen. Bei Markteinführung wurden die ersten 100 produzierten Flaschen in besonders gestalteten Geschenkkartons verpackt, vom Braumeister handsigniert und nummeriert und mit Wachssiegel verschlossen.

Single Source de Monteith's est une bière blonde néozélandaise qui respecte la tradition — elle est fidèle à la terre et à ses gens, et est brassée par lots avec des ingrédients soigneusement sélectionnés. La bouteille noire aide à conserver la fraîcheur de son contenu en bloquant la lumière du jour, mais permet également au produit de se démarquer des autres bières tout en créant un contraste tranché avec l'étiquetage. La silhouette caractéristique des bouteilles de la marque a été conservée afin de favoriser l'association du produit avec la famille de bières de Monteith's. Pour le lancement, un coffret-cadeau spécial a été conçu pour les 100 premières bouteilles produites, signé et numéroté par le brasseur et fermé par un sceau en cire.

MONTEITH'S SINGLE SOURCE

Creative Strategy: Michael Crampin
Creative Direction: Jef Wong
Design Lead: Damian Alexander
Company: Designworks
Country: New Zealand
Category: Beer, ciders and low-alcohol drinks

GOLD PENTAWARD 2011

SAN MIGUEL 1516

Creative Direction: Antonia Hayward, Matt Thompson
Project Direction: Edward Mitchell
Design Direction: Emma Follet
Design: Sarah Bustin, Hayley Barrett
3D Creative Direction: Laurent Robin-Prevallee
3D Design: Ben Davey
Company: Design Bridge
Country: UK
Category: Beer

SILVER PENTAWARD 2012

San Miguel 1516 is founded on the principles of the Germanic beer purity law of 1516 and is produced only with water, malt, hops and yeast. To avoid confusion with a strong beer and instead convey its purity and carve out a position in the premium beer market, the brewer required an appropriate new packaging design. The bottle's smooth new profile echoes the San Miguel logo and in place of a label "1516" has been formed in the glass itself along with the message "according to the law of purity" — a self-assured bespoke finish to appeal to the brand's consumers. Each bottle carries a red seal, certifying the simplicity of its ingredients.

San Miguel 1516 wird, basierend auf den Prinzipien des deutschen Reinheitsgebots von 1516, nur aus Wasser, Malz, Hopfen und Hefe gebraut. Um sich vom Starkbier abzugrenzen und vor allem die Reinheit des Bieres zu betonen, wünschte die Brauerei ein passendes neues Verpackungsdesign, mit dem man sich eine gute Position im Markt der Premiumbiere erkämpfen wollte. Im glatten, neuen Profil der Flasche klingt das Logo von San Miguel an. Das „1516" erscheint ohne Etikett auf dem Glas selbst, ebenso die Botschaft „Nach dem Reinheitsgebot gebraut". Diese maßgeschneidert selbstbewusste Lösung spricht die Zielgruppe besonders an. Jede Flasche ziert ein rotes Siegel als Zertifikat für die Reinheit seiner Inhaltsstoffe.

San Miguel 1516 est fondée sur les principes de la loi germanique de 1516 sur la pureté de la bière et est produite uniquement avec de l'eau, du malt, du houblon et de la levure. Pour éviter toute confusion avec une bière forte, transmettre l'idée de pureté et se faire une place sur le marché de la bière haut de gamme, le brasseur avait besoin d'une nouvelle bouteille. Son nouveau profil lisse fait écho au logo de San Miguel, et au lieu d'une étiquette, « 1516 » a été travaillé en relief directement dans le verre avec le message « conformément à la loi sur la pureté ». C'est une touche finale pleine d'assurance pour séduire les consommateurs de la marque. Chaque bouteille est garnie d'un sceau rouge qui certifie la simplicité de ses ingrédients.

MILLER 64

Design: Adam Ferguson, Justin Berglund
Company: Soulsight
Country: USA
Category: Beer

GOLD PENTAWARD 2012

VICTORIA PALE LAGER

Creative Design: Julian Ditchburn (O-I)
Concept Design: Cowan Design
Company: O-I
Country: USA
Category: Beer

BRONZE PENTAWARD 2012

TUBORG BOTTLE

Creative Direction: David Turner, Bruce Duckworth
Design Direction: Clem Halpin
Design: Miles Marshall, Buzz Burman
Structural Design: Andre Message
Visualisation: Peter Ruane
Artwork: James Norris
Company: Turner Duckworth, London & San Francisco
Country: UK
Category: Beer

BRONZE PENTAWARD 2012

DOSS BLOCKOS

Creative Direction: Josh Lefers, Stephen Wools
Design: Kane Marevich
Company: Big Dog Creative
Country: Australia
Category: Beer, ciders
and low-alcohol drinks

SILVER PENTAWARD 2011

BOHEMIA

Design Direction: Will Parr, Tim Vary
Creative Direction: David Annetts
3D Design Direction: Laurent Robin-Prevalle
Design: Claire Smith
Company: Design Bridge
Country: UK
Category: Beer, ciders and low-alcohol drinks

BRONZE PENTAWARD 2011

OXOTA DARK

Creative Direction: Andrey Kugaevskikh
Company: Svoe Mnenie Branding Agency
Country: Russia
Category: Beer, ciders and low-alcohol drinks

BRONZE PENTAWARD 2011

GOOD CHEER BEER

Design Direction: Ben Greengrass, Chris Jackson
Group Design Direction: Torben Dunn
Head of Creative Services: Mark O'Donnell
Writer: Natalie Woodhead
Account Direction: Caroline Dilloway
Chairman: Jonathan Sands
Company: Elmwood
Country: UK
Category: Beer, ciders and low-alcohol drinks

SILVER PENTAWARD 2011

MATEO & BERNABÉ AND FRIENDS

Design: Javier Euba, Daniel Morales
Company: Moruba
Country: Spain
Category: Beer

SILVER PENTAWARD 2012

BASSANO HARD SODA

Creative Direction: Don Chisholm
Creative Strategy: Patrick Ho
Design: Pat Smith
Production Design: Rob Sunderland
Implementation Management: Reg Dick
Company: Dossier Creative Inc.
Country: Canada
Category: Beer, ciders and low-alcohol drinks

BRONZE PENTAWARD 2011

JAW DROP COOLERS

Design: Laurie Millotte, Bernie Hadley-Beauregard
Illustration: Gary Bullock
3D: Paul Sherstobitoff
Company: Brandever
Country: Canada
Category: Ciders and low-alcohol drinks
BRONZE PENTAWARD 2012

On a cool spring morning in 1929, a small crew from Okanagan Falls set off to a deserted mining camp some 16 miles away. An old wooden church was to be dismantled and brought back to the town, which called for a controlled blast of four dynamite sticks inside the church in order to "loosen the nails". Odd as it may seem, the explosion spared the wood from damage during the subsequent dismantling and save for losing the steeple, the plan succeeded. Today, the 120-year-old wooden church stands proudly in its second home of Okanagan Falls. In naming these Vintners Quality Alliance wines **Blasted Church** the ingenuity of this initiative is celebrated, honouring the pioneers for their vision, steadfastness and craftsmanship.

An einem kühlen Frühlingsmorgen des Jahres 1929 machte sich ein kleiner Trupp aus Okanagan Falls auf den Weg zu einem etwa 25 km entfernten verlassenen Minenarbeiterlager. Eine alte Holzkirche sollte abgetragen und in der Stadt wiederaufgebaut werden. Dafür war im Gebäude eine kontrollierte Sprengung mit vier Dynamitstäben nötig, um „die Nägel zu lockern". So merkwürdig das klingen mag, die Explosion bewahrte bei der anschließenden Wiedererrichtung das Holz vor Schäden, und abgesehen davon, dass der Kirchturm nicht zu retten war, wurde der Plan erfolgreich umgesetzt. Heute steht die 120 Jahre alte hölzerne Kirche stolz in ihrer zweiten Heimat Okanagan Falls. Die Weine der Vintners Quality Alliance feiern den Einfallsreichtum dieser Initiative mit **Blasted Church**, und die Pioniere werden für ihre Vision, Standhaftigkeit und Handwerkskunst geehrt.

Un frais matin de printemps en 1929, une petite équipe d'Okanagan Falls se mit en route pour un camp minier déserté situé à 25 km de distance. Une vieille église en bois devait être démontée et ramenée en ville, ce qui impliquait l'explosion contrôlée de quatre bâtons de dynamite à l'intérieur de l'église pour « desserrer les clous ». Aussi étrange que cela puisse paraître, l'explosion permit d'éviter d'endommager le bois pendant le démontage qui suivit, et bien que la flèche n'ait pas pu être sauvée, le plan a fonctionné. Aujourd'hui, cette église en bois vieille de 120 ans se dresse fièrement dans sa deuxième demeure d'Okanagan Falls. Le fait d'avoir baptisé ces vins Vintners Quality Alliance **Blasted Church** (« église dynamitée ») rend hommage à l'ingéniosité de cette initiative ainsi qu'à la vision, la ténacité et les talents manuels des pionniers.

BLASTED CHURCH VINEYARDS

Art Direction: Bernie Hadley-Beauregard,
Laurie Millotte
Illustration: Chris Sickel (Red Nose Studio)
Photography: Laurie Millotte
Company: Brandever
Country: Canada
Category: Wines

GOLD PENTAWARD 2011
AVERY DENNISON PRIZE

PLAGIOS WINE
KTIMA BIBLIA CHORA WINES

Design: Yiannis Charalambopoulos,
Alexis Nikou, Vaggelis Liakos
Photography: Kostas Pappas
Company: Beetroot Design Group
Country: Greece
Category: Wines

GOLD PENTAWARD 2012

TRUETT HURST DRY CREEK VALLEY
DEARLY BELOVED

Design: Kevin Shaw
Company: Stranger & Stranger
Country: USA
Category: Wines

SILVER PENTAWARD 2012

WISHBONE
SAINT CLAIR FAMILY ESTATE

Creative Direction: Tony Ibbotson
Design: Mayra Monobe
Artwork: Greg Coles
Company: The Creative Method
Country: Australia
Category: Wines

BRONZE PENTAWARD 2011

**LONGVIEW VINEYARD
W. WAGTAIL**

Creative Direction: Anthony De Leo
Design: Shane Keane
Company: Voice
Country: Australia
Category: Wines

SILVER PENTAWARD 2012

Mistress Pinot Gris
Assertive & Alluring
Divine Pleasure Can Be Yours
JUST TXT 'GRIS' TO
0458 263 309
Fresh from Tasmania

750mL   2010

Generous Full-bodied Deeply Sumptuous
Syrah
Ripe & Juicy
Deliciously Lusty Ripe & Inviting

TXT 'SYRAH' TO
0458 263 398
STRICTLY McLAREN VALE 2007

750mL

2010
ADELAIDE HILLS
SAVVY BLANC
YOUNG, FRESH, FRUITY & PLAYFUL

TXT 'BLANC'
0428696729

750mL

Cabernet Sauvignon
Indulgent Luscious
Intense & Totally Seductive
Txt 'Cabernet' to
0428 256 918
EXCLUSIVELY WRATTONBULLY 2006

750mL

Ripe,
Sensual,
Velvety,
Enticingly Earthy
Spicy Temptation
Meet Pinot Noir
Long Lasting
Impression Guaranteed
TXT 'pinot' 0428848696
XXX

750mL

LONGVIEW VINEYARD
THE PIECE

Creative Direction: Anthony De Leo,
Scott Carslake
Design: Tom Crosby, Shane Keane
Art: Vans the Omega
Company: Voice
Country: Australia
Category: Wines

BRONZE PENTAWARD 2012

SAINT & SINNER
CALLING CARD

Design: Edouard Ball, Jon Clark, Jodi Hooker,
Pamela Partridge, Ico Hernandez
Company: Boldincreative Pty Ltd.
Country: Australia
Category: Wines

SILVER PENTAWARD 2011

ESPORÃO
RESERVA & PRIVATE SELECTION

Design: Eduardo Aires
Company: White Studio
Country: Portugal
Category: Wines

BRONZE PENTAWARD 2012

FORANELL
JOAQUIM BATLLE

Art Direction: Els Neirinckx
Brand Consultancy: Adri Ardenuy
Company: Carré Noir Barcelona
Country: Spain
Category: Wines

BRONZE PENTAWARD 2011

KORLAT

Design/Art Direction: Vanja Cuculic
Company: Studio Cuculic
Country: Croatia
Category: Wines

BRONZE PENTAWARD 2011

WINEBOW
24 KNOTS PINOT NOIR

Creative Direction: Stan Church
Design: Lou Antonucci
Company: Wallace Church, Inc.
Country: USA
Category: Wines

BRONZE PENTAWARD 2012

In developing a high-class organically cultivated wine to be sold, straight from the vintner, in a new-generation bag-in-box, crisp design helps with costs and wastage compared to traditional glass bottles — all for an attractive **10 euros**. This revitalised packaging was also intended to attract younger, design-orientated people who value sustainability, whilst elevating the familiar wine-box from its discounted image. With reasons for saving money and ecological resources being ever present, examples were employed in the wording on the boxes themselves: the 2009 crisis box, the climate conference of 2010, etc. Each box thus constitutes a particular campaign and thereby advertises itself, boxes also being sent with corresponding press material to all German newspapers and magazines.

Dieser erstklassige, organisch angebaute Wein wird direkt ab Winzerei in einer Bag-in-Box-Verpackung der neuen Generation verkauft. Das knackig-frische Design sorgt, verglichen mit traditionellen Glasflaschen, für niedrige Kosten und geringen Abfall — und alles für attraktive **10 Euro**. Die revitalisierte Verpackungsform soll auch jüngere, designorientierte Leute ansprechen, die Wert auf Nachhaltigkeit legen. Gleichzeitig löst sich der altbekannte Weinkarton von seinem Discounter-image. Sparen bei Geld und ökologischen Ressourcen ist ein ständig präsentes Thema, das zeigt sich auch in den Texten auf den Kartons selbst: der Krisenkarton des Jahres 2009, die Klimakonferenz 2010 usw. Jeder Karton steht für eine bestimmte Kampagne und wirbt somit für sich selbst. Zusammen mit entsprechendem Presse-material wurden die Kartons an alle deutschen Zeitungen und Magazine verschickt.

Pour ce vin écologique haut de gamme, vendu directement par le viticulteur dans un conditionnement de nouvelle génération consistant en un sachet dans une boîte, la conception aide à économiser sur les coûts et le gaspillage par rapport aux bouteilles de verre traditionnelles, et tout cela pour **10 euros** seulement. Cet emballage redynamisé devait également attirer un public plus jeune, sensible au design, qui accorde de l'importance à la durabilité, tout en élevant le bon vieux cubi au-dessus de son image bas de gamme. Avec de bonnes raisons pour économiser à la fois l'argent et les ressources environnementales, les bons exemples sont appliqués sur les emballages directement : la crise de 2009, la conférence sur le climat de 2010, etc. Chaque carton constitue donc une campagne particulière et assure ainsi sa propre publicité, car les cartons sont également envoyés, accompagnés de leur dossier de presse, à tous les journaux et magazines allemands.

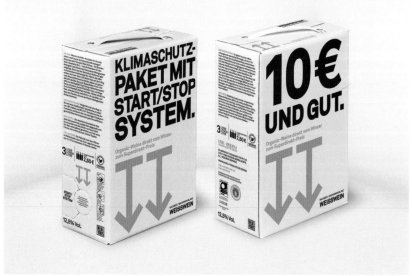

10 EUROS AND GOOD!
CRISIS BOX, CLIMATE BOX, INFLATION BOX

Creative Direction: Roman Ruska, Francisca Martín
Design: Roman Ruska, Alexander Ahlert, Axel Ganser
Copy Text: Roman Ruska, Francisca Martín, Jurg Horn, Jochen Blass
Company: Ruska, Martín, Associates GmbH
Country: Germany
Category: Wine as bag-in-box

GOLD PENTAWARD 2011

DIE IDEE: In der Krise sollen wir den Gürtel enger schnallen? Auf guten Wein verzichten? Oh nein! Wein & Vinos – Ihr Spanien-Wein-Spezialist No.1 – hat die Weinbox für den krisengeschüttelten Weingourmet kreiert. Denn auf der Iberischen Halbinsel gibt es Top-Weine zu Best-Preisen! Und damit diese auf dem Weg nach Deutschland nicht unnötig in die Höhe schießen, haben wir gehandelt. Mit der Krisenbox zum Superdirekt-Preis. Hier zählt nur die Qualität des Weines: Kein Design-Schnickschnack! Keine schweren, teuren Flaschen! Kein unnötiger Zwischenhandel! Einfach vom Winzer direkt ins Glas! Und das Ganze natürlich in 1A-Qualität und dazu aus Trauben, die aus zertifiziert ökologischem Anbau stammen! Da kann die Krise einpacken.

DER VORTEIL: Der elastische Innenteil der Box zieht sich zusammen, sobald Wein abgezapft wird. So vermeidet man die Zufuhr von Sauerstoff. Der Wein wird optimal geschützt und hält seine Frische vom ersten bis zum letzten Tropfen.

DIE UMWELTBILANZ: Vergleicht man eine Bag-in-Box mit einer traditionellen Glasflasche, so spart man 85% Abfall und 55% CO$_2$-Emissionen (bei der Produktion und durch das viel niedrigere Transportgewicht). Eine bemerkenswert gute Umweltbilanz.

DIE LAGERUNG: Der Wein ist nach dem Öffnen im Kühlschrank oder bei einer Lagertemperatur von 12–15°C mindestens 8 Wochen haltbar.

KRISEN BEWÄLTIGUNG OHNE NEU-VERSCHULDUNG.

Organic-Weine direkt vom Winzer
zum Superdirekt-Preis

3 LITER LITROS LITRE

FLASCHENPREIS 0,75L 2,50 €

ORGANIC GROWN GRAPES

Anleitung auf dem Boden der Box

100% MONASTRELL
ROTWEIN

14% Vol.

WEIN & VINOS

DER WEINMACHER: Er gehört zu jenen zähen unbeugsamen spanischen Önologen, die sich mit Haut und Haar dem Qualitätsweinbau verschrieben haben: Manuel Olmo, der in der spanischen unbekannten D.O. Utiel-Requena im hochgelegenen Hinterland von Valencia das Musterweingut Sierra Norte aufgebaut hat. Hier liegt und pflegt er uralte Rebstöcke und baut dabei auf autochthone Reben wie Macabeo, hat aber auch keine Scheu, hochwertige Zuzügler wie Sauvignon Blanc auf seinen kargen Boden zu kultivieren. Und das natürlich in zertifiziertem Bio-Anbau! So ist er der Protagonist einer neuen Generation von Önologen, die weltoffen in der Provinz für frischen Wind sorgen und dabei blitzsaubere ökologischen Wein keltern!

DER WEIN: Köstliche Cuvée aus der urspanischen Rebsorte Macabeo (80%), die milde, mediterrane Weißweine hervorbringt, und Sauvignon Blanc (20%), die Frucht, feine Weinsäure und Struktur hinzufügt. Daraus ist ein Wein entstanden, der mit feiner Aromatik, herrlich duftendem Bouquet, großer Ausgewogenheit am Gaumen und bester Bekömmlichkeit keinen Vergleich mit weit teureren Weißen scheuen muss.

10€ UND GUT.

Organic-Weine direkt vom Winzer
zum Superdirekt-Preis

3 LITER LITROS LITRE

FLASCHENPREIS 0,75L 2,50 €

ORGANIC GROWN GRAPES

UTIEL - REQUENA
DENOMINACIÓN DE ORIGEN

ELABORADO Y ENVASADO POR R.E.IS
3701/V PARA BODEGA SIERRA NORTE,
S.L. / REQUENA (ESPAÑA)

VINO BLANCO / PRODUCTO DE ESPAÑA
WWW.VINOS.DE

CONTIENE SULFITOS / ENTHÄLT SULFITE
CONTIENT SULFITES / CONTAINS SULFITES

AGRICULTURA ECOLÓGICA

VA0929E

MACABEO / SAUVIGNON BLANC
WEISSWEIN

12,5% Vol.

INDULGE

Design: Uxus Creative Team
Company: Uxus
Country: Netherlands
Category: Wine as bag-in-box

SILVER PENTAWARD 2011

MASTER'S COLLECTION

Design: Henrik Olssön, Erika Barbieri
Company: Olssön Barbieri
Country: Norway
Category: Wine as bag-in-box

BRONZE PENTAWARD 2012

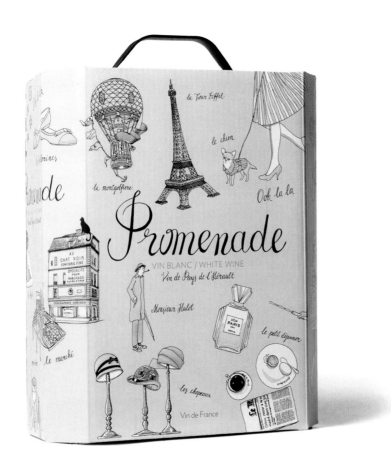

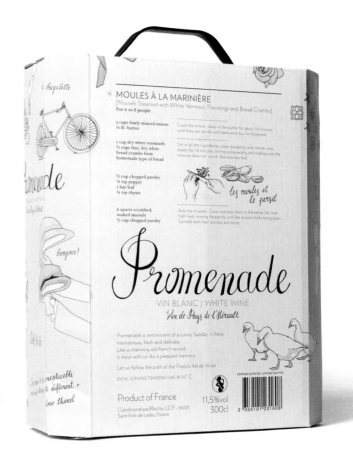

PROMENADE

Design: Henrik Olssön, Erika Barbieri
Company: Olssön Barbieri
Country: Norway
Category: Wine as bag-in-box

SILVER PENTAWARD 2011

VILLALTA RIPASSO

Design: Henrik Olssön, Erika Barbieri
Company: Olssön Barbieri
Country: Norway
Category: Wine as bag-in-box

BRONZE PENTAWARD 2011

DROP IN

Project Management: André Hindersson
Concept: Jacob Bergström
Art Direction: Ricky Tillblad
Illustration: Giorgio Cantú/Rithuset
Production Management: Therese Utterström
Production Design: Monica Holm
Company: Designkontoret Silver
Country: Sweden
Category: Wine as bag-in-box

SILVER PENTAWARD 2012

BERRY BROS. & RUDD
N°3

Design: David Beard, Bronwen Edwards,
Pip Dale, Keely Jackman
Company: Brandhouse
Country: UK
Category: Spirits

GOLD PENTAWARD 2011

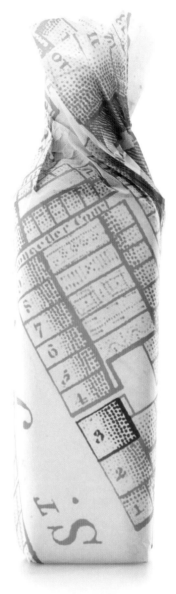

In an increasingly fashionable market, presentation is essential when seeking to create the ultimate luxury London Dry Gin for Britain's oldest wine and spirit merchant and supplier to the Queen. **N°3** is named after the address Berry Bros. & Rudd have occupied since the 17th century (3, St. James's), whilst in designing the complete branding identity the bottle form itself is based on early gin bottles shipped from Holland, with a tipped-in aged-metal key, wrapped in paper showing a 17th-century map of the location, all housed in a luxurious die-cut and embossed gift box. Every element of the identity is based on threes, from the trefoil in the top of the key to the key itself, the repeat of the logo round the foiling and the branded copy.

In einem zunehmend fashionaffinen Markt ist Präsentation der zentrale Punkt, wenn es um die Kreation des ultimativ luxuriösen London Dry Gin des ältesten Wein- und Spirituosenhändlers Großbritanniens und Hoflieferanten der Queen geht. **N°3** erhielt seinen Namen nach der Adresse, unter der die Berry Bros. & Rudd seit dem 17. Jahrhundert zu finden sind (3, St. James's). Beim Design der gesamten Markenidentität basiert die Flaschenform auf den ersten aus Holland importierten Ginflaschen. Darauf eingelassen ein Schlüssel aus verwittertem Metall, die Flasche selbst verpackt in Papier, das eine Karte aus dem 17. Jahrhundert mit erwähnter Adresse zeigt — alles in einem gestanzten und geprägten luxuriösen Geschenkkarton untergebracht. Jedes Element der Identität basiert auf der 3: das Dreiblatt oben im Schlüssel und auch der Schlüsselbart selbst, das sich wiederholende Logo der Deckelfolie und der Text.

Sur un marché de plus en plus régi par la mode, la présentation est essentielle lorsque l'on veut créer le London Dry Gin de luxe suprême pour le plus ancien marchand de vins et spiritueux de Grande-Bretagne et fournisseur de la reine. **N°3** tient son nom de l'adresse que Berry Bros. & Rudd occupe depuis le XVIIᵉ siècle (3, St. James's). En ce qui concerne l'identité de marque, la forme de la bouteille est basée sur les bouteilles de gin qui étaient importées de Hollande à l'époque, avec une clé en métal vieilli incrustée. Elle est emballée dans un papier qui porte une carte du XVIIᵉ siècle de l'endroit, le tout dans un coffret-cadeau luxueux avec des détails découpés et estampés. Chaque élément de l'identité est basé sur le nombre trois, depuis le trèfle de la clef jusqu'à la clef elle-même, la répétition du logo et du texte.

GREENHOOK GINSMITHS

Associated Design Direction: Fiona Scott
Direction: Gary Fortune-Smith
Company: Threebrand
Country: UK
Category: Spirits

GOLD PENTAWARD 2012

PAZO DE VALDOMIÑO

Design: Series Nemo team
Company: Series Nemo
Country: Spain
Category: Spirits

SILVER PENTAWARD 2011

BROOKLYN GIN

Creative Direction: Ron Wong
Design: Spring Design Partners staff
Strategy Direction: Susan Federspiel
Account Management: Jaime Niederman
Production Management: Arwen Kassebaum
Photography: Livio Dimulescu
Company: Spring Design Partners, Inc.
Country: USA
Category: Spirits

SILVER PENTAWARD 2011

COMPASS BOX WHISKY CO. GREAT KING STREET

Design: Kevin Shaw, Guy Pratt
Company: Stranger & Stranger
Country: USA
Category: Spirits

SILVER PENTAWARD 2012

REYKA

Creative Partnership: Kate Marlow
Design: Sarah Carr
Company: Here Design
Country: UK
Category: Spirits

BRONZE PENTAWARD 2011

CENTOPERCENTO
3.39

Design: Franco Vendramin
Company: Novaidea
Country: Italy
Category: Spirits

BRONZE PENTAWARD 2012

SKYY SPIRITS
EL ESPOLÓN

Executive Creative Direction: Nicolas Aparicio
Design: Anastasia Laksmi (senior designer),
Tony Rastatter
Company: Landor Associates
Country: USA
Category: Spirits

BRONZE PENTAWARD 2011

SX LATIN LIQUORS
SXSAMBA, SXCHA CHA CHA, SXCALYPSO

Design: David Knight (SX Latin Liquors)
Structure: Stuart Leslie, David Shor (4sight Inc.)
Graphics: Greg Stewart (Ingenuity Design)
Company: 4sight Inc.
Country: USA
Category: Spirits

BRONZE PENTAWARD 2011

CAVÔDA VODKA

Design: Linea design team
Company: Linea
Country: France
Category: Spirits

SILVER PENTAWARD 2012

CLAN CAMPBELL
4 ELEMENTS

Creative Direction: Raphael Riffe, Vincent Lebrun
Design: Julien Prabel
Company: The Brand Union, Paris
Country: France
Category: Spirits

BRONZE PENTAWARD 2012

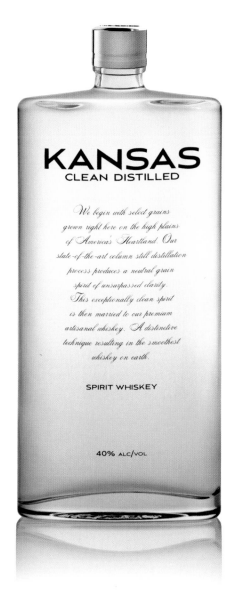

KANSAS CLEAN
DISTILLED WHISKEY

Creative Design: Paul Goldman
Bottle Design: O-I NA product
development team
Company: O-I
Country: USA
Category: Spirits

BRONZE PENTAWARD 2012

COCA-COLA
SUMMER 2010 PACKAGING

Creative Direction: David Turner, Bruce Duckworth, Sarah Moffat
Design: Emily Charette, Josh Michels
Design Direction: Pio Schunker, Vince Voron,
Frederic Kahn (Coca-Cola North America)
Company: Turner Duckworth, London & San Francisco
Country: USA
Category: Limited editions, limited series, collectors' items

GOLD PENTAWARD 2011

MILLERCOORS
COORS LIGHT

Creative Direction: Tosh Hall
Account Direction: J.P. Sabarots
Design Direction: Ryin Kobza
Client Management: Allison Hung, Adam Weiner
Design: Tosh Hall, Ryin Kobza, Erik Gomez,
Daniel D'Arcy
Typography: Ian Brignell
Illustration: Chris Mitchell
Photography: Timothy Hogan
Company: Landor Associates, San Francisco
Country: USA
Category: Limited editions,
limited series, collectors' items

BRONZE PENTAWARD 2012

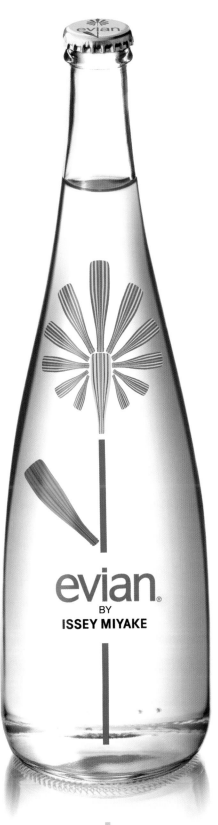

EVIAN
BY ISSEY MIYAKE

Design: Issey Miyake
Company: Danone Waters
Country: France
Category: Limited editions,
limited series, collectors' items

BRONZE PENTAWARD 2011

ORANGINA

Design: Fabrice Peltier
Company: P'référence
Country: France
Category: Limited editions,
limited series, collectors' items

SILVER PENTAWARD 2011

ORANGINA
MISS O

Design: Fabrice Peltier and team
Company: Diadeis
Country: France
Category: Limited editions,
limited series, collectors' items

BRONZE PENTAWARD 2012

BAILEYS
STEPHEN WEBSTER

Design Direction: Mary Lewis
Design: Silja Holm
Company: Lewis Moberly
Country: UK
Category: Limited editions,
limited series, collectors' items

GOLD PENTAWARD 2012

Baileys Limited Edition Russia was conceived to celebrate a collaboration between its owner Diageo and jeweller Stephen Webster. The stylish design for the brand's well-known Original Irish Cream is here based around an exquisite Webster creation layered in gold and sprinkled with diamonds. Since this Limited Edition was to sell at a considerable premium, it was possible to experiment with various decorative printing techniques and the use of precious metals. To achieve the optimum effect, proofing trials tested three "real gold" colours, white, yellow and red.

Die **Baileys** Limited Edition Russia wurde zur Würdigung der Kooperation zwischen dem Getränkekonzern Diageo, zu dem Baileys gehört, und dem Juwelier Stephen Webster auf den Markt gebracht. Das stilvolle Design für die bekannte Original Irish Cream der Marke basiert hier auf einer exquisiten Schöpfung von Webster und ist mit Gold beschichtet und mit Diamanten bestückt. Weil diese Limited Edition mit beträchtlichem Aufschlag angeboten werden sollte, konnte man mit verschiedenen dekorativen Drucktechniken experimentieren und wertvolle Metalle verwenden. Für den optimalen Effekt wurden in Tests drei Farben für den echten Goldeffekt getestet, also Weiß, Gelb und Rot.

L'édition limitée Russie de **Baileys** a été conçue pour célébrer la collaboration entre son propriétaire Diageo et le joaillier Stephen Webster. Le graphisme élégant de la célèbre Original Irish Cream est ici basé sur une création tout en délicatesse de Webster en à-plats dorés parsemés de diamants. Comme cette édition limitée devait être vendue à un prix considérablement plus élevé, il a été possible d'expérimenter différentes techniques d'impression décoratives avec les métaux précieux. Pour obtenir le meilleur effet, des essais ont été réalisés sur trois couleurs de « vrai or », blanc, jaune et rose.

HEINEKEN
DESPERADOS

Design: Stéphane Ricou,
The Brand Union creative team
Company: The Brand Union, Paris
Country: France
Category: Limited editions,
limited series, collectors' items

SILVER PENTAWARD 2011

HEINEKEN'S BIERBROUWERIJ MAATSCHAPPIJ

HEINEKEN
BIER.

GEBOTTELD DOOR

"N.V. DIE PORT VAN CLEVE"
v.h. Gebrs Hulscher

AMSTERDAM

AMSTERDAM
1873

ORIGINAL RECIPE

HEINEKEN LAGER BEER

DIPLOME D'HONNEUR AMSTERDAM 1883

TRADE ★ MARK

Heineken

MEDAILLE D'OR PARIS 1875
GRAND PRIX PARIS 1889

EST.

HORS CONCOURS MEMBRE DU JURY PARIS 1900

PREMIUM QUALITY

BREWED WITH PASSION FOR QUALITY

WORLD
2012

Heineken

Heineken

THE
FUTURE

AT HEINEKEN'S BREWERY

HEINEKEN'S LAGER BEER

HOPS CONCOURS MEMBRE DU JURY PARIS 1900

TRADE HBM MARK

GRAND PRIX PARIS 1889

HEINEKEN'S
BREWED IN HOLLAND

DIPLOME D'HONNEUR
Amsterdam 1883

AMSTERDAM-ROTTERDAM

MEDAILLE D'OR
PARIS 1875

CONTENTS FULL 16 FL. OZ.

NEW YORK
1933

**HEINEKEN
THE 2012 HEINEKEN
LIMITED EDITION GIFT-PACK**

Art Direction: Ramses Dingenouts (dBOD),
Pascal Duval (Iris Amsterdam)
Design: Janneke Visser (dBOD),
Glenn Doherty (Iris Amsterdam)
Copy: Ady Thomas (Iris Amsterdam)
Account Direction: Evelyn Hille (dBOD)
Project Management: Kim Hogenbirk (dBOD)
Account: Chris Friends, Matt Atherton (Iris Amsterdam)
Company: dBOD
Country: Netherlands
Category: Limited editions,
limited series, collectors' items

SILVER PENTAWARD 2012

HEINEKEN SPECIAL EDITION

Creative Direction: Yan Chiabai
Art Direction: Hélène Colin, Jérémy Vince, Wonki Kim
Account Management: Franck D'Andrea
Company: Raison Pure International
Country: France
Category: Limited editions,
limited series, collectors' items

BRONZE PENTAWARD 2011

BEEFEATER INSIDE LONDON

Design Direction: Stuart Humm
Company: Coley Porter Bell
Country: UK
Category: Limited editions, limited series, collectors' items

BRONZE PENTAWARD 2012

BRAHMA CARNAVAL

Design: Adrian Pierini
Company: Pierini Partners
Country: Argentina
Category: Limited editions, limited series, collectors' items

BRONZE PENTAWARD 2011

J&B
RARE EDITION 2011

Creative Direction: Laurent Hainaut,
Lorena Seminario
Design: Kristin Kohlmyer
Production Management: Linda Tseng
Marketing Direction: Steve White (GTME Diageo)
Design Management: Steve Honour (Diageo)
Company: Raison Pure International
Country: USA
Category: Limited editions,
limited series, collectors' items

SILVER PENTAWARD 2012

Coca-Cola
daftcoke.com
Coca-Cola
Inspired by
DAFT PUNK's
original bottle*
daftcoke.com
Coca-Cola
daftcoke.com
Coca-Cola
Inspired by
DAFT PUNK's
original bottle*
daftcoke.com

COCA-COLA CLUB COKE

Design Direction: Laurent Moreau,
Virgil Reboul (Pixelis)
Design: Brice Marchelidon (Pixelis)
Company: Coca-Cola France
Country: France
Category: Limited editions,
limited series, collectors' items
BRONZE PENTAWARD 2011

COCA-COLA
HISTORIC GLASS BOTTLES

Design: Mia Vojnic, Thomas Portenseigne,
Eric Kaddari, Argiris Dabanlis,
Daniela Zahariea, Saskia Goeteyns
Company: Coca-Cola Services
Country: Belgium
Category: Limited editions,
limited series, collectors' items
BRONZE PENTAWARD 2012

In 2010, Milwaukee-based Roundy's opened its flagship store, Mariano's Fresh Market, in the Chicago suburb of Arlington Heights. The in-store café would sell authentic Italian gelato and coffee, and this formed the basis for a full re-branding from the name itself to the graphics, which needed to suit the whole café environment, to staff uniforms and packaging. The name **Vero** ("true" in Italian) was chosen to represent the "True Taste of Italy". The logo, heart-shaped to show the passion behind the brand, works in conjunction with simple black and white photography, presenting a sophisticated yet warm design which also keeps a strong shelf presence.

2010 eröffnete die Supermarktkette Roundy's aus Milwaukee ihren Flagship-Store Mariano's Fresh Market im Vorort Arlington Heights von Chicago. Im ladeneigenen Café werden authentisches italienisches Eis und Kaffee angeboten. Das bildete die Basis für ein umfassendes Re-branding: Angefangen beim Namen bis hin zur Bildgebung musste alles zum Café-Ambiente passen, auch Verpackungen und Angestelltenbekleidung. Der Name **Vero** (italienisch „wahr") soll für den „wahren Geschmack Italiens" stehen. Das herzförmige Logo verdeutlicht die Leidenschaft hinter der Marke. Zusammen mit den einfachen Schwarz-Weiß-Fotos wird ein anspruchsvolles und doch warmes Design präsentiert, das auch im Regal starke Wirkung zeigt.

En 2010, Roundy's, entreprise basée à Milwaukee, a ouvert son flagship store, Mariano's Fresh Market, dans la banlieue de Chicago à Arlington Heights. Le café du magasin vend des glaces et du café italiens, ce qui a motivé la révision complète de l'image de la marque, depuis le nom lui-même jusqu'au graphisme, qu'il fallait adapter à l'environnement du café, jusqu'aux uniformes du personnel et à l'emballage. Le nom **Vero** (« vrai » en italien) a été choisi pour représenter « le vrai goût de l'Italie ». Le logo en forme de cœur, pour montrer la passion qui sous-tend la marque, s'allie à une simple photographie en noir et blanc pour présenter un graphisme sophistiqué mais chaleureux qui assure également une bonne visibilité dans les rayons.

VERO

Creative Direction: Michael Duffy
Design: Nick Wright, Derek Massey
Company: equator
Country: USA
Category: Distributors'/Retailers' own brands
GOLD PENTAWARD 2011

vero
SPECIALTY COFFEE

GROUND

True Espresso
Authentic

light | | | dark

12 OZ (340g)

DELHAIZE
365

Design: Nacho Lavernia, Alberto Cienfuegos
Company: Lavernia & Cienfuegos
Country: Spain
Category: Distributors'/Retailers' own brands

GOLD PENTAWARD 2012

Australian
White Wine · Chardonnay

Chardonnay
White Wine of California

Coteaux d'Aix en Provence
Appellation d'Origine Contrôlée

Bergerac
Appellation d'Origine Contrôlée

Côtes du Rhône
Appellation d'Origine Contrôlée

TESCO
SPANISH JUICES

Creative Direction: Simon Pemberton
Graphic Design: Iain Dobson
Company: P&W Design Consultants
Country: UK
Category: Distributors'/Retailers' own brands

SILVER PENTAWARD 2012

ICA
LACTOSE-FREE DAIRY PRODUCTS

Concept Direction: Ulf Berlin
Art Direction: Steven Webb, Niclas Öster
Illustration: Bo Lundberg
Design: Malin Mortensen
Production Management: Christine Schönborg
Production Design: Monica Holm
Company: Designkontoret Silver
Country: Sweden
Category: Distributors'/Retailers' own brands

SILVER PENTAWARD 2011

SAFEWAY
REFRESHE

Account Direction: Mark Hamilton
Creative Direction: Brian Lovell, Philip VanDusen
Design Direction: Sean Baca
Design: Mike Johnson, Seth Coronis
Company: Anthem Worldwide, San Francisco
Country: USA
Category: Distributors'/Retailers' own brands

BRONZE PENTAWARD 2011

**DELHAIZE
HOP BEERS**

Creative Direction: Patrick De Grande
Design: Jos Notteboom
Company: Quatre Mains
Country: Belgium
Category: Distributors'/Retailers' own brands

SILVER PENTAWARD 2012

FRESH & EASY
SPARKLING CIDERS

Design: Jamie Saunderson,
Simon Pemberton, Adrian Whiteford
Company: P&W Design Consultants
Country: UK
Category: Distributors'/Retailers' own brands

BRONZE PENTAWARD 2011

JUMBO

Creative Strategy/Concept: OD
Art Direction: Niels Alkema, Oscar van Geesbergen
Artwork: Niels Alkema
Company: OD
Country: Netherlands
Category: Distributors'/Retailers' own brands

BRONZE PENTAWARD 2011

For its 12th Christmas gift **Stranger & Stranger** chose to resurrect the glory days of absinthe and created a bespoke single batch of only 250 bottles. To produce the desired labelling they dug up some old-school printers who worked their craft die-stamping the inks and embossing pure cotton-fibre paper. "Absinthe, mother of all happiness, O infinite liquor, you glint in my glass green and pale like the eyes of the mistress I once loved..." (Gustave Kahn).

Stranger & Stranger entschieden sich, für ihr 12. Weihnachtsgeschenk die glorreichen Tage des Absinths wiederauferstehen zu lassen, und gaben eine maßgeschneiderte Einzelcharge mit 250 Flaschen in Auftrag. Für die gewünschte Etikettierung wurden ein paar altmodische Drucker mit Die-Stamping-Technik ausgegraben und so die reine Baumwollpapierfaser bedruckt. „Absinth, Mutter allen Glücks, oh endlose Spirituose, funkelst in meinem Glase grün und bleich wie die Augen jener, die ich einst liebte ..." (Gustave Kahn).

Pour son 12ᵉ cadeau de Noël, **Stranger & Stranger** a choisi de ressusciter la grande époque de l'absinthe et a créé un lot unique et sur mesure de seulement 250 bouteilles. Pour l'étiquette, l'entreprise est allée chercher des imprimeurs à l'ancienne qui estampent l'encre et travaillent en relief le papier en pures fibres de coton. « Absinthe, mère des bonheurs, ô liqueur infinie, tu miroites en mon verre comme les yeux verts et pâles de la maîtresse que jadis j'aimais ... » (Gustave Kahn).

CHRISTMAS ABSINTHE 2010

Design: Kevin Shaw
Company: Stranger & Stranger
Country: UK
Category: Self-promotion

GOLD PENTAWARD 2011
AVERY DENNISON PRIZE

STRANGER & STR

Nº 12

Nº 12

HANDMADE IN A SINGLE BATCH

AFTER ONE GLASS YOU SEE THINGS
AS YOU WISH THEY WERE.

STRANGER & STRANGER
LONDON · NEW YORK

CHRISTMAS
ABSINTHE

BEAUTIFUL, HIDEOUS, ANGELIC, DEVILISH.

ALL NATURAL AND ORGANIC

To reinforce its reputation for creativity and "out of the box" design solutions, **Ampro Design** developed this special holiday gift for its clients. With many of its international trade customers not being allowed to receive gifts for various reasons, this was neatly circumvented by asking: "who would be upset to receive a bottle of milk?" Of course, no client would expect to receive a gift like this, even more so when it was discovered that the bottle in fact contains a fine Pinot Noir.

Ampro Design schuf dieses ganz spezielle Urlaubsgeschenk für seine Kunden und bekräftigte damit die eigene Reputation für Kreativität und ideenreiches Querdenken in Designlösungen. Zwar dürfen viele internationale Kunden keine Geschenke annehmen, aber man umging dies geschickt durch die Frage „Wer hätte schon etwas dagegen, eine Milchflasche zu erhalten?". Natürlich hatte kein Kunde ein Präsent wie dieses erwartet. Für eine noch größere Überraschung sorgte der Inhalt: ein ausgezeichneter Pinot Noir.

Ampro Design a créé ce cadeau de Noël spécial pour ses clients dans le but de renforcer sa réputation basée sur la créativité et les solutions originales. Nombre de ses clients internationaux n'étant pas autorisés à recevoir des cadeaux, pour des raisons diverses, ce problème a été astucieusement contourné en posant la question : « quel problème pourrait-il y avoir à recevoir une bouteille de lait ? » Évidemment, aucun client ne pourrait s'attendre à recevoir un cadeau comme celui-ci. Surtout que la bouteille contient en fait un grand Pinot Noir.

Milk*

A milk bottle?
Yes, we know that you have never received this kind of gift. That's why we've packed our finest Pinot Noir in this bottle of milk.
Enjoy it!

ampro design

AMPRO DESIGN

Creative Direction: Irinel Ionescu
Design/3D: Alin Patru
Art Direction/Copy: Francesca Muresan
Production: Danubiu Birzu
Company: Ampro Design Consultants
Country: Romania
Category: Self-promotion

GOLD PENTAWARD 2012

STOCKING FILLER
CHRISTMAS WINE

Design: Tim Wilson, Ash Higginbotham,
Stephnie Croft, Gary Scott, Tim Warren
Company: Cowan Design
Country: Australia
Category: Self-promotion

GOLD PENTAWARD 2011

ALTERNATIVE

Creative Direction/Design: Tony Ibbotson
Design/Illustration: Tim Heyer
Company: The Creative Method
Country: Australia
Category: Self-promotion

SILVER PENTAWARD 2011

MUSEUM OF ART
OPENING MEMORIAL WHISKY

Creative Direction: Shizuko Ushijima
Art Direction: Yoshio Kato
Design: Satoshi Ito
Company: Suntory
Country: Japan
Category: Self-promotion

BRONZE PENTAWARD 2011

**STRANGER & STRANGER
SPIRIT NO. 13**

Design: Kevin Shaw, Cosimo Surace, Guy Pratt
Company: Stranger & Stranger
Country: USA
Category: Self-promotion

SILVER PENTAWARD 2012

Add a touch of colour to your cheeks this season, with a glass (or two) of mulled wine.

Warmer wishes from Designers Anonymous®

DESIGNERS ANONYMOUS CHRISTMAS GIFT

Design: Darren Barber
Creative Direction: Darren Barber,
Christian Eager
Company: Designers Anonymous
Country: UK
Category: Self-promotion

SILVER PENTAWARD 2012

CIULLA
HOLIDAY WINE

Design: Sam J. Ciulla
Company: Ciulla Assoc.
Country: USA
Category: Self-promotion

BRONZE PENTAWARD 2012

THANKSGIVING WINE
BOTTOMS UP

Creative Direction/Design: Stan Church
Company: Wallace Church, Inc.
Country: USA
Category: Self-promotion

BRONZE PENTAWARD 2011

FACTOR TRES
SUN, MOON & TRUTH

Creative Direction: Rodrigo Cordova
Illustration: Flavia Zorrilla Diafla
Account Direction: Malena Gutierrez
Design Direction: Angel Gonzalez
Company: Factor Tres
Country: Mexico
Category: Self-promotion

BRONZE PENTAWARD 2012

HAPPY NEW YEAR
2011 SPECIAL EDITION WINE

Art Direction: Arthur Schreiber
Design: Maria Ponomareva
Visualisation: Anastasia Chamkina
Company: StudioIN
Country: Russia
Category: Self-promotion

BRONZE PENTAWARD 2011

KEEP ON PLAYING TOGETHER
TA TE TI

Design: Cecilia Iuvaro, Silvia Keil,
Celia Grezzi, Agustina Romero, Julia Godoy
Company: Estudio Iuvaro
Country: Argentina
Category: Self-promotion

BRONZE PENTAWARD 2011

HOLY WATER LABEL

Design: Tony Ibbotson
Artwork: Greg Coles
Account Direction: Jess McElhone
Creative Direction: Tony Ibbotson
Illustration: Jason Paulos (The Drawing Book)
Company: The Creative Method
Country: Australia
Category: Self-promotion

BRONZE PENTAWARD 2012

CREATIVITY ON YOUR DOORSTEP

Design: Shaun Green
Company: SMR Creative
Country: UK
Category: Self-promotion

BRONZE PENTAWARD 2011

TEA IN A BOX

Design: Jure Leko
Company: The Grain
Country: Australia
Category: Self-promotion

BRONZE PENTAWARD 2011

With a more than 40-year track record in helping to rehydrate athletes and people in physical training, **Gatorade**'s specially designed formula is a proven sports drink. By taking the brand's identity and literally putting it in the hands of the consumer, a smart re-working of the initial "G" of the logo has produced a unique structural design with instant recognition and a team of walking (well, running) advertising boards for the drink. Whether you're an amateur, athlete or pro, now you can recover on the go.

Mit seiner über 40-jährigen Erfolgsbilanz als isotonisches Sportlergetränk hat sich die speziell entwickelte Formel von **Gatorade** wahrhaft bewährt. Die Identität der Marke wird dem Verbraucher buchstäblich in die Hand gegeben: Man setzte den Anfangsbuchstaben des Logos pfiffig in ein unverwechselbar strukturiertes Design um. So auffällig wird es sofort erkannt, und die Verbraucher laufen buchstäblich Werbung für das Getränk. Egal ob Sie Amateur, Athlet oder Profi sind — nun können Sie sich schon beim Laufen erholen.

Avec plus de 40 ans d'expérience dans le domaine de la réhydratation des athlètes, la formule spéciale de **Gatorade** a fait ses preuves dans le secteur des boissons de sport. Le « G » du logo a été astucieusement retravaillé : l'identité de la marque est littéralement mise entre les mains du consommateur. Ce design structurel donne une reconnaissance instantanée et produit une armée de panneaux publicitaires vivants pour la boisson. Que vous soyez amateur, athlète confirmé ou pro, vous pouvez maintenant reprendre des forces n'importe où, n'importe quand.

GATORADE ON THE GO

Design: Cadú Gomes
Company: Cadú Gomes Design
Country: UK
Category: Packaging concept (beverages)

GOLD PENTAWARD 2012

DAILY DOSE

Design: Ivan Pierre,
Laurent Lepoitevin, Damien Bourne
Company: Sidel
Country: France
Category: Packaging concept (beverages)

SILVER PENTAWARD 2012

NUDE
JR FLAVOURED MILK

Design: Andrianto Kwan (student)
School: Billy Blue College of Design
Country: Australia
Category: Packaging concept (beverages)

SILVER PENTAWARD 2012

CRAID
BEER FOR BUDDIES

Design: Merwyn Wijaya (student)
Project Supervision: Jeffrey Hong
School: Nanyang Technological University
Country: Singapore
Category: Packaging concept (beverages)

BRONZE PENTAWARD 2012

JAPAN STYLE GREEN TEA

Creative/Art Direction: Yoshio Kato (Suntory)
Design: Kotobuki Seihan Printing Co., Ltd.
Company: Kotobuki Seihan Printing Co., Ltd.
Country: Japan
Category: Packaging concept (beverages)

BRONZE PENTAWARD 2012

ONE-PIECE BOTTLE

Design: Rolf Hering
Company: Hering's Büro
Country: Germany
Category: Ecological concept (beverages)

BRONZE PENTAWARD 2012

REFILLABLE SPRAY

Design: Elen Provost (student)
School: L'École de Design Nantes Atlantique
Country: France
Category: Ecological concept (beverages)

BRONZE PENTAWARD 2012

EAT.

PARSNIP BEETROOT & CARROT CRISPS

100% NATURAL INGREDIENTS

40g ℮

Best of the category

Cereals

Dairy products

Spices, oils & sauces

Fish, meat, poultry

Fruit & vegetables

Soups, ready-to-eat dishes

food

Confectionery & sweet snacks

Savoury snacks

Pastry, biscuits, ice-cream, desserts, sugar

Food trends

Limited editions, limited series, collectors' items

Distributors'/Retailers' own brands

Packaging concept

Ecological concept

Essay by

TEDDY FALKENEK & SOFIA OLSSON

Teddy Falkenek, Brand Executive Officer at ICA, Sweden
Sofia Olsson, Brand Manager at ICA, Sweden

The evolution of the private label — from me-too to category hero

Private or own-labels are no longer about being the cheaper alternative in the category — the ambition should be to become the leader in the category! And the simple strategy to get there is to see each and every one of the products as a strong individual character player in the private-label team.

In Sweden, the general level of private labels is lower than in the rest of Europe, on average 15% among leading retailers. There is a strong perception among grocers that consumers think too many private-label products in stores reduces choice. ICA is the leading Swedish grocery retailer with a 48.8% market share (the number two, Coop, has 21.7% of the market) and launched its first private-label product back in 1922: coffee, under the brand name "Luxus". It was a huge success and paved the way for many subsequent launches. In 2000, the switch was made to a master brand strategy and all private-label products were henceforth launched under the ICA brand.

The secret of building private-label success is to work from the belief that every individual private-label product should add something to its category, rather than reducing consumer choice. And when it comes to packaging communication (we prefer to see it as "communication", not just as design), you need to let the product be the hero, not the brand. Another part of building private-label success is to keep constant track of consumers' needs and behaviour in order to be able to respond: don't be afraid to launch new ranges that address consumers' express needs.

Playing in the Premium League

When it comes to premium private, private labels really need to rethink. For the consumer, premium is no longer about luxury, but rather about origin and authenticity. This means that the traditional, horizontal approach to private-label range design won't do the trick, so the task is to develop packaging communication that can convey each separate product's unique story and values. For instance, when we developed the design for the re-launch of our premium range, we put ourselves in the shoes of small local producers and created a "home-designed" expression with simple packaging in rustic and tactile materials. Each product has its own unique expression, but all of the packaging designs are based on the same idea: using a no-frills visual style to communicate the story behind the product and highlight its producer.

Opposites attract — private-label marketing

When working with private-label products in different parts of the value chain, always think that you are building a unified whole. By re-launching two ranges simultaneously — our premium and value range — we were able not only to clarify the two different value propositions for consumers, but also to let the two opposites shine a light on the full range of our private-label goods. Some of our premium selection products doubled their sales and the negative trend for our low-price products turned into a 15% rise in sales.

Always remember: private-label products are one of the most important instruments we have for building brand equity. They create customer loyalty, make stores even more attractive and, perhaps most importantly, they are a representation of everything we stand for in the heart of the consumer's private sphere, their home, their daily lives. We believe packaging communication is the key to achieving this and so far, we seem to be right.

Die Evolution der Eigenmarken — vom „Ich auch" zum Helden der Kategorie

Bei Eigenmarken oder Handelsmarken geht es nicht länger darum, die preisgünstigere Alternative einer Kategorie zu sein — man sollte so ambitioniert sein, zum Anführer derselben zu werden! Die einfache Strategie lautet, jedes einzelne Produkt als einen starken, charaktervollen Einzelspieler im Team der Eigenmarke zu betrachten.

In Schweden ist der allgemeine Anteil von Eigenmarken mit durchschnittlich 15 % bei führenden Einzelhändlern geringer als im restlichen Europa. Lebensmittelhändler gehen von der Annahme des Verbrauchers aus, dass die Auswahl geschmälert werde, wenn es in den Läden zu viele Produkte als Eigenmarken gäbe. ICA ist der führende schwedische Lebensmittelhändler mit einem Marktanteil von 48,8 % (die Nummer zwei, Coop, verfügt über 21,7 %). ICA brachte 1922 das erste Produkt als Eigenmarke auf den Markt: eine Kaffeesorte mit Markennamen „Luxus". Deren Riesenerfolg ebnete den Weg für viele nachfolgende Markteinführungen. 2000 wechselte man zur Strategie einer Hauptmarke, und demzufolge wurden alle Eigenmarken unter dem Titel ICA angeboten.

Das Erfolgsgeheimnis einer Eigenmarke besteht darin, den Verbraucher davon zu überzeugen, dass es seine Auswahlmöglichkeit erweitert anstatt verringert. Und wenn es um Verpackungskommunikation geht (wir betrachten Verpackung als „Kommunikation" und nicht einfach als Design), müssen Sie das *Produkt* und nicht die Marke zum Helden werden lassen. Außerdem gehört es zum Erfolgsaufbau, ständig auf Ansprüche und Verhalten der Kunden zu achten, um reagieren zu können: Haben Sie keine Angst, neue Produktpaletten herauszubringen, die sich an die vom Verbraucher benannten Bedürfnisse richten.

Die Teilnahme an der Premium-Liga

Hier müssen Eigenmarken wirklich umdenken. Für den Verbraucher geht es bei der Premium-Liga, also dem oberen Preissegment, nicht mehr nur um Luxus, sondern um Ursprung und Authentizität. Das bedeutet, für die Produktpalette der Eigenmarken reicht der traditionelle horizontale Ansatz beim Design nicht mehr. Also stellt sich die Aufgabe, eine Verpackungskommunikation zu entwickeln, die für jedes einzelne Produkt die jeweils eigene Geschichte und deren Werte vermittelt. Als wir beispielsweise den Relaunch unserer Premium-Produktpalette designt haben, versetzten wir uns in die Perspektive der kleinen, lokalen Produzenten: Wir schufen mit schlichter Verpackung sowie rustikalen und griffig-spannenden Materialien eine Ausdrucksmöglichkeit, die wie „zu Hause gestaltet" wirkte. Jedes Produkt bekam seine eigene Ausprägung, doch die Verpackungsdesigns insgesamt basierten auf dem gleichen Konzept: Wir wollten einen visuellen Stil ohne Schnickschnack, der die dem Produkt zugrunde liegende Story kommuniziert und dessen Produzenten hervorhebt.

Gegensätze ziehen sich an — Marketing für Eigenmarken

Wenn man mit Eigenmarkenprodukten an verschiedenen Stellen der Wertschöpfungskette arbeitet, sollte man stets daran denken, ein vereinheitlichtes Ganzes zu schaffen. Wir brachten zeitgleich zwei Produktpaletten (*Premium* und *Value*) erneut auf den Markt. So konnten wir verdeutlichen, wie die beiden unterschiedlichen Wertversprechen für den Konsumenten lauteten. Die Gegensätze beider Paletten beleuchteten auch die volle Bandbreite unseres Eigenmarkenangebotes. Manche unserer Produkte aus der Premium-Auswahl verdoppelten ihre Verkaufszahlen, und der negative Trend für unsere Niedrigpreisprodukte verwandelte sich in um 15 % erhöhte Verkaufszahlen.

Denken Sie stets daran: Eigenmarkenprodukte gehören zu den wichtigsten Instrumenten, die uns zum Aufbau des Markenwerts zur Verfügung stehen. Sie schaffen die Loyalität der Kunden, machen die Geschäfte attraktiver und — vielleicht am wichtigsten — repräsentieren alles, womit wir im Kern der Privatsphäre unserer Verbraucher, in ihrem Zuhause und ihrem Alltag, stehen. Wir glauben daran, dass Verpackungskommunikation der Schlüssel zu diesem Ziel ist, und bislang scheinen wir damit richtig zu liegen.

Essay by

TEDDY FALKENEK & SOFIA OLSSON

L'évolution de la marque de distributeur — du suivisme au vedettariat

Pour les marques de distributeur, la question n'est plus d'être l'option la moins chère de leur catégorie. Elles devraient ambitionner de devenir la meilleure option ! Et pour y arriver, la stratégie la plus simple est de considérer chaque produit comme un acteur qui joue un rôle solide et bien défini dans l'équipe de la marque de distributeur.

En Suède, le niveau général des marques de distributeur est plus faible que dans le reste de l'Europe, environ 15 % chez les principaux distributeurs. D'après les commerçants, un trop grand nombre de produits de marque de distributeur suggère aux consommateurs que le choix est plus restreint. ICA est le plus grand distributeur suédois dans le domaine de l'alimentation, avec une part de marché de 48,8 % (le numéro deux, Coop, occupe 21,7 % du marché), et a lancé le premier produit de sa propre marque en 1922 : du café, sous le nom « Luxus ». Ce produit a remporté un succès énorme, et a ouvert la voie à de nombreux autres lancements. En 2000, il a été décidé de passer à une stratégie de marque globale et tous les produits maison ont depuis lors été lancés sous la marque ICA.

Pour les marques de distributeur, le secret du succès est de travailler en partant de la conviction que chaque produit de la marque en question doit apporter quelque chose à sa catégorie, plutôt que restreindre les choix du consommateur. Et en ce qui concerne la communication sur les emballages (nous préférons considérer qu'il s'agit de « communication », et pas seulement de design), il faut que le produit, et non la marque, prenne le devant de la scène. Une autre grande composante du succès des marques de distributeur est de toujours suivre l'évolution des besoins et des comportements des consommateurs afin d'être en mesure d'y répondre : n'hésitez pas à lancer de nouvelles gammes qui correspondent aux besoins que les consommateurs expriment.

Jouer dans la cour des grands

En ce qui concerne le haut de gamme, les marques de distributeurs doivent vraiment se remettre en question. Pour le consommateur, le haut de gamme n'est plus une question de luxe, mais plutôt une question d'origine et d'authenticité. Cela veut dire que la démarche horizontale traditionnellement adoptée dans la conception des gammes des marques de distributeur n'est plus valide. Il faut mettre au point des emballages qui communiquent l'histoire personnelle et les valeurs de chaque produit. Par exemple, lorsque nous avons mis au point la conception pour le relancement de notre ligne haut de gamme, nous avons adopté le point de vue des petits producteurs locaux et avons créé un style « fait maison » avec un emballage simple fabriqué dans des matériaux rustiques et tactiles. Chaque produit est doté de sa propre voix unique, mais tous les emballages sont basés sur la même idée : un style visuel sans fioritures pour communiquer l'histoire du produit et mettre en valeur son producteur.

Les contraires s'attirent — le marketing des marques de distributeur

Lorsque vous travaillez sur des produits de marque de distributeur à différents points de la chaîne de valeur, gardez toujours à l'esprit que vous voulez construire un ensemble unifié. En relançant deux lignes simultanément — notre ligne haut de gamme et notre ligne bon marché — nous avons pu non seulement clarifier les deux propositions distinctes faites aux consommateurs en termes de valeur, mais aussi nous servir de ces deux contraires pour attirer l'attention sur toute notre gamme de produits de marque de distributeur. Certains de nos produits haut de gamme ont vu leurs ventes doubler, et la tendance négative de nos produits bon marché s'est transformée en une augmentation des ventes de 15 %.

N'oubliez pas : les produits de marque de distributeur sont l'un des meilleurs instruments que nous ayons pour construire le capital de la marque. Ils fidélisent les consommateurs, rendent les magasins encore plus attrayants et, surtout, ils incarnent tout ce que nous représentons au cœur de la sphère privée du consommateur, son foyer, sa vie quotidienne. Nous pensons que la communication à travers l'emballage est la clé de ce processus et, pour l'instant, il semble que nous ayons raison.

PANDA LIQUORICE

Design: David Pearman, Hayley Bishop
Company: Cowan Design
Country: UK
Category: Best of the category food

PLATINUM PENTAWARD 2011

The **Panda** brand was established in Finland in 1927 and has been available in the UK for 25 years, chiefly in health food outlets. To gain broader appeal in a wider market two traditional soft liquorice varieties were launched, Original Black and Raspberry. To stand out from other 'traditional' brands and the more mainstream sweetie players, the image of the panda bear was developed to become the face of the brand — conveying a sense of familiarity and nostalgia as well as softness through clear design and distinctive packaging.

Die Marke **Panda**, 1927 in Finnland eingeführt, ist seit 25 Jahren in Großbritannien vor allem in Reformhäusern erhältlich. Um einen größeren Markt zu erreichen, wurden zwei traditionelle Geschmacksrichtungen der Weichlakritze eingeführt: Original Black und Raspberry. Damit man sich von anderen „traditionellen" Marken und etablierten Süßwaren abheben konnte, wurde der Pandabär als Gesicht der Marke entwickelt. Klares Design und eine markante Verpackung vermitteln das Gefühl von Vertrautheit und Nostalgie, aber auch von Weichheit.

La marque **Panda** est née en Finlande en 1927 et est disponible au Royaume-Uni depuis 25 ans, principalement dans les magasins de produits diététiques. Pour attirer une clientèle plus large sur un marché plus étendu, deux variétés traditionnelles de réglisse à mâcher ont été lancées, Original Black et Raspberry (framboise). Pour se distinguer des autres marques « traditionnelles » et des acteurs plus connus de la confiserie, l'image du panda a été développée pour donner un visage à la marque. Elle véhicule un sentiment de familiarité, de nostalgie et de douceur grâce à un graphisme clair et à un emballage original.

The introduction of a new brand of eggs into the market also offered through its design an opportunity to help raise awareness for the Help for Heroes charity. By calling them **Eggs for Soldiers** the familiar way of eating boiled eggs with toast soldiers also referred to the charitable intent. Strong use of colouring helps with identification, along with the weave of military uniforms, while the photographic image doubles in its suggestion of a medal. After a successful launch in May 2011, the brand is now worth £2.3m and has so far donated £250,000 to its charity.

Bei der Lancierung dieser neuen Eiermarke sollte über das Design auf die Charity-Organisation Help for Heroes aufmerksam gemacht werden. Die Bezeichnung **Eggs for Soldiers** spielt einerseits auf den typisch englischen Snack an, bei dem man Toaststifte in ein weichgekochtes Ei dippt (die sogenannten Toast Soldiers), zugleich wird für den karitativen Zweck geworben. Die kraftvolle Farbgebung und die militärisch anmutende Gewebeart verstärken die Identifikation, die Abbildung des Eis spielt deutlich auf militärische Orden an. Nach dem erfolgreichen Start im Mai 2011 ist die Marke nun 2,3 Millionen Pfund wert und hat bisher 250.000 Pfund an Spenden eingebracht.

Le lancement d'une nouvelle marque d'œufs a également été l'occasion, à travers la conception de son emballage, de contribuer à faire connaître l'organisation caritative Help for Heroes. Le nom **Eggs for Soldiers** fait référence aux « mouillettes » trempées dans l'oeuf bouilli, appelées « soldiers » en Angleterre, fait également référence à cette cause charitable. La couleur très présente facilite l'identification, tout comme la trame de toile militaire, tandis que la photographie de l'œuf évoque également une médaille. Après un lancement réussi en mai 2011, la marque vaut aujourd'hui 2,3 M £, et a pour l'instant reversé 250 000 £ à la cause qu'elle défend.

EGGS FOR SOLDIERS

Creative Direction: Moyra Casey
Design: Jon Vallance
Company: Springetts Brand Design Consultants
Country: UK
Category: Best of the category food

PLATINUM PENTAWARD 2012

Julia Barclay's **Love 2 Bake** kit combines the finest pre-measured ingredients to make baking as simple as possible. To express this quality in the product and at the same time to promote it as a premium brand a design was developed that was "blissfully simple" just like the ingredients. By taking a mirror-image of the number 2, the new heart-shaped space in the middle of the logo links the brand name with the simplicity of starting with just two ingredients while also reflecting the warmth of the brand's personality. Using traditional techniques, the new logo and its typeface is letter-pressed from hand-drawn calligraphy on to uncoated paper, before each pack is hand-sealed to create a beautifully crafted design.

Das **Love 2 Bake** Kit von Julia Barclay kombiniert nur allerbeste abgemessene Zutaten, damit das Backen so einfach wie möglich wird. Um die Qualität dieses Produkts zu verdeutlichen und es gleichzeitig als Premiummarke zu bewerben, wurde ein Design entwickelt, das so „herrlich einfach" wie die Zutaten ist. Durch Spiegelung der Zahl 2 entsteht eine Herzform in der Mitte des Logos. Der Markenname verlinkt so zwei Botschaften: die Einfachheit — nur zwei Zutaten sind nötig, um loszulegen — und die Liebenswürdigkeit der Markenpersönlichkeit. Mittels traditioneller Techniken werden das neue Logo und der Text aus einer handgemalten Kalligrafie auf unbeschichtetes Papier geprägt. Anschließend wird jede Packung von Hand versiegelt — so entsteht wunderschönes handgemachtes Design.

Le kit **Love 2 Bake** de Julia Barclay contient des ingrédients prémesurés de la meilleure qualité afin que réaliser un gâteau soit aussi simple que possible. Pour exprimer cette idée de qualité tout en mettant en valeur le positionnement haut de gamme de la marque, l'emballage est « d'une simplicité suprême », tout comme les ingrédients. Avec l'image inversée du chiffre 2, l'espace en forme de coeur associe la marque à la simplicité pour commencer un gâteau avec juste deux ingrédients, tout en reflétant la personnalité chaleureuse de la marque. Le nouveau logo et sa police de caractères, dessinés à la main, sont imprimés à la presse typographique sur du papier brut, puis chaque paquet est fermé à la main pour obtenir le superbe résultat final.

LOVE 2 BAKE

Design Direction: Asa Cook
Design: Casey Sampson
Lettering: Frederick Marns
Company: Design Bridge
Country: UK
Category: Cereals

GOLD PENTAWARD 2012

RICE GARDEN EIGHT TREASURES OF HAPPINESS

Design: Victor Branding creative team
Company: Victor Branding Design Corp.
Country: Taiwan
Category: Cereals

GOLD PENTAWARD 2011

Eight Treasures of Happiness was the theme chosen for the packaging for this range of different flavoured rice, personified through eight different experts in the business of rice production: grain-polisher, quality-controller, supervisor for organic standards, environmental protection officer, simple farmer, and so on. With these eight all contributing their expertise to the process, excellent quality rice is the result, delivering the taste of happiness to consumers. To bring this process home each package was personalised with one of the key production personnel, using cartoon-style illustrations for the design.

Die **Acht Schätze des Glücks** waren das auserwählte Thema für die Verpackungen dieser Produktpalette Reis der verschiedenen Geschmacksrichtungen, personifiziert durch acht Experten der Reisproduktion: den Entspelzer, den Qualitätskontrolleur, den Kontrolleur für die organischen Standards, den Umweltschutzbeamten, den einfachen Bauern usw. Weil alle acht ihr Fachwissen in den Prozess einbringen, entsteht ein hervorragender Qualitätsreis und schenkt den Konsumenten den „Geschmack des Glücks". Um diesen auch bis ins eigene Heim spürbar zu machen, wurden alle Packungen durch Illustrationen im Cartoonstil von Schlüsselfiguren der Produktion personalisiert.

Huit trésors du bonheur est le thème choisi pour l'emballage de cette gamme de riz parfumé, personnifiée par huit experts de la production du riz : polisseur de grain, contrôleur qualité, superviseur des normes biologiques, agent de protection de l'environnement, simple fermier, etc. Avec l'expertise de ces huit métiers, le résultat est un riz d'excellente qualité qui a le goût du bonheur. Pour communiquer cette idée, chaque paquet a été personnalisé avec l'un de ces métiers clés de la production à l'aide d'illustrations dans un style proche de celui des dessins animés.

JIN MAI LANG
LANDSCAPE VERMICELLI

Design: Xiaohui Xi
Company: CAC 110 Creativity Advertising Co., Ltd.
Country: China
Category: Cereals

SILVER PENTAWARD 2011

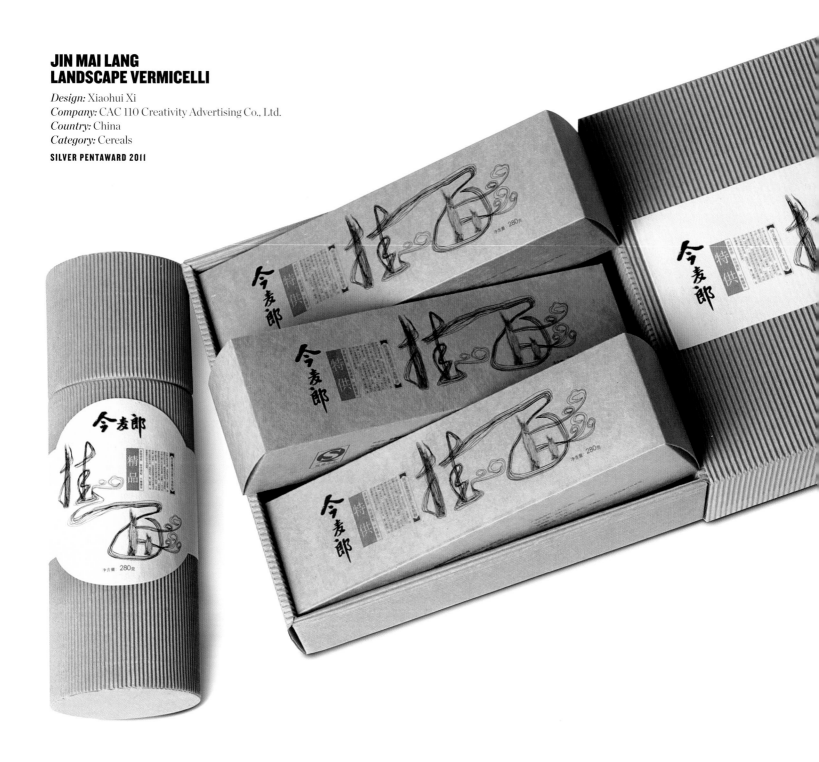

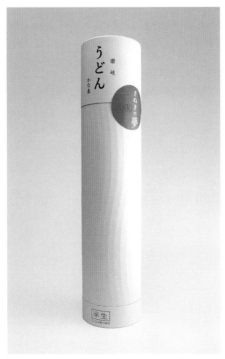

KANAIZUMI — SANUKI UDON
SANUKI-NO-YUME 2000

Design: Jun Kuroyanagi
Box Manufacturing: Akiyoshi Yamada
Project Management: Kosuke Kuwabara
Country: Japan
Category: Cereals

SILVER PENTAWARD 2011

GRAN CEREALE

Creative Direction: Gianni Tozzi,
Chiara Sozzi Pomati
Design: Marta Mapelli
Company: CMGRP Italia/FutureBrand
Country: Italy
Category: Cereals

SILVER PENTAWARD 2012

NATURE'S PATH
LOVE CRUNCH

Creative Direction: Stan Church
Design Direction: Kevin Sams
Design: Ithinand Tubkam
Company: Wallace Church, Inc.
Country: USA
Category: Cereals

SILVER PENTAWARD 2012

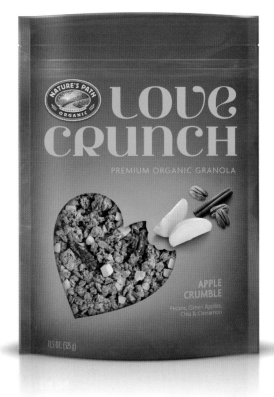

ALLINSON BREAD

Creative Direction: Alex Durbridge
Creative Partnership: Derek Johnston
Design: Stephen Sheffield, Dan Kimmins
Company: Family (and friends)
Country: UK
Category: Cereals

BRONZE PENTAWARD 2012

QUAKER RICE CAKES

Design Direction: Jose Parado
Company: Haugaard Creative Group
Country: USA
Category: Cereals

BRONZE PENTAWARD 2012

SANITARIUM
LIGHT 'N' TASTY

Management Direction: Chris Chong
Account Direction: Kate Imlach
Creative Direction: Catherine Baker
Design: Rebecca Charlton
Production: Nicola Kearns
Photography: Charlie Smith
Company: Redcactus Design
Country: New Zealand
Category: Cereals

BRONZE PENTAWARD 2012

The pasteurised milk produced at the Abe dairy farm, in **Aso** in Kumamoto, is delivered without any involvement from middlemen, with the milk going directly from the farm to the consumer. It is delivered daily, with the empty bottles being collected, so to distinguish it the design concentrates on the bottle itself — it has a simple, classic shape, easily identifiable, but made individual by the red stripe design which forms a red cross when the bottle is empty!

Die pasteurisierte Milch aus dem Abe-Milchbetrieb der Stadt **Aso** in der Präfektur Kumamoto gelangt ohne Zwischenhandel direkt vom Bauernhof zum Konsumenten. Die Milchflaschen werden täglich ausgeliefert und geleert abgeholt. Um beides zu unterscheiden, konzentriert sich das Design auf die Flasche selbst: Sie hat eine einfache, klassische Form und ist leicht identifizierbar — aber das Design mit den roten Balken, die bei leerer Flasche zu einem roten Kreuz werden, macht sie individuell.

Le lait pasteurisé produit à la laiterie Abe, à **Aso**, dans la préfecture de Kumamoto, est livré sans aucun intermédiaire, directement de la ferme au consommateur. Il est livré chaque jour et les bouteilles sont consignées. Afin de mieux les distinguer, le concept est centré sur la bouteille elle-même : sa forme simple et classique est facilement reconnaissable, et individualisée grâce aux bandes rouges qui forment une croix lorsqu'elle est vide !

MLK
ORGANIC DAIRY RANGE

Creative Direction: Alexey Fadeev
Strategic Planning Direction: Inna Likhacheva
Art Direction: Aram Mirzoyants, Vadim Briksin
Company: Depot WPF
Country: Russia
Category: Dairy products

SILVER PENTAWARD 2011

ASO MILK

Design: Hideaki Iwai
Company: Ohesono Design Works
Country: Japan
Category: Dairy products

GOLD PENTAWARD 2011

KALATHAKI LEMNOS

Creative Direction: Yiannis Charalambopoulos,
Alexis Nikou, Vaggelis Liakos
Photography: Kostas Pappas
Company: Beetroot Design Group
Country: Greece
Category: Dairy products

SILVER PENTAWARD 2011

This new premium brand of speciality and rare-breed eggs was launched with the aim of making this niche category more accessible to mainstream shoppers. Its cheeky name, **Posh Birds**, suits its position as best in class, rather than a class above. The choice of wording on the box is intended to drive consumption amongst those unused to speciality eggs, with tips such as duck eggs being great for baking. Launched early in 2012, the range comprises 6 Free Range Duck Eggs, 12 Free to Fly Quail Eggs, 6 Speciality Brown Hen Eggs and 6 Speciality Blue Hen Eggs.

Diese neue Premiummarke für besondere Eier seltener Rassen will Mainstreamkunden ein Nischenprodukt zugänglicher machen. Der freche Name **Posh Birds** passt zur Positionierung als Beste ihrer Klasse, anstatt sich auf eine Stufe darüber zu stellen. Die Wortwahl auf den Verpackungstexten soll all jene zum Kauf motivieren, die keine Eierspezialitäten gewöhnt sind, z.B. durch den Tipp, wie hervorragend sich Enteneier zum Backen eignen. Zu der Anfang 2012 erschienenen Produktpalette gehören sechs Freiland-Enteneier, zwölf Eier von frei fliegenden Wachteln, sechs Eierspezialitäten von Brown-Hen-Eiern und sechs von Blue-Hen-Eiern.

Cette nouvelle marque premium d'oeufs spéciaux a été lancée afin de rendre cette catégorie « de niche » plus accessible à un plus large public de consommateurs. Son nom, **Posh Birds** (« Oiseaux chics »), le positionne comme le meilleur plutôt que le plus cher. Les textes figurant sur l'emballage encouragent l'utilisation de ces oeufs inhabituels, avec par exemple des conseils sur l'emploi des œufs de canard dans la pâtisserie. Lancée au début de l'année 2012, la gamme comprend 6 œufs de canards en liberté, 12 œufs de cailles en liberté, 6 œufs de poule marron et 6 œufs de poules bleues.

POSH BIRDS

Creative Direction: Moyra Casey
Design: Chris McDonald, Kelly Bennett, Karina Monger
Company: Springetts Brand Design Consultants
Country: UK
Category: Dairy products

GOLD PENTAWARD 2012

THE COLLECTIVE

Design: Karl O'Connell, Bella Akroyd
Company: pHd3 Limited
Country: New Zealand
Category: Dairy products

BRONZE PENTAWARD 2011

ZUIVELRIJCK MILK

Design: Rene Gruijs
Company: Brandnew
Country: Netherlands
Category: Dairy products

BRONZE PENTAWARD 2012

NESTLÉ BABYNES

Creative Direction: Béatrice Mariotti
Art Direction: Frédérique Lyard
Account Direction: Clémentine Segard,
Justine Guicherd
Company: Carré Noir
Country: France
Category: Dairy products

SILVER PENTAWARD 2012

DEUNDEUNHAN BEANS

Design: Choi Jin-kyu, Lee Sang-hee,
Heo In-sung, Lee you-na, Back Shin-young
Company: Woongjin Foods
Country: South Korea
Category: Dairy products

SILVER PENTAWARD 2012

PURE DAIRY FREE

Creative Direction: Alex Durbridge
Copy Text: Derek Johnston
Design: Malcolm Phipps
Photography: Howard Shooter
Company: Family (and friends)
Country: UK
Category: Dairy products

BRONZE PENTAWARD 2011

Rustic Apple Crumble
The ultimate heartwarming pudding.

For the full recipe visit
puredairyfree.co.uk

Mediterranean Herb Scones
A delicious twist on a traditional favourite.

For the full recipe visit
puredairyfree.co.uk

Chunky Choc Nut Cookies
An irresistably perfect teatime treat.

For the full recipe visit
puredairyfree.co.uk

MAMMOTH SUPPLY CO.

Creative Direction: Lucien Law
Art Direction/Design: Noah Butcher
Illustration: Mat Hunkin
Contributing Design: George Goldsack
Company: Shine Limited
Country: New Zealand
Category: Dairy products

BRONZE PENTAWARD 2011

**YOPLAIT
NATURLIG LETT**

Creative Direction: Morten Throndsen
Design: Sandro Kvernmo
Company: Strømme Throndsen Design
Country: Norway
Category: Dairy products

SILVER PENTAWARD 2012

ONKEN

Design Direction: Asa Cook
Design: Sapphire Wosko
Project Implementation: David Benjamin
Client Direction: Rebecca Wood
Client Management: Rachel Gotts
Company: Design Bridge
Country: UK
Category: Dairy products

BRONZE PENTAWARD 2012

KSW LATTE
1.5 % / 3.5 %

Design: Sándor Suha
Company: KSW Latte Kft
Country: Hungary
Category: Dairy products

BRONZE PENTAWARD 2012

New Zealand-born **Bob** makes alcoholic bitters for culinary usage, employing single ingredients that add specific flavour to drinks, such as tangerine or lavender. To establish a strong identity for the range, interest was stirred by telling a brand story to customers, both existing and new. Bob's Kiwi roots were then made central to the graphic identity used on the bottles and all associated material. A single label design that could be used on all variants lowered production costs and reduced waste, and to make a virtue of Bob's craft and personal touch, each label left space for a hand-written batch number and bottling date with the flavour's name being added using a custom rubber stamp.

Bob aus Neuseeland stellt Bitterspirituosen her. Die Zutaten verleihen den Drinks einen bestimmten Geschmack, etwa Mandarine oder Lavendel. Um eine starke Produktgruppenidentität zu etablieren, reizt man das Interesse der Kunden und erzählt ihnen alte und auch neue Geschichten über die Marke. Bobs „Kiwi"-Wurzeln wurden ins Zentrum der Grafik bei den Flaschen und allen dazugehörigen Materialien gerückt. Die Gestaltung mit nur einem Etikett wurde für alle Varianten verwendet und senkte sowohl Produktionskosten als auch Abfallmenge. Um das Handgemachte und die persönliche Note bei Bob wirkungsvoll herauszustellen, lässt jedes Etikett Platz für eine handgeschriebene Chargennummer und das Abfülldatum. Der Name der Geschmacksvariante wird mit einem handelsüblichen Stempel aufgebracht.

Le Néozélandais **Bob** fait des bitters alcoolisés à usage culinaire, et leur ajoute un ingrédient unique pour parfumer les boissons, comme la mandarine ou la lavande. L'idée de raconter l'histoire de la marque aux clients, habituels et nouveaux venus, a retenu l'intérêt pour donner à la gamme une identité forte. Les racines néozélandaises de Bob ont donc pris le devant de la scène dans l'identité graphique utilisée sur les flacons et sur tous les supports associés. C'est la même étiquette qui est utilisée sur toutes les variantes, ce qui permet de réduire les coûts de production, et pour ajouter une touche artisanale et personnelle, chaque étiquette laisse assez d'espace pour écrire à la main le numéro de lot et la date de mise en bouteille. Le nom du parfum est ajouté à l'aide d'un tampon encreur.

BOB'S BITTERS

Design Direction/Creative Direction: Dave Thomson
Design: John Hughes, Digby Gall
Account Direction: Sarah Wade
Management Direction: Elliot Wilson
Company: Elmwood
Country: UK
Category: Spices, oils & sauces
GOLD PENTAWARD 2011

ZEST
PASTA SAUCES

Design/Creative Direction:
Christian Eager, Darren Barber
Company: Designers Anonymous
Country: UK
Category: Spices, oils & sauces
BRONZE PENTAWARD 2012

HEINZ FIRST HARVEST

Creative Direction: Claire Parker
Design Direction: Zayne Dagher
Design: Joeri Florin (senior), Wouter Friso
Client Management: Sandy Beltman
Client Services Direction: Bas van Herten
Company: Design Bridge, Amsterdam
Country: Netherlands
Category: Spices, oils & sauces
SILVER PENTAWARD 2012

KRAFT FOODS
MIRACLE WHIP

Creative Direction: David Turner, Bruce Duckworth
Design Direction: Sarah Moffat
Design: Tanawat Pisanuwongse
Lettering: David Bateman
Production: Craig Snelgrove
Company: Turner Duckworth, London & San Francisco
Country: USA
Category: Spices, oils & sauces

SILVER PENTAWARD 2011

MARZETTI
SIMPLY DRESSED

Design: Geralyn Curtis
Company: The Chesapeake Group
Country: USA
Category: Spices, oils & sauces

SILVER PENTAWARD 2011

KRAFT FOODS
MAYO SANDWICH SHOP

Creative Direction: David Turner,
Bruce Duckworth
Design Direction: Sarah Moffat
Design: Tanawat Pisanuwongse
Photography: Scott Peterson
Lettering: Dan Becker
Production: Craig Snelgrove
Company: Turner Duckworth,
London & San Francisco
Country: USA
Category: Spices, oils & sauces

BRONZE PENTAWARD 2011

LIMA
SOYA DRESSINGS

Creative Direction: Patrick De Grande
Art Direction: Jurgen Huughe
Design: Hendrik Colenbier
Food Styling: Els Goethals
Photography: Quatre Etoiles
Company: Quatre Mains
Country: Belgium
Category: Spices, oils & sauces

BRONZE PENTAWARD 2012

**TARARUA
VOILÁ**

Management Direction: Chris Chong
Account Direction: Kristen Marks
Creative Direction: Catherine Baker
Design: Margaux Shand
Production: Nicola Kearns
Photography: Shaun Cato-Symonds
Company: Redcactus Design
Country: New Zealand
Category: Spices, oils & sauces

BRONZE PENTAWARD 2012

AUGUSTE

Creative Direction: Patrick De Grande
Design: Kobe De Keyzer
Company: Quatre Mains
Country: Belgium
Category: Spices, oils & sauces

BRONZE PENTAWARD 2012

ROYAL GREEN
FLAVOURED COCONUT OIL

Design: Joep Janssen
Company: PROUDdesign
Country: Netherlands
Category: Spices, oils & sauces

BRONZE PENTAWARD 2011

Jens Eide, a well-known butcher's in Agder, Norway, offers high-quality meat and sausages but lacked the means to communicate this added value to the consumer and so missed out on doing better business. To convey this sense of quality the shop was re-branded as a specialist outlet, offering expert skills and knowledge, and a wide variety of meat products. The design was based on the values of competence, quality and local pride and resulted in a simple yet powerful identity that stated "Butcher handcraft from the heart of Agder".

Jens Eide aus dem norwegischen Agder ist ein bekannter Fleischereibetrieb, der hohe Qualität anbietet. Aber es fehlten die finanziellen Mittel, um das zu kommunizieren, und der Umsatz stagnierte. Um diesen Qualitätsanspruch zu transportieren, wurden die Filialen als Fachgeschäfte neu definiert, in denen man Qualitäts-arbeit und Fachberatung findet, außerdem ein breites Angebot. Das Design basiert auf den Werten Kompetenz, Qualität und Lokalstolz und führt zu der einfachen und doch kraftvollen Identität mit der Aussage „Fleischerhandwerk aus dem Zentrum von Agder".

Jens Eide, un boucher renommé à Agder, en Norvège, vend de la viande et des saucisses de qualité, mais n'avait pas les moyens de communiquer cette valeur ajoutée aux consommateurs et perdait donc l'occasion de faire croître son activité. Pour transmettre cette idée de qualité, la stratégie de marque a été revue afin de faire de la boucherie un magasin spécialisé offrant des compétences et connaissances d'expert ainsi qu'une grande variété de produits de boucherie. Le graphisme est basé sur les valeurs de la compétence, de la qualité et de la fierté locale, et a pour résultat une identité simple mais efficace qui indique « Boucher artisanal du cœur d'Agder ».

JENS EIDE

Design: Eia Grødal
Creative Lead/Design: Morten Throndsen
Company: Strømme Throndsen Design
Country: Norway
Category: Fish, meat, poultry

GOLD PENTAWARD 2011

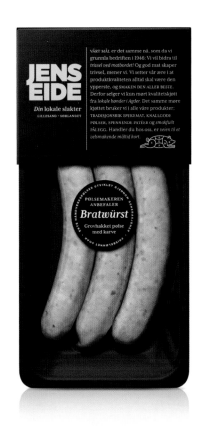

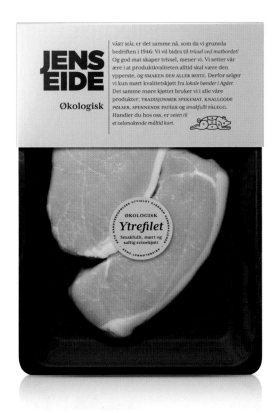

KEFALONIA FISHERIES

Creative Direction: Gregory Tsaknakis
Illustration: Ioanna Papaioannou
Food Styling: Tina Webb
Photography: Dimitris Poupalos
Company: Mousegraphics
Country: Greece
Category: Fish, meat, poultry

GOLD PENTAWARD 2012

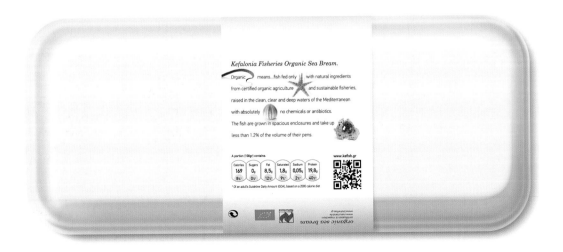

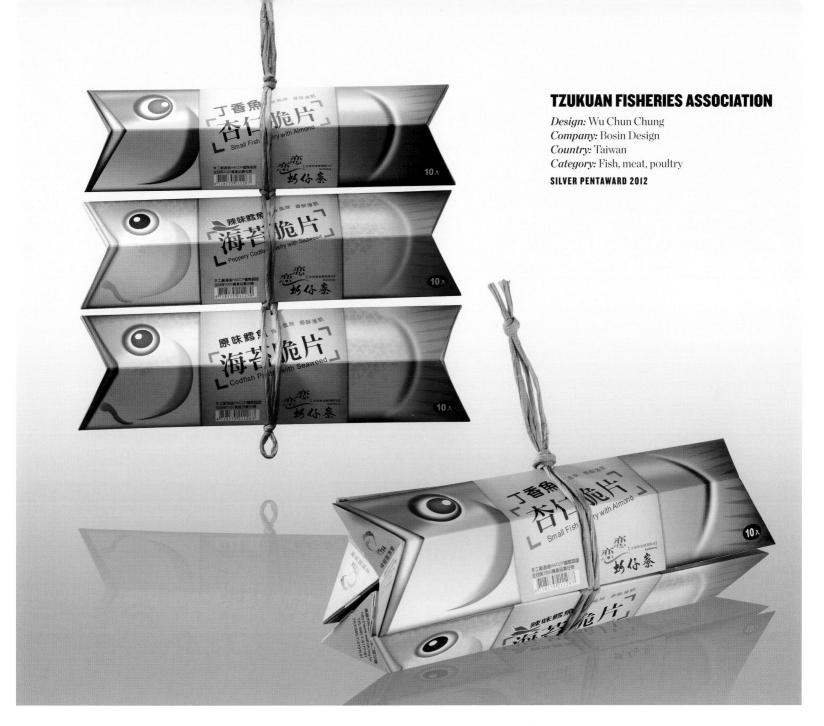

TZUKUAN FISHERIES ASSOCIATION

Design: Wu Chun Chung
Company: Bosin Design
Country: Taiwan
Category: Fish, meat, poultry

SILVER PENTAWARD 2012

In designing the packaging for this seafood pastry the main motif was fishing culture, with each design shaped like a different fish or shrimp, which also helps protect the fragile contents nicely. The sectional shape allows two or three to be bundled together with twine as a gift set, or packaged just as fishermen in olden days put the dry fish together for sharing with friends and family. In the same way that **Tzukuan** is a fishing village rich in both harvest and happiness, in which the fishermen shared along with their catch, nowadays people can enjoy that too by sharing this delicious seafood pastry.

Das Verpackungsdesign dieser Pasteten aus Meeresspezialitäten bezieht seine Hauptmotive aus der Fischereikultur. Jede Verpackung zeigt dem Inhalt entsprechend unterschiedliche Fisch- oder Shrimpsorten und schützt gleichzeitig die Ware sehr gut. Wegen der angeschnittenen Form können zwei oder drei Packungen mit einer Schnur als Geschenk zusammengebunden oder so verschnürt werden, wie früher die Fischer ihren getrockneten Fisch an Freunde und Familie weitergereicht haben. **Tzukuan** ist ein fröhliches Fischerdorf mit reichhaltigem Fangergebnis, in dem alle Fischer ihren Ertrag miteinander teilten. Auf gleiche Weise können heutzutage andere Menschen diese köstlichen Pasteten gemeinsam genießen.

Pour la conception de cet emballage pour des spécialités aux fruits de mer, le thème principal est la culture de la pêche. Chaque élément est en forme de poisson ou de crevette, ce qui aide aussi à protéger le fragile contenu. La forme modulaire permet d'attacher deux ou trois éléments ensemble avec de la ficelle pour faire un cadeau, tout comme les pêcheurs d'antan attachaient les poissons séchés pour les partager avec leurs amis et leur famille. **Tzukuan** est un village où les pêcheurs avaient la coutume de partager leurs prises. Aujourd'hui nous pouvons faire de même en partageant ces délicieuses spécialités aux fruits de mer.

PATAKUKKONEN

Design: Packlab team
Company: Packlab Partners
Country: Finland
Category: Fish, meat, poultry

BRONZE PENTAWARD 2012

DEN STOLTE HANE
HELT RÅ

Creative Lead: Helge Persen
Graphic Design: Tina T. Aasvestad
Company: Tank Design
Country: Norway
Category: Fish, meat, poultry

BRONZE PENTAWARD 2012

AHTI

Design/Creative Direction: David Pearman
Company: Cowan Design, London
Country: UK
Category: Fish, meat, poultry

BRONZE PENTAWARD 2012

 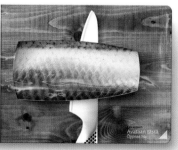 

SAUPIQUET
LES SARDINES

Creative Direction: Ruta Figarol
Design Direction: Virginie Hirsh, Brigitte de Guillebon
Company: Lonsdale
Country: France
Category: Fish, meat, poultry

SILVER PENTAWARD 2011

DINNER FOR N

Creative Direction: Belinda Lau
Design Direction: Elsie Tam
Company: Dragon Rouge, China
Country: China
Category: Fish, meat, poultry

BRONZE PENTAWARD 2011

LOFOTEN
LYNGEN REKER

Design: Eia Grødal
Creative Lead/Design: Morten Throndsen
Photography: Lisa Westgaard
Company: Strømme Throndsen Design
Country: Norway
Category: Fish, meat, poultry

SILVER PENTAWARD 2011

BONDUELLE KOOKHULP

Design: Jobert van de Bovenkamp, Danny Klein
Company: Millford Brand-id
Country: Netherlands
Category: Fruit & vegetables

SILVER PENTAWARD 2012

JA TSUGARU HIROSAKI

Design: Ai-Koike, Yusuke-Terai
Company: Rengo Co., Ltd.
Country: Japan
Category: Fruit & vegetables

BRONZE PENTAWARD 2012

Quick, the number 2 fast-food restaurant in France, needed to modernise its entire packaging line to establish a strong and consistent identity but which also showcased the range of "taste experiences" it offered and still championed its values of quality and authenticity. It was also important to retain the brand's spirit of friendliness and generous servings, and all of these elements became combined in a fresh, colourful packaging design that was both playful and encouraged customers to choose their own individual menu combinations.

Quick ist bei Frankreichs Schnellrestaurants die Nummer zwei und musste die gesamte Verpackungslinie modernisieren, um eine starke und konsistente Identität zu etablieren. Gleichzeitig sollten die ganze Palette der angebotenen „Geschmackserfahrungen" zur Schau gestellt und die Werte Qualität und Authentizität in den Vordergrund gerückt werden. Überdies war es wichtig, Freundlichkeit und großzügig bemessene Portionen als Geist der Marke zu bewahren. All diese Elemente wurden in einem frischen und farbenfrohen Verpackungsdesign kombiniert. Es wirkt spielerisch und ermutigt die Kunden, ihre Menüs selbst zusammenzustellen.

Quick, le numéro deux de la restauration rapide en France, avait besoin de moderniser toute sa gamme d'emballages afin de renforcer et d'harmoniser son identité tout en mettant en valeur la gamme de ses « expériences du goût » et en défendant ses valeurs de qualité et d'authenticité. Il était également important de conserver l'esprit de convivialité et de portions généreuses de la marque, et tous ces éléments se sont combinés dans un emballage moderne et coloré qui, tout en étant ludique, encourage les clients à choisir leur propre combinaison de menu individuelle.

QUICK RESTAURANTS

Creative Direction: Mélanie Gransart
Company: Black and Gold
Country: France
Category: Soups, ready-to-eat dishes

GOLD PENTAWARD 2011

KFC AUSTRALIA
SO GOOD

Management Direction: Chris Chong, Mike Pearce
Creative Direction: Catherine Baker
Design: Rebecca Charlton
Production: Shelley Black
Company: Redcactus Design
Country: New Zealand
Category: Soups, ready-to-eat dishes

SILVER PENTAWARD 2012

QIZINI
PREMIUM PIZZA

Design: Jeroen de Kok, Heidi Boersma
Company: Brandnew
Country: Netherlands
Category: Soups, ready-to-eat dishes

GOLD PENTAWARD 2012

Qizini recently began offering its fresh convenience products to retailers, specifically a range of premium pizzas, richly topped with fine ingredients. The "clair obscure" cover photography highlights the main ingredient, while the back of the box shows all the necessary information in the shape of a half-pizza slice, as emphasised by the pizza slicer alongside. The texture of the printed box makes the black feel almost like leather so that the overall impression conveys a real sense of quality in all the details. Beautiful ingredients combined with mysterious black designed to seduce the consumer, even in the bright light of chiller cabinets.

Qizini begann vor Kurzem, Einzelhändlern seine frischen Fertigprodukte anzubieten, insbesondere die Produktpalette der großzügig mit erlesenen Zutaten belegten Premiumpizzen. Die kraftvollen „Hell-Dunkel"-Fotos der Verpackung heben die jeweilige Hauptzutat hervor, während auf der Rückseite alle notwendigen Infos in Form eines halben Pizzastücks aufgeführt sind, besonders betont durch den Pizzaschneider daneben. In seiner Textur fühlt sich der bedruckte Karton fast wie Leder an und vermittelt damit in allen Details echte Qualität. Wunderschöne Zutaten, kombiniert mit einem geheimnisvollen Schwarz, das den Konsumenten sogar im grellen Licht des Kühlregals verführen soll.

La marque **Qizini** a récemment commencé à proposer ses produits frais cuisinés aux distributeurs, notamment une ligne de pizzas haut de gamme, généreusement garnies d'ingrédients de première qualité. Au recto, la photographie en clair-obscur met en valeur l'ingrédient principal, tandis qu'au verso, toutes les informations nécessaires sont présentées en forme de demi-pizza, accentuée par une roulette à pizza représentée à côté. La texture de la boîte imprimée donne au noir l'aspect du cuir et transmet une impression générale de qualité et d'attention aux détails. Cette combinaison d'ingrédients magnifiques et de noir mystérieux est conçue pour séduire le consommateur, même sous la lumière crue des armoires de produits frais.

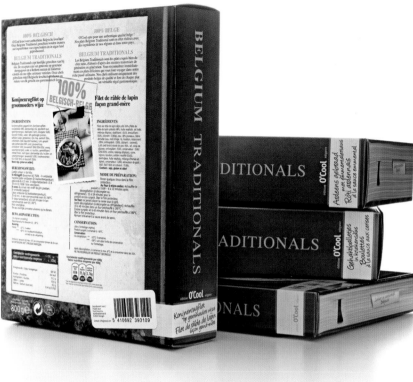

O'COOL
BELGIUM TRADITIONALS

Creative Direction: Patrick De Grande
Design: Hendrik Colenbier
Food Styling: Els Goethals
Photography: Quatre Etoiles
Company: Quatre Mains
Country: Belgium
Category: Soups, ready-to-eat dishes

SILVER PENTAWARD 2012

KABUTO NOODLES

Design: Shaun Bowen, Kerry Bolt,
George Hartley
Company: B&B studio
Country: UK
Category: Soups, ready-to-eat dishes

SILVER PENTAWARD 2011

ILLEGAL BURGER

Design: Are Kleivan,
Christian Schnitler, Frode Skaren
Company: The Metric System Design Studio
Country: Norway
Category: Soups, ready-to-eat dishes

SILVER PENTAWARD 2011

**DELISHOP
TAKE AWAY**

Design: Gaizka Ruiz
Company: Enric Aguilera Asociados
Country: Spain
Category: Soups, ready-to-eat dishes

BRONZE PENTAWARD 2011

HEALTHY CHOICE
100% NATURAL

Design: Lori Cerwin, Amy Hawker
Client Lead: Darrell Dragoo (ConAgra Foods, Inc.)
Company: Brandimage – Desgrippes & Laga
Country: USA
Category: Soups, ready-to-eat dishes

SILVER PENTAWARD 2012

KFC

Creative Direction: Tim Schultheis, Harri Lemke
Company: LSD – lemkeschultheis design
Country: Germany
Category: Soups, ready-to-eat dishes

BRONZE PENTAWARD 2012

FLEURY MICHON
5 ESSENTIELS

Design: Bernard Bertail,
Manuella Mary, Soline de la Martinière
Company: Nouveau Monde DDB, Nantes
Country: France
Category: Soups, ready-to-eat dishes

BRONZE PENTAWARD 2012

L'ARTIGIANO

Management Direction: Emmanouela Bitsaxaki
Graphic Design: Eleni Pavlaki
Studio Management: Alexandra Papaloudi
Company: 2yolk Branding & Design
Country: Greece
Category: Soups, ready-to-eat dishes

BRONZE PENTAWARD 2012

SnackWell's
WHITE FUDGE DRIZZLED
Caramel Popcorn
130 CALORIE PACK

SnackWell's
FUDGE DRIZZLED
Double Chocolate
Chip Cookies
100 CALORIE PACK

SnackWell's
RICH VANILLA CRÈME
Brownie Bites

NABISCO SNACKWELL'S

Design: Heather Miehm
Account Direction: Chris Thalgott, Anne Lawrence
Company: Davis
Country: Canada
Category: Confectionery & sweet snacks

GOLD PENTAWARD 2011

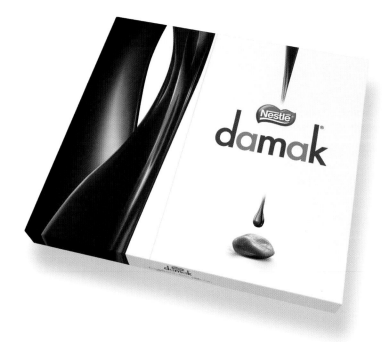

NESTLÉ DAMAK

Design: Jérôme Lecabellec
Company: CB'a Turkey
Country: Turkey
Category: Confectionery & sweet snacks

BRONZE PENTAWARD 2011

TOBLERONE
SPECIAL EDITION

Creative Direction: Richard Cleveland
Design: Stephen McDavid
Company: LPK
Country: Switzerland
Category: Confectionery & sweet snacks

SILVER PENTAWARD 2011

With a product so strange and quite likely unique, its packaging should attract the bolder and braver consumer, with a sweet tooth and a nose for discoveries. Playing on the relationship between medium and message, the eccentric coupling of package and product presents an "outer-inner" game of illusions especially for the eyes of the curious. The paradox of a sweet, edible, even appetising pebble, the beautiful image of an open crop, with its startlingly realistic flesh, fake cherries which can fool birds into coming down to nibble at them like in the ancient paintings of Zeuxis: all these are mind-treats concocted for the consumer within a heightened-reality design environment.

Bei diesem so eigenartigen und höchstwahrscheinlich einzigartigen Produkt spricht die Verpackung eher mutige und tapfere Verbraucher mit süßem Zahn und Entdeckernase an. Die exzentrische Kombination von Verpackung und Produkt spielt mit Medium und Botschaft. Sie präsentiert vor allem für neugierige Augen ein „Außen-Drinnen"-Spiel der Illusionen. Ein paradoxerweise süßer, essbarer, sogar appetitlicher Kieselstein, das wunderschöne Bild einer offenen Frucht mit ihrem verblüffend realistischen Fruchtfleisch, echt wirkende Kirschen, die wie auf den antiken Gemälden des Zeuxis sogar die Vögel verlocken, an ihnen zu knabbern — all dies ein Hochgenuss für den Geist und ersonnen für Verbraucher in einer Umgebung der durchs Design gesteigerten Realität.

Avec un produit aussi étrange, et certainement unique, l'emballage doit attirer les consommateurs les plus audacieux, portés sur les sucreries et avides de découvertes. L'association excentrique de l'emballage et du produit joue sur la relation entre le support et le message et présente un jeu d'illusions « intérieur-extérieur » à l'intention des curieux. Le paradoxe d'un galet sucré, comestible, et même appétissant, la superbe image d'un fruit ouvert, avec sa chair étonnamment réaliste, de fausses cerises qui peuvent tromper les oiseaux et les inviter à les grignoter, comme dans les peintures antiques de Zeuxis : toutes ces friandises de l'esprit ont été concoctées pour le consommateur dans un environnement graphique en réalité augmentée.

HATZIYIANNAKIS DRAGEES

Creative Direction: Gregory Tsaknakis
Art Direction: Kostas Vlachakis
Illustration: Ioanna Papaioannou
Company: Mousegraphics
Country: Greece
Category: Confectionery & sweet snacks

GOLD PENTAWARD 2012

LOTTE
BLACK BLACK FLAVONO

Art Direction: Yoichi Kondo
Creative Direction: Yukio Okada
Copy Text: Endoh 2nd
Design: Yoichi Kondo, Kaoru Ogawa, Kana Mashiko
Planning Direction: Seiichi Nishikawa
Production: Isao Tomizawa
Company: Enjin Inc.
Country: Japan
Category: Confectionery & sweet snacks

BRONZE PENTAWARD 2011

BIOKIA

Creative Direction/Concept: Renne Angelvuo
Graphic Design: Tiina Achrén
Illustration: Mikael Achrén
Company: Win Win Branding
Country: Finland
Category: Confectionery & sweet snacks

SILVER PENTAWARD 2012

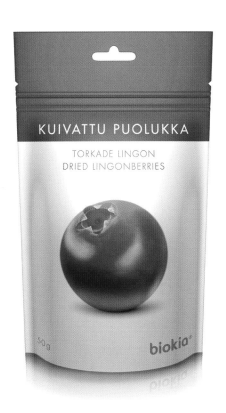

MAROU
FAISEURS DE CHOCOLAT

Design: Chi-An De Leo, Joshua Breidenbach
Company: Rice Creative
Country: Vietnam
Category: Confectionery & sweet snacks

BRONZE PENTAWARD 2012

BRIGADERIA

Creative Direction: Gustavo Piqueira, Samia Jacintho
Design: Ana Lobo, Danilo Helvadjian
Design Assistance: Caroline Vapsys, Marianne Meni
Company: Casa Rex
Country: Brazil
Category: Confectionery & sweet snacks

BRONZE PENTAWARD 2012

CHUPA CHUPS
GIFT PACK

Design: Bak Sang-hee, Oh Hye-mi, Bae Hong-cheol
Company: Nongshim Communications
Country: South Korea
Category: Confectionery & sweet snacks

SILVER PENTAWARD 2012

PIPERS CRISP CO.

Creative Direction: Paul Taylor
Account Direction: Avril Tooley
Design: Rachel Bright
Account Management: Lydia De'Ath
Company: BrandOpus
Country: UK
Category: Savoury snacks

SILVER PENTAWARD 2012

**ZWEIFEL
POPCORN**

Design: ARD design team
Company: ARD Design Switzerland
Country: Switzerland
Category: Savoury snacks

SILVER PENTAWARD 2012

KIYU TARO
METEOROLOGICAL STATION

Design: Victor Branding creative team
Company: Victor Branding Design Corp.
Country: Taiwan
Category: Savoury snacks
GOLD PENTAWARD 2012

X SNACKS

Creative Direction: Irinel Ionescu
Design: Oliwer Iovanovici
DTP: Danubiu Birzu
Illustration/3D: Alin Patru
Company: Ampro Design Consultants
Country: Romania
Category: Savoury snacks

SILVER PENTAWARD 2011

STEGEMAN

Design Strategy/Packaging Concept: OD
Direction: Menno Mulder, Oscar van Geesbergen
Artwork: Super-A (Shop-Around)
Company: OD
Country: Netherlands
Category: Savoury snacks

SILVER PENTAWARD 2011

MICHAEL'S FARM

Design: Eia Grødal
Creative Direction: Morten Throndsen
Company: Strømme Throndsen Design
Country: Norway
Category: Savoury snacks

BRONZE PENTAWARD 2011

AOZASHI KARARI

Art Direction: Akihiro Nishizawa
Design: Kanako Narita
Company: Eight Branding Design Co., Ltd.
Country: Japan
Category: Savoury snacks

BRONZE PENTAWARD 2012

EAT.
CRISPS RANGE

Creative Direction: Natalie Chung
Design: Will Gladden
Account Management: Erin Tucker
Company: Pearlfisher
Country: UK
Category: Savoury snacks

BRONZE PENTAWARD 2011

A new brand of premium goat-milk ice cream and sorbets, **La Luna**, was developed for the American market. Goats' milk is a more ecologically conscious and healthier alternative to cows' milk, and yet it was decided not to use a goat as the brand image but to keep this key detail on the back of the packaging, in the dark as it were. The reason for this was to emphasise the brand values other than the ingredients: mystery, special quality and a magical taste, and so the image of the moon was chosen — also showing just one side and happily too being the same shape as a scoop of ice cream.

La Luna, die neue Premium-Marke für Eiscreme und Sorbets aus Ziegenmilch, wurde für den amerikanischen Markt entwickelt. Ziegenmilch ist die ökologisch bewusste und gesündere Alternative zu Kuhmilch. Aber eine Ziege sollte nicht das Markenimage zieren, sondern dieses Schlüsseldetail sollte auf der Verpackungsrückseite erscheinen, sozusagen auf der dunklen Seite. Neben den Zutaten sollten nämlich auch andere Markenwerte betont werden: das Geheimnis, die besondere Qualität, der magische Geschmack. Für diesen Zweck entschied man sich für das Bild des Mondes — auch hier wird nur die eine Seite gezeigt. Wie ein glücklicher Zufall es wollte, weist diese Seite die gleiche Form auf wie eine Kugel Eiscreme.

Une nouvelle marque de glaces et sorbets haut de gamme au lait de chèvre, **La Luna**, a été développée pour le marché américain. Le lait de chèvre est une option plus écologique et plus saine que le lait de vache, et pourtant il a été décidé de ne pas utiliser de chèvre dans l'image de la marque, et de reléguer ce détail essentiel au dos de l'emballage, pour ainsi dire dans l'ombre. La raison était de mettre en avant les valeurs de marque autres que les ingrédients : mystère, qualité spéciale et goût magique. C'est donc l'image de la lune qui a été retenue, qui elle aussi ne se montre que d'un côté, et qui, heureux hasard, a la même forme qu'une boule de glace.

LA LUNA
GOAT-MILK ICE CREAM

Design: Baruch Nae
Company: Baruch Nae Creative Branding Ltd.
Country: Israel
Category: Pastry, biscuits, ice-cream, desserts, sugar

GOLD PENTAWARD 2011

HÄAGEN-DAZS

Design Direction: Mary Lewis
Company: Lewis Moberly
Country: UK
Category: Pastry, biscuits, ice-cream, desserts, sugar
GOLD PENTAWARD 2012

MORARITA

Creative Direction: Irinel Ionescu
Design: Francesca Muresan
Illustration: Alin Patru
DTP/Production: Danubiu Birzu
Company: Ampro Design Consultants
Country: Romania
Category: Pastry, biscuits, ice-cream, desserts, sugar

SILVER PENTAWARD 2012

BUCKWUD
CANADIAN MAPLE SYRUP

Creative Direction: Paul Taylor
Design: Caroline Gates
Account Direction: Avril Tooley
Account Management: Sarah Starck
Company: BrandOpus
Country: UK
Category: Pastry, biscuits,
ice-cream, desserts, sugar

SILVER PENTAWARD 2012

**FOXY'S FOODS
ICE CREAM**

Design: Mel Dickinson
Company: Channelzero
Country: Australia
Category: Pastry, biscuits,
ice-cream, desserts, sugar

BRONZE PENTAWARD 2011

**BETTY CROCKER
SEASONAL COOKIES**

Design: Walter Perlowski, Krystina Porcaro
Company: Brandimage – Desgrippes & Laga
Country: USA
Category: Pastry, biscuits, ice-cream, desserts, sugar

SILVER PENTAWARD 2011

JOHN ALTMAN COOKIES

Creative Direction: Hajo de Boer
Illustration: Jeroen Klaver
Copy Text: William Georgi
Company: Gummo
Country: Netherlands
Category: Pastry, biscuits, ice-cream, desserts, sugar

BRONZE PENTAWARD 2011

TK FOOD
ASSORTED FLAVOUR GIFT BOX

Design: Victor Branding creative team
Company: Victor Branding Design Corp.
Country: Taiwan
Category: Pastry, biscuits, ice-cream, desserts, sugar

SILVER PENTAWARD 2011

**CISHAN FOCUS
BANANA PIE**

Design: Wu Chun Chung
Company: Bosin Design
Country: Taiwan
Category: Pastry, biscuits,
ice-cream, desserts, sugar

BRONZE PENTAWARD 2011

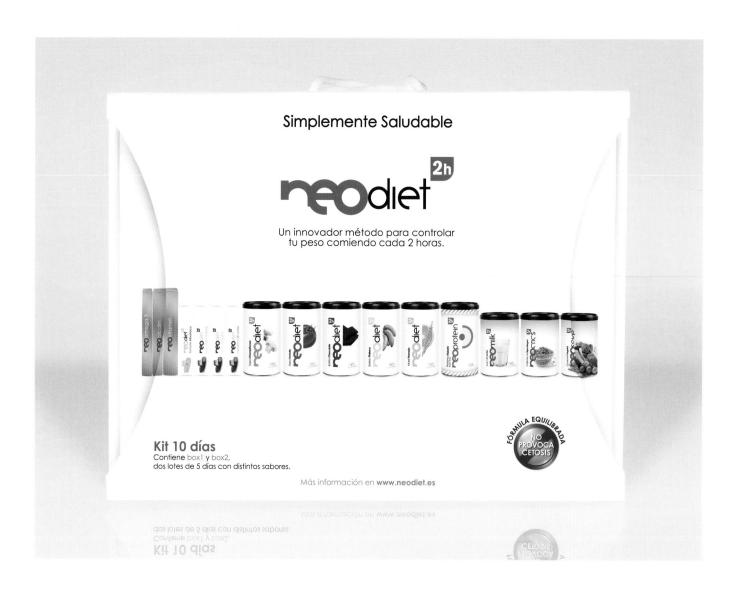

Simplemente Saludable

neodiet 2h

Un innovador método para controlar
tu peso comiendo cada 2 horas.

Kit 10 días
Contiene box1 y box2,
dos lotes de 5 días con distintos sabores.

FÓRMULA EQUILIBRADA
NO PROVOCA CETOSIS

Más información en **www.neodiet.es**

NEODIET

Design: Aïda Font Garcia,
Jordi Ferrandiz Fernandez
Company: Orange BCN
Country: Spain
Category: Food trends

SILVER PENTAWARD 2011

AURA HEALTH & WELLBEING

Brand Identity/Graphic Design/Artwork/
Structural Packaging Design: Burgopak
Company: Burgopak
Country: UK
Category: Food trends

BRONZE PENTAWARD 2011

RITTER SPORT

Design: Roman Klis, Elisabeth Eschbach,
Frank Zinkewitz, Sibel Yücesoy
Company: Roman Klis Design
Country: Germany
Category: Limited editions,
limited series, collectors' items

GOLD PENTAWARD 2011

CAMINO
CHOCOLATE RANGE

Creative Direction: James Bateman
Copy Text: Jeff Galbraith
Art Direction/Design: Dan O'Leary
Account Direction: Megan McCord
Production: Courtney Smith
Illustration: Chris Haughton
Digital Art: Mark Finn
Company: DDB Canada/Karacters Vancouver
Country: Canada
Category: Food trends

SILVER PENTAWARD 2011

LYLE'S GOLDEN SYRUP

Group Creative Direction: Graham Shearsby
Design Direction: Asa Cook
Design: Sarah Bustin (senior),
Jonathan Ferriday (junior)
Company: Design Bridge, London
Country: UK
Category: Limited editions,
limited series, collectors' items

SILVER PENTAWARD 2012

KANNISTON LEIPOMO

Design: Janne Asikainen, Tony Dianoff,
Per-Oskar Joenpelto, Marika Luoto,
Ian Rooney, Juho Viironen
Company: Packlab Partners
Country: Finland
Category: Limited editions,
limited series, collectors' items

SILVER PENTAWARD 2011

THINK GLOBAL TASTE LOCAL

Design: Guilherme Jardim, Pedro André,
Mar Hernandez, Maio Belèm, Mauro de Donatis
Company: NTGJ
Country: Portugal
Category: Limited editions,
limited series, collectors' items

SILVER PENTAWARD 2011

COMILFO

Creative Direction: Alexey Fadeev
Copy Text: Kirill Rizhkov
Art Direction: Aram Mirzoyants, Julia Zhdanova
Illustration: Olga Fedosova
Account Direction: Anastasia Razumova
Company: Depot WPF
Country: Russia
Category: Limited editions,
limited series, collectors' items

BRONZE PENTAWARD 2011

MONT BLANC
LIMITED EDITION RANGE

Art Direction: Haleh Madani
Graphic Design: Marjolaine Jacques
Account Direction: Estelle Pillet
Company: Raison Pure International
Country: France
Category: Limited editions,
limited series, collectors' items

BRONZE PENTAWARD 2011

HALLOWEEN CRUNCH

Design Direction: Jose Parado
Design: Ron Szafarczyk
Illustration: Chris Nolan, Ed Griffin
Company: Haugaard Creative Group
Country: USA
Category: Limited editions,
limited series, collectors' items

BRONZE PENTAWARD 2011

Waitrose

LOMBARDIA INSPIRED
PIZZA WITH SALAME
BRIANZA DOP*, BLUE
CHEESE AND PEAR

INSPIRED BY THE ROBUST, HEARTY FLAVOURS OF ITALY'S
LOMBARDIA REGION, WITH CREAMY WHITE SAUCE,
SUCCULENT LOCALLY-PRODUCED SALAME BRIANZA DOP*,
ITALIAN BLUE CHEESE AND PEAR PUREE, ON A THIN,
CRISP BASE, HAND-STRETCHED FROM THE CENTRE
FOR A LIGHT, PUFFY EDGE AND CHARRED IN
A HOT OVEN FOR EXTRA FLAVOUR.

DISPLAY UNTIL/USE BY

Keep refrigerated below 5°C

PER ½ PIZZA		GDA
calories	327	16%
sugars	3.7g	4%
fat	12.8g	18%
saturates	5.8g	29%
salt	1.54g	26%

WAITROSE REGIONAL PIZZAS

Creative Direction: David Turner, Bruce Duckworth
Design Direction: Clem Halpin
Design: Jamie McCathie, David Blakemore
Retouching: Andy Burton
Photography: Gareth Sambidge
Artwork: James Norris
Company: Turner Duckworth, London & San Francisco
Country: UK
Category: Distributors'/Retailers' own brands

GOLD PENTAWARD 2011

Waitrose

CAMPANIA INSPIRED
PIZZA WITH TOMATO,
BASIL AND BUFFALO
MOZZARELLA

Waitrose

PUGLIA INSPIRED
PIZZA WITH CHARGRILLED
PEPPERS, SPINACH AND
SAINT' AGOSTINO OLIVES

WAITROSE LOVE LIFE

Creative Direction: Natalie Chung
Creative Partnership: Jonathan Ford
Strategy Direction: Yael Alaton
Design Direction: Poppy Stedman
Design: Vicki Willatts
Company: Pearlfisher
Country: UK
Category: Distributors'/Retailers' own brands

SILVER PENTAWARD 2012

With consumers becoming increasingly health-conscious, Waitrose sought a mid-tier range that offered varied food choices to help customers live a healthier, happier life, and packaged to celebrate freshness and naturalness. If our natural instincts about what is good to eat have faded with food commercialisation, a design approach that reaffirms the pleasure of food and importance of health should appeal more to today's shoppers. Consequently, an identity, name and packaging were established, with a vibrant colour palette, to celebrate positivity and the benefits of healthy eating. The food photography showed how ingredients combined to create appetising, tasty and healthy choices, and **Waitrose LOVE life** has achieved astronomical success.

Weil das Gesundheitsbewusstsein der Verbraucher stetig steigt, bietet Waitrose diese Produktpalette im mittleren Marktsegment an. Damit sollen Kunden ein gesünderes, zufriedeneres Leben führen, und schon die Verpackung zelebriert Frische und Natürlichkeit. Weil durch die Kommerzialisierung von Nahrung unser natürlicher Instinkt für gutes Essen nachgelassen hat, sollte dieser Designansatz, der die Freuden des Essens und den Wert der Gesundheit beteuert, den modernen Kunden ansprechen. Konsequent wird dies durch Identität, Namensgebung und Verpackung in kraftvollen Farben umgesetzt, um die positive Einstellung und die Vorzüge gesunder Speisen zu feiern. Die Fotos der Lebensmittel zeigen, wie die Zutaten in Kombination ein appetitliches, leckeres und gesundes Angebot ergeben. Infolgedessen verzeichnet **Waitrose LOVE life** astronomische Erfolge.

Les consommateurs sont de plus en plus préoccupés par leur santé, c'est pourquoi Waitrose a voulu créer une ligne de milieu de gamme offrant des choix variés pour aider ses clients à mener une vie plus saine et plus heureuse, avec des emballages centrés sur la fraîcheur et le naturel. Nos instincts naturels sur ce qu'il est bon de manger se sont émoussés avec le marketing, mais une approche graphique qui réaffirme le plaisir de la nourriture et l'importance de la santé devrait plaire davantage aux acheteurs d'aujourd'hui. Une identité, un nom et un emballage ont donc été créés autour d'une palette de couleurs vives pour célébrer la positivité et les avantages d'une alimentation saine. Les photographies montrent comment les ingrédients se combinent pour composer des choix sains, appétissants et savoureux, et **Waitrose LOVE life** a récolté un succès astronomique.

MORRISONS SAVERS

Creative Direction: Stephen Bell
Design: Craig Barnes, Carolyn Sweet
Account Management: Andy Hellmuth
Company: Coley Porter Bell
Country: UK
Category: Distributors'/Retailers' own brands

GOLD PENTAWARD 2012

12 Fairy Cakes
Ready to decorate

Seasonal Salad

savers

14 Normal Incontinence Pads

savers

4 Jumbo Toilet Rolls

savers

14 Ultra Towels

savers

30 Refuse Sacks

Sweetcorn
32oz℮

savers
Whisky

savers
Vodka

savers
Brandy

savers
Gin

savers

40 Plasters

savers

3 Jumbo Kitchen Towels

Orange Juice
from concentrate
1 Litre ℮

savers
Carbon Zinc
D
batteries

savers
Carbon Zinc
AAA
batteries

savers
Carbon Zinc
9v
batteries

savers

10 All Purpose Cloths

savers

Washing Up Liquid
500ml℮

savers
Soap

savers

Gel Air Freshener

savers

20 Nappies
Size 4

savers

72 Fragrance Free Baby Wipes

savers

Shaving Foam
250ml℮

savers

Hair Mousse
400ml℮

savers

Bath Foam
1 Litre℮

savers

10 Disposable Razors
Twin Blade

THE FOOD DOCTOR

Creative Direction: Natalie Chung
Creative Partnership: Jonathan Ford
Design Direction: Sarah Pidgeon
Strategy: Georgia Levison
Company: Pearlfisher
Country: UK
Category: Distributors'/Retailers' own brands

BRONZE PENTAWARD 2012

JUMBO
BABY NUTRITION

Creative Strategy/Concept: OD
Art Direction: Menno Mulder, Oscar van Geesbergen
Artwork: Tummy (Shop-Around)
Company: OD
Country: Netherlands
Category: Distributors'/Retailers' own brands

SILVER PENTAWARD 2011

SPAR
VEROPOULOI BROS S.A.

Creative Direction: Marina Gioti
Marketing Direction: Konstantinos Kavalaris
Art Direction: Victoria Sakka
Brand Management: Sotiris Tavoularis
Printing: Mesogeiaki Ektipotiki
Company: Sonar Marketing Consulting
Country: Greece
Category: Distributors'/Retailers' own brands

BRONZE PENTAWARD 2011

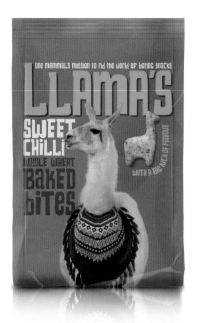

LLAMA'S

Creative Planning: Tamara Williams
Creative Direction: Jo Saker
Design: Ellen Munro
Company: Parker Williams Design
Country: UK
Category: Distributors'/
Retailers' own brands

BRONZE PENTAWARD 2012

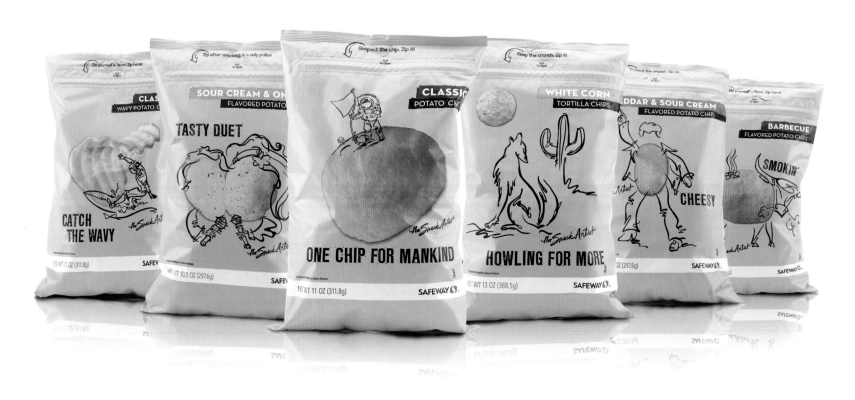

SAFEWAY
THE SNACK ARTIST

Account Direction: Mark Hamilton,
Jeanne Gavenda
Creative Direction: Brian Lovell
Design Direction: Sean Baca
Design: Chris Waddell
Illustration: John Worthen
Company: Anthem Worldwide,
San Francisco Office
Country: USA
Category: Distributors'/
Retailers' own brands

SILVER PENTAWARD 2011

CHOKABLOK

Creative Direction: Barry Gillibrand
Design: Roger Akroyd
Copy: Michael Harvey
Photography: Jess Koppel
Account Direction: Katherine Greenwood
Company: Mayday
Country: UK
Category: Distributors'/Retailers' own brands

SILVER PENTAWARD 2012

CHOKA BLOK
GOLD DIGGER DYNAMITE
CARAMEL & VANILLA ICE CREAMS CHARGED WITH
CHUNKS OF SWEET HONEYCOMB, REAL CHOCOLATE
CARAMEL CUPS & OUR SILKY SWEET CARAMEL SAUCE

CHOKA BLOK
COOKIE DOUGH MON-STAR
CHUNKS OF CHOC CHIP COOKIE DOUGH &
REAL CHOCOLATE STARS DROWNED IN OUR SILKY
SWEET CARAMEL SAUCE WITH CREAMY ICE CREAM

CHOKA BLOK
CHERRY BOMB BROWNIE
CHERRY ICE CREAM PACKED WITH TANGY,
CHEWY CHERRIES, GOOEY CHOCOLATE BROWNIES
REAL CHOCOLATE FLAKES & SWEET CHERRY SAUCE

CHOKA BLOK
BILLIONAIRES SHORTCAKE
SMOOTH & CREAMY CARAMEL ICE CREAM, WITH CHUNKS
OF SWEET & CHEWY CARAMEL FUDGE, REAL CHOCOLATE
COVERED SHORTCAKE & SWIRLS OF CARAMEL SAUCE

CHOKA BLOK
AMERICAN DREAMCAKE
A RICH AND CREAMY MIX OF CHEESECAKE & DARK
CHOCOLATE ICE CREAMS SWIRLED WITH CHOCOLATE FROSTING,
CHUNKS OF CHEESECAKE & CHOCOLATE BROWNIE PIECES

CHOKA BLOK
ROCKY ROAD OF LOVE
RICH CHOCOLATE & MARSHMALLOW ICE CREAMS, PACKED WITH
MILK CHOCOLATE HEARTS, CHUNKS OF CRUNCHY BISCUIT,
MINI MARSHMALLOWS & SWIRLS OF STICKY TOFFEE SAUCE

FRESH & EASY
COOKIE CRÈMES

Design: Jonathan Sleeman,
Simon Pemberton, Adrian Whitefoord
Company: P&W Design Consultants
Country: UK
Category: Distributors'/Retailers' own brands

BRONZE PENTAWARD 2011

ICA
CRISPS, CHEESE DOODLES
AND PARTY SNACKS

Concept Direction: Ulf Berlin
Art Direction: Niclas Öster, Steven Webb
Design: Niclas Öster
Design Assistance: Rasmus Enström
Illustration/Handmade Fonts: Vladimir Loginov
Production Management: Christine Schönborg
Production Design: Monica Holm
Company: Designkontoret Silver
Country: Sweden
Category: Distributors'/Retailers' own brands

BRONZE PENTAWARD 2011

ICA
ICE CREAM

Design: Jimmy Petersson Chan
Design Assistance: Emil Söderberg
Art Direction: Eddoe Löthman
Project Management: Susanne Jerdenius
Company: ICA Sverige AB
Country: Sweden
Category: Distributors'/Retailers' own brands

BRONZE PENTAWARD 2012

CORA DÉGUSTATION

Design: Jérôme Lanoy, Fabrice Renard, Cyriaque Porte
Company: Logic Design
Country: France
Category: Distributors'/Retailers' own brands

BRONZE PENTAWARD 2011

ZERO% PACKAGING
ONLY SOUP

Creative Direction: Catherine Faucheux,
Dimitri Castrique
Art Direction: Stephane Kimpe,
Michael Vandendael
Company: Monalisa
Country: Belgium
Category: Ecological concept (food)

SILVER PENTAWARD 2012

Zero% Packaging gets the last word on being as environmentally friendly as possible. Here is an organic product that is made of soup (consisting of fresh vegetables), contained in a pack made from pure corn and with an external design printed in organic ink. Nothing else! A 100% cradle 2 cradle product solution. Furthermore, it is as easy to use as 1–2–3: 1. Wash the pack gently under running cold water; 2. spread it into a bowl; 3. heat in the microwave.

Zero% Packaging will bei der Frage, wie man möglichst umweltfreundlich sein kann, die ultimative Aussage treffen. Diese Suppe ist ein organisches Produkt (aus frischem Gemüse zubereitet) in einer Verpackung aus reinem Mais, dessen externes Design mit organischen Farben aufgedruckt ist. Das war's — mehr nicht! Eine zu 100 % ökoeffektive Produktlösung. Obendrein ist sie kinderleicht zu verwenden: Die Packung wird unter fließend kaltem Wasser abgespült, in eine Schale gegeben und in der Mikrowelle erhitzt.

Zero% Packaging bat tous les records en matière de respect de l'environnement. Voici un produit organique, une soupe composée de légumes frais, conditionné dans un emballage entièrement composé de maïs, avec un graphisme imprimé à l'encre organique. Et rien d'autre ! Une solution 100 % « berceau à berceau ». De plus, l'utilisation est on ne peut plus simple : 1. laver le pack délicatement sous de l'eau courante froide ; 2. placer dans un bol ; 3. réchauffer au four à microondes.

With **gogol mogol** eggs an ambitious project for the future introduces a new way of cooking, storing and packing eggs. Sold in shops on a three-storey pedestal, this also takes up less space in a shopping-bag. Each egg is packaged individually in recycled cardboard with further layers beneath — the second constitutes the catalyst, beneath which is a membrane separating it from a third layer made of smart material. When the membrane is pulled out (by means of a tag), a chemical reaction occurs between the catalyst and the smart material, and the egg begins to heat up. After a few minutes, when the lid of the packaging is lifted off, a boiled egg is ready for an easy breakfast.

Die **gogol mogol**-Eier führen ein ehrgeiziges zukunftsorientiertes Projekt ein, das neue Wege beim Zubereiten, Lagern und Verpacken von Eiern vorstellt. In den Läden werden sie in einer Art dreiteiligen Säule verkauft, die auch in Einkaufstüten weniger Platz benötigt. Jedes Ei wird einzeln in recyceltem Karton verpackt. In der Schicht darunter befindet sich der Katalysator und darunter, getrennt durch eine Membran, eine dritte Schicht aus einem intelligenten Material. Wenn die Membran mittels eines kleinen Etiketts herausgezogen wird, löst das eine chemische Reaktion zwischen Katalysator und intelligentem Material aus, und das Ei wird erhitzt. Nach wenigen Minuten kann man den Deckel der Verpackung öffnen und erhält ein perfektes Frühstücksei.

Les œufs **gogol mogol** sont un projet d'avenir ambitieux qui présente une nouvelle façon de cuire, stocker et emballer les œufs. Vendus en magasin sur un présentoir à trois étages, ils prennent aussi moins de place dans les sacs à provisions. Chaque œuf est emballé individuellement dans du carton recyclé avec plusieurs couches internes : la deuxième est le catalyseur, et une membrane la sépare d'une troisième couche faite d'un matériau intelligent. Lorsqu'on ouvre la membrane (à l'aide d'une languette), une réaction chimique se produit entre le catalyseur et le matériau intelligent, et l'œuf commence à chauffer. Quelques minutes plus tard, lorsqu'on soulève le couvercle, l'œuf à la coque est prêt pour le petit-déjeuner.

GOGOL MOGOL

Creative Direction: Kirill Konstantinov
Design: Evgeny Morgalev
Company: Kian Branding Agency
Country: Russia
Category: Packaging concept (food)

GOLD PENTAWARD 2012

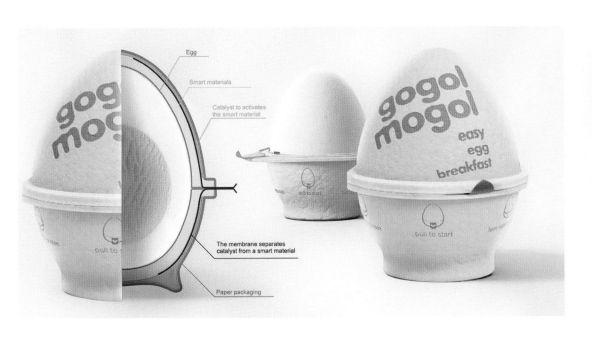

The traditional packaging of flour, as in 1kg paper bags, could certainly be updated both for a less utilitarian design and out of practical considerations. A new approach to packing might also prove easier to open, use or close, and improve storage. The design settled on here makes use of rubber balloons instead of bags, with a plastic cork on top. As a bonus, the playful packaging makes flour less a simple commodity and more an appealing branded product, with a range for cakes and pastry. If there isn't much space on the kitchen shelf, the rubber means the pack can be squeezed into a new shape to fit, while the kids can play with it while you cook.

Die traditionelle Verpackung von Mehl in 1-kg-Papier-tüten hat es sicher verdient, zugunsten eines weniger nutzwertorientierten Designs und aus praktischen Erwägungen heraus modernisiert zu werden. Mit diesem Designansatz soll man die Verpackung auch einfacher öffnen, verwenden und verschließen können, obendrein wird die Aufbewahrungsmöglichkeit verbessert. Man entschied sich für ein Design, das mit Gummiballons statt Tüten arbeitet und oben einen Plastikkorken aufweist. Als zusätzlicher Bonus ist das Mehl durch die spielerische Verpackung nun weniger Grundnahrungsmittel, sondern eher ein ansprechendes Markenprodukt. Sowohl eine Mehlmischung für Kuchen als auch Teige ist erhältlich. Falls im Küchenregal zu wenig Platz ist, kann die Packung durch das flexible Gummimaterial so verformt werden, dass sie überall hineinpasst. Außerdem können Kinder damit spielen, während Sie kochen.

Le traditionnel sac en papier d'1 kg de farine avait certainement besoin d'être remis à jour, en faveur d'un design moins utilitariste, mais aussi pour des raisons pratiques. Le nouvel emballage pouvait améliorer l'ouverture, la fermeture et l'utilisation, ainsi que le stockage. La solution choisie ici utilise des ballons en caoutchouc fermés par des bouchons en liège. En bonus, cet emballage ludique transforme une simple marchan-dise générique en produit de marque séduisant, avec une gamme pour la pâtisserie. Si l'on manque d'espace dans les placards, on peut presser le caoutchouc pour lui donner une forme qui prend moins de place, et les enfants peuvent jouer avec pendant que vous cuisinez.

THE FLOUR MODELLINO

Creative Direction: Irinel Ionescu
3D/Illustration: Alin Patru
Project Management: Mihaela Dumitrescu
Company: Ampro Design Consultants
Country: Romania
Category: Packaging concept (food)

SILVER PENTAWARD 2012

**TRUE
AIR FRESHENERS**

Design: Berik Yergaliyev
Company: Good!
Country: Kazakhstan
Category: Packaging concept (food)

SILVER PENTAWARD 2012

When squeezing a lemon, the half-fruit is pressed down with the fingers to release the stream of fragrant juice — an action essentially the same as operating an air-freshener. Thus was born the idea to replace the boring spray-top with a half of fruit for this new range. The effect is much more psychologically pleasing than pressing on a piece of hard plastic and the smell of the air-freshener this way is perceived as being more organic and natural. The cap simulates the fruit in colour and texture and is made from thick rubber which keeps its shape but is sufficiently elastic to allow pressing on the sprayer freely, giving users the impression they are squeezing the actual fruit.

Will man eine Zitrone ausdrücken, presst man die halbierte Frucht mit Fingern und setzt so einen Strom duftenden Safts frei — im Wesentlichen werden auf diese Weise auch Lufterfrischer benutzt. Dieses Prinzip stand Pate bei der Idee zu einer neuen Produktpalette, die das langweilige Oberteil einer Sprühdose durch eine halbierte Frucht ersetzt. Der Effekt ist psychologisch weitaus befriedigender als das Drücken eines harten Plastik-stücks. Auch wird der Geruch des Lufterfrischers so eher als organisch und natürlich wahrgenommen. Der Deckel simuliert in Farbe und Beschaffenheit eine Frucht und wird aus dickem Gummi hergestellt, das formbeständig aber gleichzeitig elastisch genug ist, um einfach auf den Sprayer drücken zu können. So kommt es dem Verbrau-cher vor, als würde er die Frucht tatsächlich auspressen.

Lorsqu'on presse un citron, on appuie sur la moitié de fruit avec les doigts pour en faire couler le jus parfumé. Ce geste s'apparente beaucoup à celui qu'on fait pour pulvériser un désodorisant. C'est ainsi qu'est née l'idée de remplacer l'embout pulvérisateur trop familier par une moitié de fruit pour cette nouvelle gamme. L'effet est bien plus agréable psychologiquement que d'appuyer sur un morceau de plastique dur, et le parfum du désodorisant est perçu comme plus organique et plus naturel. Le bouchon simule la couleur et la texture du fruit. Il est fabriqué dans un caoutchouc épais qui conserve sa forme, mais est suffisamment élastique pour que l'utilisateur puisse presser en toute liberté, ce qui lui donne l'impres-sion de toucher un fruit.

Best of the category

Clothing

Health care

body

Body care

Beauty

Distributors'/Retailers' own brands

Essay by

BRIAN HOUCK

Director, Visual Brand Communications at Henkel Consumer Goods, Inc. USA

At some level we would all love to work on brands that have huge marketing budgets, witty advertising campaigns and sexy endorsements. The reality is that the majority of us work on brands with smaller budgets which require their more limited consumer touch-points to work harder to convince the overwhelmed consumer to notice, consider and, hopefully, purchase our products. We have several of these brands within our Henkel North American portfolio, including Dial soap and Right Guard antiperspirant, but the one that's seen the most dramatic turnaround after reinventing itself recently is our Tone brand, which was reintroduced in 2010.

Tone was first launched in 1973 and has gone through several relaunches and redesigns since, even one during the exercise craze of the 1980s that resulted in the unfortunate tagline of "Tone Up With Tone". A consumer-driven message? Probably not. Playing second fiddle most of its life to bigger brands in our portfolio, Tone received the attention it deserved in 2008 when a project was undertaken to find out who our target consumer really was, or could be, and to use this to drive a design project that helped transform the brand. A true coming-out story.

Armed with research that helped identify our new consumer target and with the freedom to reach beyond most of the restrictions that cause many brands to "refresh" versus "reinvent", we embarked on an entirely new image and personality for the brand including new bottles, caps and dynamic graphics. Our target consumer is confident, fun-loving and thinks for herself. She is excited to try new things, loves great fragrances and delights in finding little hidden treasures. All of these traits drove the design process and were kept front and center in each design review.

Collaborating with a trusted design partner, Ciulla Associates in Chicago, and our fantastic graphics and industrial designer Scott Liu, who created our elegant and flowing bottle shape, we established an entirely new personality and design language for the brand. To keep costs in line, we chose a stock cap, but with color being so crucial to success, each fragrance variant would have its own signature color palette. The result is an elegant but approachable silhouette, reminiscent of a draped and flowing gown, in a range of rich jewel tones and cheerful pastels, inspired by premium cosmetics, all glimmering with pearlescence and adorned with illustrations that include scent and

ingredient cues, as well as little visual treats, or those little hidden treasures our consumer loves so much.

The results are stunning and have resulted in double-digit growth each year since its launch, including incremental distribution at key retailers, significant gains in household penetration and stronger equity for the brand. All this was achieved through the marriage of consumer-driven insights and a focused design effort that kept the consumer first at all stages. Since no major product improvements or investments in higher levels of marketing were made, this was a truly design-driven solution.

Design is the great equalizer and the package is the embodiment of the brand. At least it should be. The temptation is too often to "save" on development time and investment in the best package or to avoid "unnecessary" costs in implementation. Instead, we should be investing just as much energy and resources in the right package for all of our brands, particularly those that rely so heavily on its voice. Tone is one small example why.

In gewisser Hinsicht würden wir alle es lieben, für Brands mit riesigen Marketingbudgets und geistreichen Werbekampagnen zu arbeiten, deren allgemeine Wertschätzung wirklich sexy ist. Die Realität ist aber, dass die Mehrheit von uns für Marken mit kleineren Budgets tätig ist, die wegen eher eingeschränkter Berührungspunkte mit Kunden härter dafür arbeiten müssen, den überwältigten Verbraucher dahin zu bringen, seine Produkte wahrzunehmen, sich mit ihnen zu beschäftigen und dann hoffentlich auch zu kaufen. Wir besitzen in unserem Portfolio für Henkel North America einige solcher Marken, darunter die Seife Dial und das Deo Right Guard. Doch die wirklich dramatische Wende in letzter Zeit hat unsere Marke Tone genommen, nachdem das Produkt sich selbst neu erfunden hat und 2010 wieder eingeführt wurde.

Tone kam erstmals 1973 auf den Markt und wurde seither mehrmals erneut gestartet und umgestaltet — sogar während der Fitnesswelle der 1980er-Jahre, was zu dem unglücklichen Slogan „Tone Up With Tone" führte. Eine vom Konsumenten gesteuerte Botschaft? Wahrscheinlich nicht. Neben den größeren Marken in unserem Portfolio spielte Tone die meiste Zeit seines Daseins eher die zweite Geige, bekam aber 2008 die verdiente Aufmerksamkeit, als man anhand eines Projekts herausfinden wollte, wer denn tatsächlich Zielgruppe ist oder dazugehören könnte. Mit diesem Wissen wollte man dann ein Designprojekt steuern, um die Marke zu transformieren. Ein echtes Debüt!

Wir schufen für Tone ein völlig neues Image und eine neue Persönlichkeit, darunter auch neue Flaschen, Deckel und dynamische Grafiken. Dazu bewaffneten wir uns mit Recherchen, um unsere neuen Zielkonsumenten zu identifizieren, und bekamen die Freiheit, über die meisten Einschränkungen hinauszugehen, die bei vielen Marken dafür sorgt, sich lieber „aufzufrischen", statt „neu zu erfinden". Unsere Zielkonsumentin ist selbstbewusst, liebt Spaß und macht sich ihre eigenen Gedanken. Sie probiert gerne spannende neue Dinge aus, liebt tolle Düfte und freut sich ausnehmend darüber, kleine versteckte Schätze zu entdecken. All diese Eigenschaften steuerten den Designprozess und wurden bei jeder Designprüfung in den Mittelpunkt gerückt.

Wir arbeiteten mit Ciulla Associates, unserem vertrauten Designpartner in Chicago, und unserem fantastischen Grafik- und Industriedesigner Scott Liu zusammen, der diese elegante und fließende Flaschenform schuf. So etablierten wir für die Marke eine völlig neue Persönlichkeit und Designsprache. Damit

die Kosten nicht explodierten, entschieden wir uns für einen Standarddeckel, aber weil die Farbe für den Erfolg absolut zentral ist, sollte jede Duftnote ihre eigene kennzeichnende Farbpalette bekommen. Das Ergebnis ist eine elegante, aber zugängliche Silhouette, die an ein drapiertes und fließendes Gewand erinnert und reichhaltige edle Farbnuancen und heiter-verspielte Pastelltöne zeigt. Es ist inspiriert von herausragender Kosmetik, schimmernd im Perlglanz und verziert mit Illustrationen voller Anspielungen auf Düfte und deren Ingredienzen oder auch jene kleinen, verborgenen Schätze, die unsere Käuferinnen so lieben.

Die Ergebnisse sind verblüffend und haben seit dem Launch jährlich zu einer zweistelligen Wachstumssteigerung geführt, dazu auch einer steigenden Distribution bei zentralen Einzelhändlern, wesentlichen Zuwächsen in der Durchsetzung der Haushalte und einem deutlich ausgebauten Markenwert. All dies erzielten wir durch die Verschmelzung der durch Verbraucher gewonnenen Erkenntnisse und einem Aufwand für das Design, bei dem auf allen Ebenen der Konsument an vorderster Stelle stand. Da keine weiteren größeren Produktverbesserungen oder Investitionen auf höherer Marketingebene durchgeführt wurden, war dies eine wirklich durch Design gesteuerte Lösung.

Design ist ein hervorragend ausgleichender Faktor, und die Verpackung verkörpert die Marke. Zumindest sollte das so sein. Die Versuchung besteht zu oft darin, an der Entwicklungszeit und den Investitionen für die beste Verpackung zu „sparen" oder „unnötige Kosten" bei der Umsetzung zu vermeiden. Stattdessen sollten wir viel Energie und Ressourcen in die richtige Verpackung all unserer Marken investieren — vor allem jene, die so sehr auf ihre eigene Stimme angewiesen sind. Tone dient als kleines Beispiel, warum man es genau so machen sollte.

Essay by

BRIAN HOUCK

À un certain niveau, nous aimerions tous travailler sur des marques qui disposent d'énormes budgets marketing, de campagnes de publicité pleines d'esprit et de célébrités sexy qui les approuvent. En réalité, la plupart d'entre nous travaillent sur des marques qui ont des budgets plus modestes. Cela exige un travail plus intense sur les points de contact plus limités avec la clientèle afin de convaincre le consommateur sollicité de toutes parts de remarquer nos produits, d'envisager de les utiliser et, avec un peu de chance, de les acheter. Chez Henkel North American, nous avons plusieurs marques de ce type dans notre portefeuille, notamment le savon Dial et le déodorant Right Guard, mais celle qui a connu le redressement le plus radical après sa récente réinvention est la marque Tone, qui a été réintroduite en 2010.

Tone a été commercialisée pour la première fois en 1973, et a connu plusieurs relancements et révisions depuis, notamment dans les années 1980 lors de la grande folie du fitness, ce qui s'est soldé par le fâcheux slogan « Tone Up With Tone » (Tonifiez-vous avec Tone). Était-ce un message axé sur le consommateur ? Probablement pas. Ayant joué les seconds rôles la plus grande partie de son existence dans l'ombre des grandes marques de notre portefeuille, Tone a enfin reçu l'attention qu'elle méritait en 2008 lorsqu'un projet a été lancé pour découvrir qui était vraiment notre consommateur cible, ou qui il pouvait être, et utiliser ces informations pour un projet de design qui aiderait à transformer la marque. Cela a été une vraie révélation.

Armés d'une étude qui nous aidait à identifier notre nouvelle cible, et de la liberté de dépasser la plupart des restrictions qui obligent de nombreuses marques à se « rafraîchir » au lieu de se « réinventer », nous avons entrepris de donner à la marque une image et une personnalité complètement nouvelles, ce qui comprenait de nouvelles bouteilles, de nouveaux bouchons et un graphisme dynamique. Notre consommatrice cible est sûre d'elle, aime s'amuser et pense par elle-même. Elle adore la nouveauté, les parfums agréables et trouver de petits trésors cachés. Tous ces traits de caractère ont guidé le processus de conception et étaient au centre de chaque évaluation.

En collaboration avec un partenaire de confiance pour le design, Ciulla Associates à Chicago, et notre fantastique graphiste et concepteur industriel Scott Liu, qui a créé la forme fluide et élégante de notre bouteille, nous avons mis en place une toute nouvelle personnalité et un nouveau langage visuel pour la marque. Pour limiter les coûts, nous avons choisi un bouchon standard, mais la couleur étant essentielle pour la réussite du projet, chaque parfum devait avoir sa propre palette de couleurs. Le résultat est une silhouette élégante mais accessible, qui évoque une robe fluide drapée, dans une gamme de tons précieux et de pastels enjoués inspirés des cosmétiques haut de gamme, avec une finition opalescente et des illustrations qui donnent des indications sur le parfum et les ingrédients, ainsi que de petites surprises visuelles, qui correspondent aux petits trésors cachés que notre consommatrice aime tant.

Le résultat est superbe, et s'est soldé par une croissance à double chiffre chaque année depuis le lancement, une augmentation de la distribution chez nos détaillants stratégiques, une importante progression en termes de pénétration dans les ménages et une revalorisation du capital de la marque. Tout cela grâce à l'alliance d'informations sur nos consommatrices et d'un projet de design ciblé dont chaque étape était axée sur elles. Puisqu'aucune grande amélioration n'a été apportée au produit, et qu'aucun investissement n'a été réalisé plus haut sur l'échelle du marketing, il s'agit bel et bien d'une solution entièrement axée sur le design.

Le design est le meilleur facteur d'égalisation, et l'emballage est l'incarnation de la marque. Ou du moins, c'est ainsi que les choses devraient être. On est souvent tenté « d'économiser » sur le temps de développement et l'investissement dans un meilleur emballage ou d'éviter des coûts « inutiles » de mise en œuvre. Nous devrions plutôt investir autant d'énergie et de ressources dans l'emballage idéal pour chacune de nos marques, particulièrement pour celles dont le succès en dépend tellement. Tone n'en est qu'un exemple parmi d'autres.

Görtz 17 sought an innovative packaging design for its Converse Collection that would engage consumers at the point of sale, knowing that its line of stylish shoes was already something of a cult product. To boost sales and make the brand even more desirable a recyclable shoebox that makes plastic bags unnecessary was developed, the first of its kind. Its minimalist design draws attention to the handles, which can be removed and used as an extra pair of shoelaces. The series consists of five lace-colour designs that can be worn with any of the shoes in the collection.

Görtz 17 suchte für die Converse-Kollektion nach einem innovativen Verpackungsdesign, das Konsumenten am Point of Sale ansprechen sollte — wohl wissend, dass die Linie dieser stylishen Schuhe selbst bereits ein Kultprodukt ist. Um dem Verkauf nachzuhelfen und die Marke noch begehrenswerter erscheinen zu lassen, wurde als erstes Werk dieser Art ein recycelbares Schuhbehältnis entwickelt, das Plastiktüten überflüssig macht. Das minimalistische Design lenkt das Augenmerk auf die Tragegriffe, die man herausziehen und als zusätzliches Paar Schnürsenkel verwenden kann. Die Serie besteht aus fünf farbigen Schnürsenkeldesigns, die zu jedem der Schuhe aus der Kollektion passen.

Görtz 17 voulait pour sa collection Converse un emballage innovant qui attirerait l'attention des consommateurs sur le lieu de vente, sachant que sa ligne de chaussures était déjà un produit culte. Pour stimuler les ventes et rendre la marque encore plus séduisante, une boîte à chaussures recyclable qui rend les sacs en plastique inutiles a été mise au point. C'est la première en son genre. Son graphisme minimaliste attire l'attention sur les anses, que l'ont peut détacher et utiliser comme paire de lacets supplémentaire. La série se compose de cinq couleurs de lacets qui peuvent être portés avec n'importe quelle paire de chaussures de la collection.

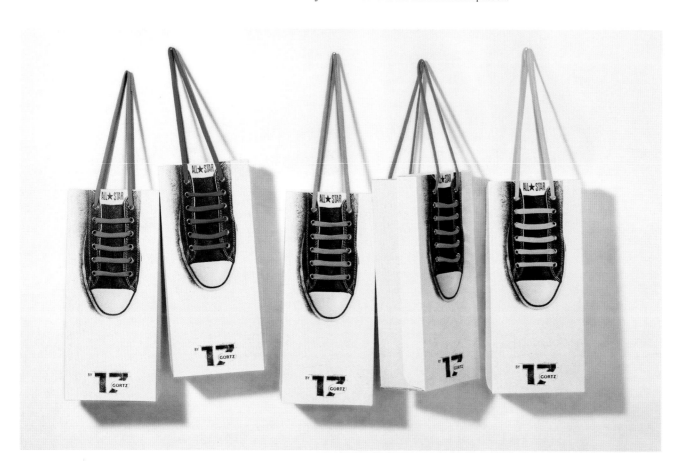

GÖRTZ 17
SHOELACE BOX

Design: Loved GmbH, Co-Agency Heiko Freyland
Creative Direction: Tim Belser, Heiko Freyland
Copy: Tim Belser
Design: Christiane Eckhardt, Peter Ruessmann
Photography: Alexander Kate (cmp)
Company: Kempertrautmann GmbH
Country: Germany
Category: Best of the category body

PLATINUM PENTAWARD 2011

ETUDE HOUSE
HANDS UP DEODORANT/DEPILATORY

Design: Jung Mi Jung, Sul Se Mi, Lee Mi Jin (Etude),
Kim Hee, Kim Jeun (Purun Image)
Company: Etude
Country: South Korea
Category: Best of the category body

PLATINUM PENTAWARD 2012

Etude is a beauty and cosmetic brand with nearly 30 years' experience in catering for girls in the 16-22 age-group. The various products in the Hands Up range have all been designed with an arm-shaped outer casing to express the message that users can raise their arms with full confidence. An extra detail is found in the tear-off strip when customers first open the container, a humorous reference to depilatory waxing. The range is sold through outlets in about a dozen countries in Asia, and at reasonable prices, with the younger customers in mind.

Etude besitzt als Beauty- und Kosmetikmarke eine fast 30-jährige Erfahrung mit Angeboten für junge Frauen zwischen 16 und 22. Den Verpackungen der verschiedenen Produkte aus der Palette Hands Up entwachsen Arme und vermitteln so die Botschaft, dass Verbraucher vertrauensvoll ihre Arme hochnehmen können. Der Abreißstreifen, mit dem das Behältnis beim ersten Mal geöffnet wird, liefert dem Kunden eine humorvolle Anspielung auf die Enthaarung mit Wachs. Die in Asien in etwa einem Dutzend Ländern erhältliche Produktserie nimmt durch ihre vernünftige Preisgestaltung Rücksicht auf die jüngere Zielgruppe.

Etude est une marque de cosmétiques et de produits de beauté qui possède près de 30 ans d'expérience sur le segment des jeunes filles de 16-22 ans. Les différents produits de la gamme Hands Up ont tous été dotés d'un emballage secondaire avec des bras pour faire comprendre que les utilisatrices peuvent lever les bras en toute tranquillité. Lorsque les clientes ouvrent le produit pour la première fois, elles trouvent un détail supplémentaire, une référence humoristique à l'épilation à la cire. La gamme est vendue dans une dizaine de pays en Asie à des prix raisonnables, pensés pour les jeunes consommatrices.

AHLENS

Concept Direction: Ulf Berlin
Art Direction: Cajsa Bratt
Photography: Niclas Alm
Design: Cajsa Bratt, Henrik Billqvist
Production Management: Anna Harrysson, Ida Stagles
Production Design: Monica Holm
Company: Designkontoret Silver
Country: Sweden
Category: Clothing

GOLD PENTAWARD 2011

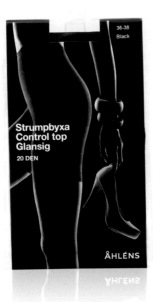
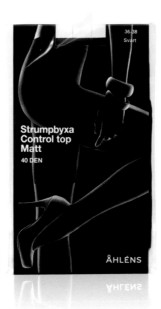
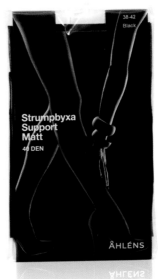

NEW BALANCE

Creative Direction: Todd Paulson
Design: Meenal Patel, Ryan Floss
Production: Neil Hagre
Account Management: Jen Kreilich
Project Management: Diana Ross-Gotta
Company: Knock Inc.
Country: USA
Category: Clothing

BRONZE PENTAWARD 2011

NOOKA
YOGURT WATCH

Design: Karim Rashid, Nooka
Company: Karim Rashid Inc.
Country: USA
Category: Clothing

BRONZE PENTAWARD 2011

AIR ASIA

Design: Somchana Kangwarnjit, Passorn
Subcharoenpun, Chidchanok Laohawattanakul,
Mathurada Bejrananda
Company: Prompt Design
Country: Thailand
Category: Clothing

BRONZE PENTAWARD 2011

BABYQSHOP

Design: Chow Kar Wo
Company: BabyQ Shop
Country: China
Category: Clothing

SILVER PENTAWARD 2011

Creative Direction: Christine Mau
Design: Jennifer Brock, Katie Hinrichs
Brand Design Management: Jody Douglas
Illustration: Hiroko Sanders
Company: Kimberly-Clark
Country: USA
Category: Health care

GOLD PENTAWARD 2011

Inner B is an inner-beauty food taken for moisturising. To express this, the design used the main motif of a water-droplet which as a pattern suggests welcome rain absorbed into the body. By selecting colours intended to appeal to women who care about beauty, and presented to give a feeling of jewellery, this was an attempt to establish a more exclusive design for the market. The container's simplicity was designed to convey trust in the product, rather than a more decorative design, while the size is small enough to be easily held in one hand and as comfortably as a droplet of water. The organic form presents a natural sense of calm, as well as closeness when it is held.

Inner B ist eine feuchtigkeitsspendende Nahrungsergänzung. Um dies zu transportieren, greift das Design das Motiv eines Wassertropfens auf, der als Muster einen wohligen Regen suggeriert, den der Körper in sich aufnimmt. Die Farbwahl soll Frauen ansprechen, denen Schönheit ein wichtiges Anliegen ist. Die wie Schmuck wirkende Präsentation legt darauf an, auf dem Markt ein sehr exklusives Design zu etablieren. Mit der Schlichtheit der Verpackung soll Vertrauen ins Produkt vermittelt werden, während das Gefäß zugleich klein genug ist, leicht und angenehm wie ein Wassertropfen in der Hand gehalten zu werden. Die organische Form vermittelt beim Anfassen einen natürlichen Sinn für Ruhe und Geschlossenheit.

Inner B est un complément alimentaire de beauté, formulé pour l'hydratation de la peau. Pour transmettre cette idée, l'élément de base du graphisme est une goutte d'eau, arrangée dans un motif qui suggère une pluie bienfaisante absorbée par la peau. Les couleurs choisies ciblent les femmes qui aiment s'occuper de leur beauté, et la présentation évoque la joaillerie pour tenter de se positionner sur un segment de marché plus exclusif. La simplicité du flacon est pensée pour inspirer confiance dans le produit, par opposition à une présentation plus décorative. De plus, il est assez petit pour tenir confortablement dans la main. Sa forme organique transmet un sentiment de calme naturel, et de proximité lorsqu'il est pris en main.

CJ CHEILJEDANG INNER B

Design: Jisun Kim, Kangkook Lee, Yuljoong Kim, Sunho Choi
Company: CJ CheilJedang Design Center
Country: South Korea
Category: Health care

GOLD PENTAWARD 2012

KLEENEX
REMOVE YOUR MASK

Design: David Jones, Mark Girvan
Company: Buddy
Country: UK
Category: Health care

SILVER PENTAWARD 2012

Simvastatin LPH 50 mg

Simvastatinum
30 comprimate filmate

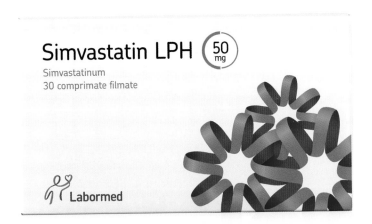

Labormed

Amoxicilină LPH 500 mg

Amoxicilină
10 capsule

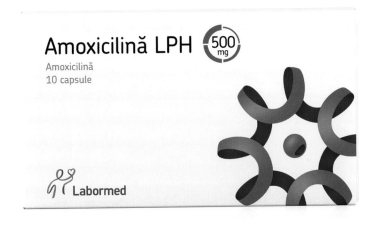

Labormed

Fluconazol LPH 50 mg

Fluconazolum
7 capsule

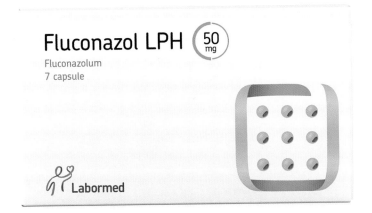

Labormed

Nopekar® 150 mg

Venlafaxinum
25 capsule

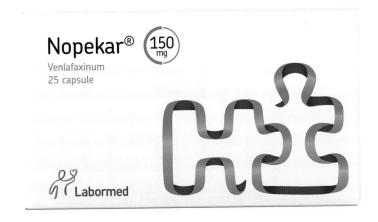

Labormed

Meloxicam LPH 15 mg

Meloxicamum
20 comprimate

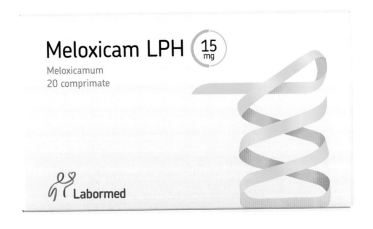

Labormed

Metformin LPH 500 mg

Metforminum
20 comprimate filmate

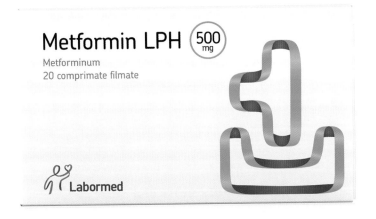

Labormed

LABORMED

Design: Liviu Maxim
Creative Direction: Marius Ursache
Company: Grapefruit
Country: Romania
Category: Health care

SILVER PENTAWARD 2011

POISE
HOURGLASS

Design: CBX creative team
Company: CBX
Country: USA
Category: Health care

BRONZE PENTAWARD 2011

KOTEX
U BY KOTEX TWEEN

Design: JooHyun, CBX team
Company: CBX
Country: USA
Category: Health care

BRONZE PENTAWARD 2011

KLEENEX HAND & AIR CARE SERIES

Design: JooHyun Sohn, BoGyeong Jung (Kimberly-Clark Design),
SangJin Kim, DongMin Kim (YuHan-Kimberly)
Company: YuHan-Kimberly
Country: South Korea
Category: Health care

SILVER PENTAWARD 2011

PUFFS
BLOSSOM

Creative Direction: Fred Richard
Art Direction: Ted Monnin
Design: Brandy Lockaby
Company: Interbrand
Country: USA
Category: Health care

BRONZE PENTAWARD 2011

KLEENEX BRAND
SPRING EDITION

Design: Christine Mau, Jody Douglas,
Jennifer Brock, Katie Hinrichs, Cinzah Merkens
Company: Kimberly-Clark
Country: USA
Category: Health care

SILVER PENTAWARD 2012

HALLS

Design: Jeff Boulton
Account Direction: Lawrence Dadds
Company: Davis
Country: Canada
Category: Health care

BRONZE PENTAWARD 2011

HVS JOWER

Art Direction: Koichi Sugiyama
Design: Koichi Sugiyama
Copy Text: Yuta Naruse
Production: Futoshi Ichii
Company: Koichi Sugiyama
Country: Japan
Category: Body care

GOLD PENTAWARD 2011

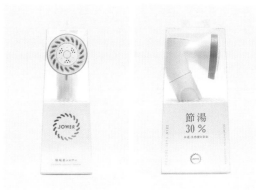

Jower is a new showerhead developed in Japan which removes chlorine and other unwanted impurities from the water by means of a replaceable fibre cartridge. It also boasts water-saving features and may be temporarily turned off directly at the showerhead, and is available with four different colour highlights. The packaging emphasises its pure action by presenting it with a clean printed design heat-stamped in silver on brilliant white, the transparent plastic making the product visible to attract customers from any angle in the store.

Jower ist ein neuer, in Japan entwickelter Duschkopf, der Chlor und andere unerwünschte Unreinheiten mit einer austauschbaren Kohlefaserkartusche aus dem Wasser filtert. Überdies wirbt das in vier verschiedenen Farben erhältliche Produkt mit seiner wassersparenden Eigenschaft, und das Gerät kann direkt am Duschkopf zeitweilig abgeschaltet werden. Die Verpackung betont diese aktive Reinigung durch ein klares Design, das im Wärmedruckverfahren in Silber auf Brillantweiß aufgebracht ist. Mit dem transparenten Plastikaufsatz macht das Produkt im Laden aus jedem Blickwinkel auf sich aufmerksam.

Jower est un nouveau pommeau de douche conçu au Japon, qui élimine le chlore et les autres impuretés indésirables de l'eau grâce à une cartouche de fibres remplaçable. Il est également doté de fonctions qui permettent d'économiser l'eau, et de la couper directement au pommeau. Il est disponible en quatre couleurs. L'emballage met en avant son action purificatrice à l'aide d'un graphisme épuré imprimé à chaud en argent sur du blanc pur, et le plastique transparent montre le produit pour attirer les clients de n'importe quel angle dans le magasin.

Bébé de forêt is a new line of organic skincare for infants, made with 99% natural ingredients. The pump-bottles are designed for effective delivery of the organic ingredients which are derived from young plants that grow in the south of France. The bud-shaped pump and smaller piece on the jar were thus designed as visualisations of newly sprouting plants bursting with energy, set in a furrowed cap representing a rich soil. The overall impression is of a fresh sprout in a pot. The package received ECOCERT accreditation for using recyclable plastic, paper materials and soya ink. It has been launched successfully as a leader in the mass-market organic skincare category.

Bébé de forêt ist eine neue Produktlinie mit organischen Hautpflegemitteln für Kleinkinder, hergestellt aus zu 99 % natürlichen Inhaltsstoffen. Die organischen Zutaten stammen von jungen Pflanzen aus Südfrankreich, effizient können sie über den Pumpspender entnommen werden. Die knospenförmige Pumpe und der recht kleine Griff auf dem Tiegeldeckel sind Nachbildungen frischer Pflanzensprossen, die vor Energie fast platzen. Der gerillte Deckel repräsentiert die fruchtbare Muttererde. Der Gesamteindruck ist der einer keimenden Knospe in einem Anzuchttopf. Der Verpackung wurde aufgrund der Verwendung von wiederverwertbarem Plastik, Papiermaterial und Sojadrucktinte die ECOCERT-Zertifizierung verliehen. Das Produkt ist führend auf dem Massenmarkt in der Kategorie organische Hauptpflegemittel.

Bébé de forêt est une nouvelle ligne de produits de soin pour les nourrissons, contenant 99 % d'ingrédients naturels. Les bouteilles à pompe sont conçues pour doser efficacement les ingrédients organiques, dérivés de jeunes plantes qui poussent dans le sud de la France. La pompe en forme de bourgeon et la petite poignée sur le pot représentent de jeunes plants vigoureux, et sont montées sur des bouchons dont les sillons représentent un riche terreau. Le tout imite une jeune plante en pot. L'emballage est certifié ECOCERT car il emploie du plastique recyclable, du papier et de l'encre de soja. Il a été lancé avec succès en tant que leader dans la catégorie des produits de soin organiques sur le marché grand public.

GREENFINGER BÉBÉ DE FORÊT

Design: JooHyun Sohn, BoGyeong Jung, Hoon Lee, JiEun Choi, Woofe Design
Marketing: JiHyun Sung
Company: YuHan-Kimberly
Country: South Korea
Category: Body care

GOLD PENTAWARD 2012

BIC
SOLEIL

Design: Bic USA Inc. design team
Illustration: Lisa Henderling
Company: Bic USA Inc.
Country: USA
Category: Body care

SILVER PENTAWARD 2012

SCHWARZKOPF OSIS+
STYLE SHIFTERS

Creative Direction: Olivier Boré
Company: Crépuscule
Country: France
Category: Body care

BRONZE PENTAWARD 2012

CHICCO ARTSANA
PURE.BIO

Creative Direction: Chiara Sozzi Pomati
Design: Marta Mapelli
Account Management: Alessandra Mauri
Company: CMGRP Italia/FutureBrand
Country: Italy
Category: Body care

SILVER PENTAWARD 2011

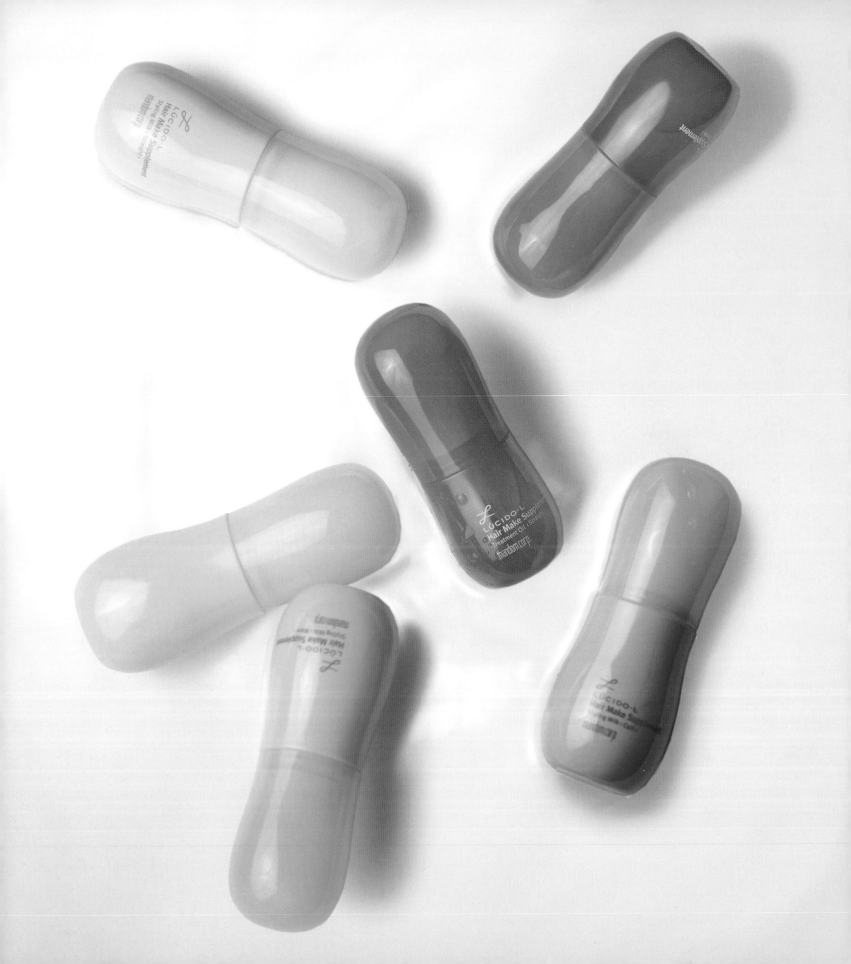

MANDOM
LUCIDO-L HAIR MAKE SUPPLEMENT

Creative Direction/Art Direction: Zenji Hashimoto
Design: Midori Hirai, Anna Kuramochi
Account Management: Koichi Furusawa
Company: Cloud8 Inc.
Country: Japan
Category: Body care

SILVER PENTAWARD 2012

EUGÈNE PERMA PRESTANCE

Design: Ruta Figarol, Virginie Hirsch
Company: Lonsdale
Country: France
Category: Body care

BRONZE PENTAWARD 2012

DIZAO ORGANICS

Creative Direction: Alexey Fadeev
Art Direction: Aram Mirzoyants, Ludmila Galchenko
Company: Depot WPF
Country: Russia
Category: Body care

BRONZE PENTAWARD 2011

ETUDE HOUSE
MILK TALK BODY WASH

Design: Jung Mi Jung, Sul Se Mi,
Kim Min Hee, Choi Ji Yee
Company: Etude
Country: South Korea
Category: Body care

BRONZE PENTAWARD 2012

SHERPA
HAIR CARE SERIES

Design: Arimino
XYZ Creation: Yasuo Kiuchi, Another Report
Company: Arimino
Country: Japan
Category: Body care

BRONZE PENTAWARD 2011

ESTHAAR
HAIR CARE RANGE

Design: Mi Young Park, Ji Hoon Jeon
Company: Aekyung Industrial
Country: South Korea
Category: Body care

BRONZE PENTAWARD 2011

COLGATE
OPTIC WHITE

Creative Direction: Peter Johnson
Design: Amy Sprague
Company: Swerve Inc.
Country: USA
Category: Body care

BRONZE PENTAWARD 2012

21 Drops is a line of therapeutic-grade essential oil blends catering for 21 universal complaints through 21 blended aromatherapy solutions. To broaden such a product's appeal to retailers as well as consumers a brand identity was developed based on qualities of transparency, quality and product design. A contemporary sensibility has been matched with the heritage of aromatherapy which helps recall the artisanal nature of the product. The packaging employs a vibrant colour palette and font-driven numerical graphics combined with embossed patterns on wholesome card, all chosen to be specifically tactile and memorable while the copy and naming system is evocative yet straightforward and informative.

21 Drops ist eine Produktlinie ätherischer Öle in therapeutischer Reinheit, die 21 universelle Beschwerden anhand von 21 Aromatherapielösungen beheben soll. Damit ein solches Produkt für Händler wie Kunden ansprechend wirkt, wurde eine Markenidentität entwickelt, die auf den Qualitäten Transparenz, Qualität und Produktdesign beruht. Neben das zeitgenössische Empfinden hat man das Erbe der Aromatherapie gestellt und die handwerkliche Natur des Produkts in Erinnerung gerufen. Für die Verpackung werden neben einer leuchtenden Farbpalette und charakteristischen Schriften für die Zahlengrafiken auch gestanzte Muster auf umweltfreundlichem Karton eingesetzt. Alles ist so gewählt, dass es besonders taktil und erinnernswert scheint, während Produkttexte und das Namenssystem aussagekräftig, aber doch unkompliziert und informativ sind.

21 Drops est une gamme de mélanges thérapeutiques d'huiles essentielles destinés à traiter 21 problèmes universels grâce à 21 solutions d'aromathérapie. Afin de rendre le produit plus attrayant pour les détaillants ainsi que pour les consommateurs, l'identité de marque a été développée autour des idées de transparence, de qualité et de conception de produit. La sensibilité contemporaine s'allie à l'héritage traditionnel de l'aromathérapie pour aider à rappeler la nature artisanale du produit. L'emballage emploie une palette de couleurs vives et différentes polices de caractères pour les numéros, combinées à des motifs en relief sur du carton brut. Tout cela a été choisi expressément pour créer une impression tactile et mémorable. Les textes et le système choisis pour les noms sont évocateurs, mais directs et informatifs.

21 DROPS

Creative Direction: Kelly Kovack, Larry Paul
Graphic Design: Mi Rae Park
Company: Purpose-Built
Country: USA
Category: Beauty

GOLD PENTAWARD 2011

ESPRIT
URBAN NATURE

Creative Direction: Sébastien Servaire
Design: Yael Bibliowicz, Juliette Lavat
Technical Development: Erwann Pivert
Company: R'Pure Studio
Country: France
Category: Beauty

SILVER PENTAWARD 2012

THE SCENT OF DEPARTURE

Design: Magali Sénéquier, Gérald Ghislain
Company: The Scent of Departure
Country: France
Category: Beauty

GOLD PENTAWARD 2012

TN — TEEN'S NATURE

Design: JooHyun Sohn, BoGyeong Jung (Kimberly-Clark Design),
JaeYong Lee (YuHan-Kimberly), KyungMi Lee (Cyphics)
Company: YuHan-Kimberly
Country: South Korea
Category: Beauty
SILVER PENTAWARD 2011

MAJOLICA MAJORCA
PUFF DE CHEEK

Creative Direction: Masato Kanazawa
Art Direction: Yoji Nobuto
Design: Kaori Kondo
Company: Shiseido Co., Ltd.
Country: Japan
Category: Beauty

SILVER PENTAWARD 2011

HARDFORD
HYPE BY MOOD

Creative Direction: André Hindersson
Design: Linus Östberg, Steven Webb
Production Management: Maja Wetterberg
Production Design: Monica Holm
Company: Designkontoret Silver
Country: Sweden
Category: Beauty

BRONZE PENTAWARD 2011

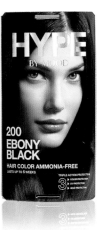

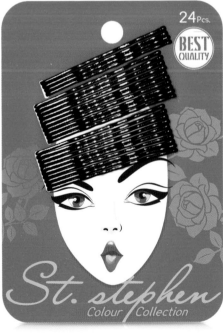

ST. STEPHEN

Creative Direction: Somchana Kangwarnjit
Design: Chalita Chaipibul
Company: Prompt Design
Country: Thailand
Category: Beauty
SILVER PENTAWARD 2012

O BOTICÁRIO EGEO CHOC

Design: Rebeca Apelbaum, Ana Luiza Bedin,
Tanea Domaradski, Daniella Rigotti, Eduardo Maldonado,
Fabio Calzavara, William Pasqualin
Company: Komm Design Strategy
Country: Brazil
Category: Beauty
BRONZE PENTAWARD 2011

CHOA

Design: Mi Young Park, Ae Ra Sin, Tae Hee Lee
Company: Aekyung Industrial
Country: South Korea
Category: Beauty
BRONZE PENTAWARD 2012

CAUDALIE
EAUX FRAICHES

Design: Bénédicte de Lescure
Company: Bénédicte de Lescure
Country: France
Category: Beauty

BRONZE PENTAWARD 2012

O BOTICÁRIO
EUDORA SOUL

Design: Luis Gustavo Bartolomei,
Rodrigo Costabeber, Alex Diniz, Hudson Abreu,
Nathalia Zupo, Nancy Stegal, Gabriela Simões
Company: B|G Designers
Country: Brazil
Category: Beauty

BRONZE PENTAWARD 2011

A re-design of this sun-care range was undertaken with an eye on optimising costs but without any perceived loss in quality or product recognition. The resulting blow-moulded bottles in two varieties may be fitted with different lids and standard dosing mechanisms: pump, spray or disc-top. This solution dealt with the logistics of production and packaging while still offering a different-iated range of products, each with its own identity. The colouring distinguishes the sub-ranges of sunscreen, tanning-aid and after-sun, supported by clean and succinct graphics. These are linked to a prominent numeral that indicates the protection factor, a key element in the purchase decision but which also strengthens the personality of the range.

Das Redesign dieser Sonnenschutzmittel berücksich-tigt die Kostenoptimierung ohne merkbare Verluste bei Qualität oder Produktwahrnehmung. Das Ergebnis sind blasgeformte Flaschen in zwei Varianten, die man mit unterschiedlichen Verschlüssen und Dosiermechanis-men ausstatten kann: Pumpe, Spray oder Disc-Top. Das löst die Logistik von Produktion und Verpackung und bietet gleichzeitig klar erkennbare Unterschiede zwischen den Produkten, die alle ihre eigene Identität aufweisen. Durch Farbgebung und die klaren, prägnanten Grafiken lassen sich die Gruppen Sonnenschutz, Bräunungsmittel und After Sun leicht unterscheiden. Bei den Grafiken wird mit prominent dargestellten Ziffern gearbeitet, die auf den Schutzfaktor verweisen. Dieses Schlüsselelement für die Kaufentscheidung stärkt auch die Persönlichkeit der Palette.

Le remodelage de cette gamme de produits solaires avait pour but d'optimiser les coûts tout en évitant toute perte de qualité perçue ou de reconnaissance du produit. Les deux modèles de bouteille soufflée peuvent être équipés de différents bouchons et de mécanismes de dosage standard : pompe, spray ou bouchon disc top. Cette solution répond aux besoins logistiques de la production et de l'emballage tout en permettant de proposer une gamme de produits différenciés qui ont chacun leur propre identité. Les sous-gammes de protection solaire, aide au bronzage et après-soleil se différencient grâce à leurs couleurs et à un graphisme épuré et succinct. Un grand chiffre indique le facteur de protection, élément essentiel dans la décision d'achat, et renforce également la personnalité de la gamme.

MERCADONA SOLCARE

Design: Nacho Lavernia,
Alberto Cienfuegos, Raul Edo
Company: Lavernia & Cienfuegos
Country: Spain
Category: Distributors'/Retailers' own brands
GOLD PENTAWARD 2012

IN-KIND

Creative Direction: Mark Christou
Client Development Direction: Cynthia Davies
Company: Pearlfisher
Country: USA
Category: Distributors'/Retailers' own brands

SILVER PENTAWARD 2011

BLEND COLLECTIVE

Creative Direction: Dave Richmond
Design: Sian Sargent
Company: R Design
Country: UK
Category: Distributors'/Retailers' own brands

SILVER PENTAWARD 2012

VS ATTRACTIONS

Creative Direction: Sandra Monteparo
Art Direction: Paulina Reyes
Design: Sunnie Guglielmo
Company: Victoria's Secret Beauty
Country: USA
Category: Distributors'/Retailers' own brands

SILVER PENTAWARD 2011

BALEA YOUNG — MADEMOISELLE CHIC

General Management: Luc Bütz
Creative Direction: Ines Jantzen
Art Direction: Jana Krüger
Customer Support: Karla König
Final Artwork: Jörg Ortmanns
Trainee Design: Helen Jahn
Production: Verena Kordes
Company: WINcommunication
Country: Germany
Category: Distributors'/Retailers' own brands

BRONZE PENTAWARD 2012

BALEA — TREND IT UP

Creative Direction: Marcus Lichte
Art Direction: Mareike Mohr, Jana Krüger,
Sebastian Hampen
Customer Services: Julia Bos
Artwork: Harald Strang
Company: WINcommunication
Country: Germany
Category: Distributors'/Retailers' own brands

BRONZE PENTAWARD 2011

IA

Creative Direction: Eduardo del Fraile
Design: Eduardo del Fraile, Manuel Quílez
Company: Eduardo del Fraile
Country: Spain
Category: Distributors'/Retailers' own brands

SILVER PENTAWARD 2012

Executive Creative Direction: Sam O'Donahue
Design/Creative Direction: Pierre Jeand'heur
Design: Felix de Voss, Valeria Bianco
Company: Established
Country: USA
Category: Distributors'/Retailers' own brands

BRONZE PENTAWARD 2012

WOMEN'SECRET FRAGRANCES

Design: Garrofé design team
Company: Garrofé Brand&Pack
Country: Spain
Category: Distributors'/Retailers' own brands

BRONZE PENTAWARD 2012

ORIFLAME
WONDER COLOUR LIPSTICK

Design: Ivan Bel Casado
Company: Ivan Bel Design
Country: Sweden
Category: Distributors'/Retailers' own brands

BRONZE PENTAWARD 2011

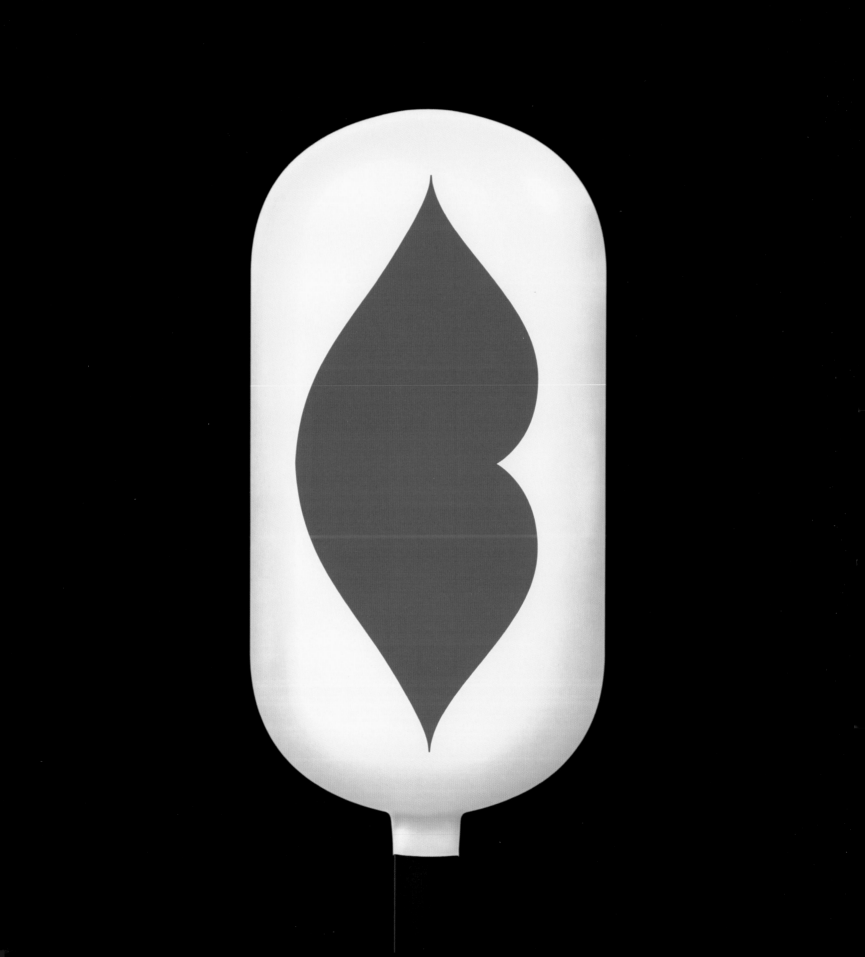

Best of the category

Perfumes

Cosmetics

Spirits

Fine wines, champagne

luxury

Casks, coffrets, gift boxes

Gourmet food

Limited editions, limited series, collectors' items

Distributors'/Retailers' own brands

Packaging concept

JOE WANG & YUAN ZONGLEI

Joe Wang, SVP at Shanghai Jahwa
Yuan Zonglei, Chief Designer at Shanghai Jahwa, Pentaward Jury Member 2010–2012

30 years ago, few people believed that China would become the second-largest economy in the world. And China as the world's second-largest luxury market was even harder to imagine. However, one should not be surprised by the second fact if the first had been accepted, or even predicted only a few years ago. Japan's role as a precedent is a useful model here. People in Asian countries (including Japan and China) have a strong desire for luxury goods in their cultural traditions. Once the economic power of these populations reached a certain level, the market for luxury goods would definitely boom, as happened with the Four Asian Tigers (Hong Kong, Singapore, South Korea and Taiwan). The reason their luxury markets were not as significant as those in Japan and China is the relatively small sizes of their population and economy.

Chinese luxury goods consumers can be grouped into three categories:

1 — The Superiority Group (or Upward-looking Group)
People seeking to demonstrate their real social status and prestige as members of upper-classes in political, economic and cultural areas.

2 — The Super-vanity Group (or Outward-looking Group)
People seeking to impress others by showing off that they can afford something not many people can.

3 — The Super-quality Group (or Inward-looking Group)
People seeking to enjoy products of superior quality and the positive, comfortable feelings associated with them, but not as status symbols.

There are also those who buy luxury goods purely for the reason of giving them as gifts to others. This is a little bit different and more common in China than in other markets. This group cares more about the different aspects of awareness, recognition and prestige of the brands they buy, so that the purpose of pleasing their recipients, be they family members, friends, government officials or *er'nai* (lovers or second wives), can be fulfilled effectively, if not perfectly.

The booming Chinese luxury market has so far been dominated by western companies and brands, except for a small number of categories where Chinese companies and brands have historical or natural advantages, such as *baijiu*

(a Chinese alcoholic spirit, with Moutai and Wu Liang Ye as the most famous brands), cigarettes, teas, rare furniture etc. However, more and more Chinese companies have made the decision to stop kowtowing to western companies, to dispense with the "cheap" image of low-end manufacturing, or to transform "Made in China" to "Made by China". One of the pioneers here is the re-emergence of Shanghai Jahwa's Shanghai Vive. The art deco style brand is Jahwa's oldest brand and has a literal meaning of "two beautiful girls" in Chinese. Shanghai Vive, having disappeared from the market for a few decades, opened its first store in the legendary Peace Hotel near Shanghai Bund followed by more outlets in other high-end shopping destinations in Shanghai and Beijing.

With formal training in arts and design, especially the unique perspective of Chinese aesthetics, Chinese designers have already been invited by western luxury brands to work independently or co-operate with their western peers in designing products for China's market as well as for international markets. These designers are the ones who create and establish the function, quality, style, taste, aesthetics, as well as the character, spirit and soul of luxury products. Any Chinese company that wants to play in the field of luxury goods must understand the important role of designers and invest heavily in their development and growth while leveraging their talents. Compared with their western counterparts, Chinese designers need to have a deeper understanding of the very essence of luxury goods.

The question for both Chinese companies and Chinese designers is: "Are You Ready?"

Noch vor 30 Jahren hätten nur wenige Menschen angenommen, dass China zur zweitgrößten Wirtschaft der Welt werden könnte. Und sich China als den zweitgrößten Markt weltweit für Luxusgüter vorzustellen, war noch schwieriger. Allerdings sollte einen die zweite Tatsache nicht überraschen, wäre die erste wenige Jahre zuvor akzeptiert oder wenigstens vorhergesagt worden. Japan hat nun die Rolle des hilfreichen Präzedenzfalls inne. Den Menschen in asiatischen Ländern einschließlich Japan und China eignet in ihren kulturellen Traditionen ein starker Wunsch nach Luxusgütern. Wenn die ökonomische Leistung der Bevölkerung ein bestimmtes Maß erreicht hat, boomt definitiv auch der Markt für Edles — so geschehen bei den vier asiatischen Tigern Hongkong, Singapur, Südkorea und Taiwan. Deren Markt für Luxusgüter ist nur deswegen nicht so signifikant wie jener von Japan und China, weil sie über eine zahlenmäßig relativ geringe Bevölkerung und Ökonomie verfügen.

Die Konsumenten für chinesische Luxusgüter kann man in drei Kategorien gruppieren:

1 — Die Gruppe der (nach oben orientierten) Überlegenen
Diese Leute wollen ihren wahren sozialen Status und ihr Prestige als Mitglieder der Oberklasse im politischen, ökonomischen und kulturellen Bereich demonstrieren.

2 — Die Gruppe der (nach außen orientierten) Supereitlen
Diese Menschen wollen andere beeindrucken, indem sie mit dem angeben, was sich nicht viele leisten können.

3 — Die Gruppe mit der (nach innen orientierten) Superqualität
Deren Mitglieder sind bestrebt, Produkte von überlegener Qualität und die damit verknüpften positiven und komfortablen Gefühle zu genießen, aber nicht als Statussymbole.

Es gibt auch solche, die Luxusgüter einfach nur aus dem Grund kaufen, um sie anderen zu schenken. Das ist in China etwas anders und kommt hier häufiger vor als auf anderen Märkten. Diese Gruppe achtet mehr auf die Aspekte Bekanntheit, Wiedererkennungswert und Prestige, um den Zweck, den Beschenkten in höchstem Maße zu erfreuen, effektiv, wenn nicht gar perfekt zu erfüllen — egal, ob es sich um Verwandte, Freunde, Behördenmitglieder oder *er'nai* (Geliebte bzw. Nebenfrauen) handeln mag.

Der boomende chinesische Luxusgütermarkt war bisher von westlichen Unternehmen und Marken dominiert, außer bei einer kleinen Anzahl von Kategorien, in denen chinesische Firmen einen historischen oder natürlichen Vorteil aufweisen, wie etwa *Baijiu* (die bekanntesten Marken dieser chinesischen Spirituose sind Moutai und Wu Liang Ye), bei Zigaretten, Tees, seltenen Möbeln etc. Allerdings beschließen immer mehr chinesische Unternehmen, ihren Kotau vor westlichen Firmen aufzugeben und sich vom billigen Image der geringwertigen Herstellung zu distanzieren oder das „Made in China" in ein „Made by China" zu verwandeln. Einer der Pioniere dafür ist das neuerliche Erscheinen von Shanghai Vive aus unserer Firma Shanghai Jahwa. Diese Marke im Art-déco-Stil ist Jahwas älteste Marke und bedeutet auf Chinesisch wörtlich „zwei schöne Frauen". Shanghai Vive war zwar einige Jahrzehnte vom Markt verschwunden, aber eröffnete nun das erste Geschäft im legendären Peace Hotel in der Nähe des Schanghai Bunds, gefolgt von weiteren Stores in anderen hochpreisigen Einkaufszentren von Schanghai und Beijing.

Chinesische Designer mit ihrer formalen Schulung in Kunst und Design, vor allem der einzigartigen Perspektive chinesischer Ästhetik, wurden bereits von westlichen Luxusmarken eingeladen, unabhängig oder auch gemeinsam mit ihren westlichen Kollegen Produkte sowohl für den chinesischen als auch den internationalen Markt zu erarbeiten. Diese Designer erschaffen und etablieren die Funktion und Qualität, den Stil und Geschmack, die Ästhetik und auch den Charakter, den Geist und die Seele dieser Luxusprodukte. Jede chinesische Firma, die in der Sparte Luxusgüter mithalten will, muss die wichtige Rolle der Designer kennen und in hohem Maße in deren Entwicklung und Wachstum investieren, um ihre Talente zu nutzen. Verglichen mit ihren westlichen Kollegen, müssen chinesische Designer die wesentliche Essenz von Luxusgütern in viel tiefer greifender Form erfassen können.

Eine Frage stellt sich chinesischen Unternehmern und Designern gleichermaßen: „Seid ihr bereit?"

Essay by

JOE WANG & YUAN ZONGLEI

Il y a trente ans, rares étaient ceux qui pensaient que la Chine deviendrait la deuxième économie du monde. Et il était encore plus difficile d'imaginer qu'elle serait aussi le deuxième marché mondial du luxe. Pourtant, si le premier phénomène a été accepté ou même prédit il y a seulement quelques années, il ne faut pas s'étonner du deuxième. Le précédent du Japon est un modèle qui nous sera utile ici. Les habitants des pays asiatiques (notamment le Japon et la Chine) ont un profond désir pour les produits de luxe enraciné dans leurs traditions culturelles. Une fois que la puissance économique de ces populations avait atteint un certain niveau, le marché du luxe allait forcément connaître un boom, comme cela était arrivé pour les quatre dragons asiatiques (Hong Kong, Singapour, Corée du Sud et Taïwan). La raison pour laquelle leurs marchés du luxe n'étaient pas aussi importants qu'au Japon ou en Chine est que leurs populations et leurs économies sont relativement plus modestes.

Les consommateurs chinois de produits de luxe peuvent être groupés en trois catégories :

1 — Le groupe de la supériorité (ou le groupe qui regarde vers le haut)
Des personnes qui cherchent à afficher leur statut social réel et leur prestige en tant que membres des classes supérieures en termes de politique, d'économie et de culture.

2 — Le groupe de la super vanité (ou le groupe qui regarde vers l'extérieur)
Des personnes qui cherchent à impressionner les autres en montrant qu'ils peuvent se permettre quelque chose que peu de gens ont les moyens d'acheter.

3 — Le groupe de la super qualité (ou le groupe qui regarde vers l'intérieur)
Des personnes qui cherchent à jouir de produits de qualité supérieure et des sentiments positifs et confortables qui leur sont associés, mais ne sont pas attachés au symbole de statut social.

Il y a également ceux qui achètent des produits de luxe uniquement dans le but de les offrir à d'autres personnes. Cela est un peu différent, et plus courant en Chine que sur les autres marchés. Ce groupe s'intéresse davantage aux différents aspects de notoriété, reconnaissance et prestige des marques qu'ils

achètent, afin d'atteindre efficacement, voire parfaitement, leur objectif de faire plaisir au destinataire du cadeau, qu'il s'agisse de membres de la famille, d'amis, de fonctionnaires ou de leur *er'nai* (maîtresse ou deuxième épouse).

L'essor du marché du luxe chinois a jusqu'à maintenant été dominé par des entreprises et marques occidentales, sauf pour un petit nombre de catégories dans lesquelles les entreprises et marques chinoises ont un avantage historique ou naturel, comme le *baijiu* (un alcool chinois, pour lequel les marques les plus célèbres sont Moutai et Wu Liang Ye), les cigarettes, le thé, les meubles rares, etc. Cependant, de plus en plus d'entreprises chinoises ont décidé d'arrêter de courber l'échine devant les entreprises occidentales, de se défaire de leur image de fabrication bon marché et bas de gamme, et de transformer le « Made in China » en « Made by China ». L'un des pionniers de cette tendance est Shanghai Jahwa, avec la résurgence de sa marque Shanghai Vive. Cette marque de style Art déco est la plus ancienne de Jahwa, et elle signifie littéralement « deux superbes filles » en chinois. Shanghai Vive, qui avait disparu du marché pendant quelques décennies, a ouvert son premier magasin dans le légendaire hôtel Peace près du Bund de Shanghai, puis d'autres points de vente dans d'autres centres commerciaux haut de gamme à Shanghai et à Pékin.

Les designers chinois possédant une formation officielle dans le domaine de l'art et du design, et particulièrement de la perspective unique de l'esthétique chinoise, ont déjà été invités à travailler indépendamment ou à collaborer avec leurs confrères occidentaux afin de concevoir des produits pour le marché chinois ainsi que pour les marchés internationaux. Ces designers sont ceux qui créent et déterminent la fonction, la qualité, le style, le goût, l'esthétique ainsi que le caractère, l'esprit et l'âme des produits de luxe. Toute entreprise chinoise qui veut jouer sur le terrain des produits de luxe doit comprendre l'importance du rôle des designers, et investir en conséquence dans leur développement et leur croissance tout en tirant parti de leurs talents. Comparés avec leurs confrères occidentaux, les designers chinois ont besoin d'acquérir une connaissance plus profonde de l'essence même des biens de luxe.

Pour les entreprises et les designers de Chine, la question est : « Êtes-vous prêts ? »

MARC JACOBS
BANG

Design: Harry Allen
Company: Harry Allen Design
Country: USA
Category: Best of the category luxury

PLATINUM PENTAWARD 2011
LUXEPACK PRIZE

In developing a form for the new fragrance from Marc Jacobs the packaging had to reflect the brand image and stand out to the young male target audience whilst also responding to the given name, **Bang**. Metal sheets struck with hammers and rocks retain the form of the impact, a literal visualisation, and one such piece was translated by computer to produce the design for the bottle. Slightly ambiguous, masculine but not over-designed, this template was then given over to the engineering team to produce in glass, the other initial criterion.

Das Design für den neuen Duft von Marc Jacobs sollte das Image der Marke widerspiegeln und für das junge, männliche Zielpublikum hervorstechen, gleichzeitig den Namen **Bang** aufgreifen. Mit Hammer oder Stein deformiertes Metall bewahrt diese Form — eine buchstäbliche Visualisierung. Ein solches Ergebnis wurde vom Computer für das Flaschendesign umgerechnet. Dezent mehrdeutig und maskulin, aber nicht überdesignt, wurde diese Vorlage dann ans Ingenieursteam weitergegeben, um die Produktion in Glas auszuführen — das war ein weiteres Eingangskriterium.

Pour le nouveau parfum de Marc Jacobs, l'emballage devait refléter l'image de la marque et se faire remarquer auprès de sa cible d'hommes jeunes, tout en faisant écho au nom choisi, **Bang**. Une feuille de métal frappée par un marteau ou une pierre conserve la forme de l'impact. C'est cette visualisation littérale qui a été traduite numériquement pour produire la forme de la bouteille. Légèrement ambigu, masculin mais pas trop travaillé, ce modèle a ensuite été transféré à l'équipe d'ingénieurs afin de le fabriquer en verre, ce qui était une autre condition décidée dès le départ.

For a new fragrance from **Davidoff** associated with sports a bold and strikingly distinctive design was developed that was quite unlike the form of classic bottles. Taking one strong shape from the world of fitness and athletics, the bottle was given the form of a dumb-bell, as used for muscle-building by people in all manner of sporting activities. Thus clearly identifiable, the bottle's shape also conveyed associations of exercise, performance and strength represented by the original object.

Für den neuen Duft von **Davidoff**, verbunden mit der Welt des Sports, wurde ein mutiges und faszinierend charakteristisches Design entwickelt, das völlig anders war als die klassische Flakonform. Aus der Welt von Fitness und Athleten stammt das Vorbild dieses Behältnisses: Die Hantel wird bei allen möglichen sportlichen Aktivitäten für das Krafttraining verwendet. Somit ist sie klar identifizierbar, und die Form konnotiert auch Aspekte von Training, Leistungsfähigkeit und Stärke, wie sie das originale Objekt repräsentiert.

Une bouteille audacieuse et d'une originalité saisissante, très éloignée de la forme classique, a été conçue pour un nouveau parfum de **Davidoff** associé au sport. Elle est en forme d'haltère, un instrument de musculation utilisé dans toutes sortes d'activités sportives. La forme de la bouteille est donc clairement identifiable, et véhicule également des associations avec l'exercice physique, la performance et la force, notions représentées par l'objet original.

DAVIDOFF CHAMPION

Design: Alnoor Design
Company: Objets de Convoitises, Alnoor Design
Country: France
Category: Perfumes

GOLD PENTAWARD 2011

The prestige Mexican ice-cream purveyor, Advanced Ice Cream Technologies, wanted to offer its carefully crafted, luxury products on the US market. With a name that sounded more like an innovator in cold storage than a producer of artisan iced confectionery, a new name and identity was required to convey the unparalleled decadence of the product, creating a sense of luxury, sensuality and desire. Meet the world's sexiest confection. The most decadent gelato is enrobed in graphic fantasy. Consumers may pick from the line-up or design their own. To eat now — or take away in its precious box, which, with a bit of magic, keeps it at the perfect temperature. Hold it. Lick it. Love it. **Bardot**.

Der angesehene Eiscremelieferant Advanced Ice Cream Technologies aus Mexiko wollte seine sorgfältig hergestellten Luxusprodukte auch auf dem amerikanischen Markt feilbieten. Doch sein Name klingt eher nach Kühlschrankproduzent als nach dem Hersteller von kunstvollen Eisspezialitäten. So waren auch ein neuer Name und eine neue Identität fällig, um die beispiellose Dekadenz dieses Produkts und Luxus, Sinnlichkeit und Begehren zu vermitteln. Hier ist sie nun: die absolut heißeste „kalte Konfektion" der Welt. Dieses dekadenteste Gelato aller Zeiten kleidet sich in fantasievolle Zeichen und Muster. Die Kunden wählen zum Genießen ein Eis aus dem Angebot oder gestalten ihr eigenes. Zum sofortigen Verzehr oder zum Mitnehmen in der kostbaren Schachtel, in der das Eis mit nur ein bisschen Zauberei perfekt temperiert bleibt. Nimm es. Leck es. Liebe es. **Bardot**.

Le prestigieux glacier mexicain, Advanced Ice Cream Technologies, voulait proposer ses produits sophistiqués et luxueux sur le marché américain. Avec un nom qui évoque plus un fabricant de chambres froides qu'un glacier artisanal, il fallait trouver un nouveau nom et une nouvelle identité pour communiquer sur la décadence sans pareil du produit et créer une idée de luxe, de sensualité et de désir. La glace la plus sexy du monde est enrobée d'une débauche de graphisme. Les consommateurs peuvent choisir parmi les options proposées, ou concevoir leur propre motif, à manger sur place ou à emporter dans sa boîte précieuse et magique, qui conserve la température parfaite. Prenez. Léchez. Adorez. **Bardot**.

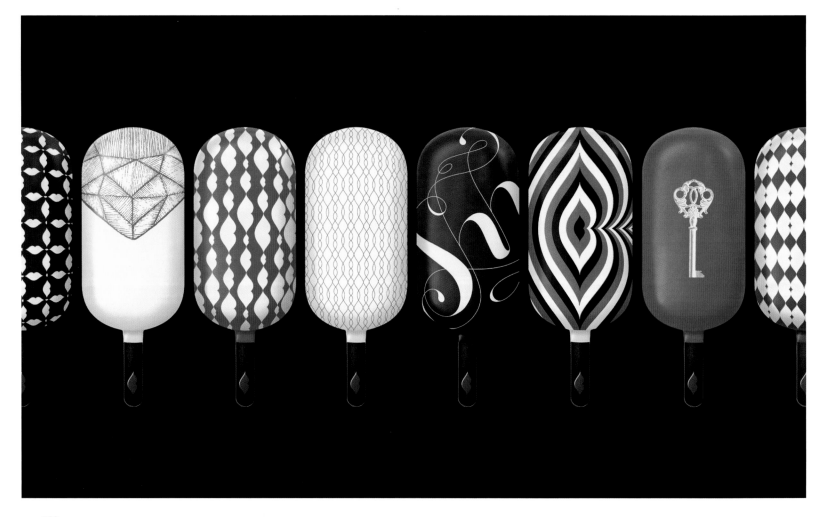

BARDOT
LUXURY ICE CREAM BARS

Creative Direction: Tosh Hall
Design: Tosh Hall, Lia Gordon
Illustration: Jessica Minn, Michael Goodman
Lettering: Jessica Minn
Naming: Jen Jordan, Jason Bice
Production: Dan Ross
Account Direction: J.P. Sabarots
Client Management: Allison Hung
Company: Landor Associates, San Francisco
Country: USA
Category: Best of the category luxury

PLATINUM PENTAWARD 2012
LUXEPACK PRIZE

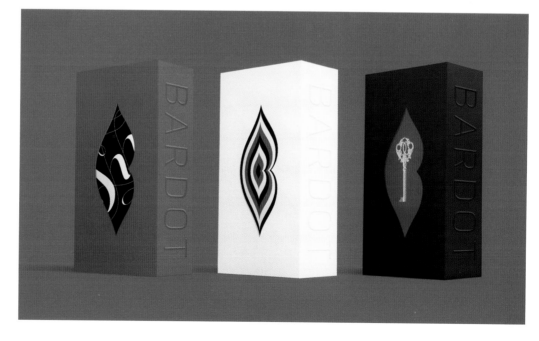

LANVIN
AVANT GARDE

Creative Direction: Elie Papiernik
Photography: Stéphane Martinelli
Company: Centdegrés
Country: France
Category: Perfumes

GOLD PENTAWARD 2012

Sophisticated manufacturing underlies the elegant simplicity of the **Avant Garde** fragrance bottle. The glass is varnished in blue with an applied metallic plating to give an inner light, over which a fine powdery layer of matte black paint is sprayed. As a finishing touch, a thin vertical strip is delicately removed from the black by laser, just like a stripe on tuxedo trousers, revealing the "juice" within through a bright blue window. It is the only technique that allows such precision and such a quality of finish. The resulting stone-like object is a pleasure to touch, with a cap that is secured to the bottle by nothing more than a strong magnet.

Der eleganten Schlichtheit des Duftflakons **Avant Garde** liegt ein anspruchsvoller Produktsvorgang zugrunde: Auf blauem Glas ist ein metallener Überzug aufgebracht. Dadurch scheint das Gefäß, auf das eine feinpudrige Schicht mattschwarzer Farbe gesprüht wurde, von innen zu leuchten. Als i-Tüpfelchen wurde ein dünner, vertikaler Streifen präzise per Laser aus dem Schwarz geschnitten, ähnlich wie der Galon einer Smokinghose. Er enthüllt wie durch ein blaues Fenster den „Saft" darin. Nur mit dieser Technik ist eine derart einzigartige Präzision möglich und erlaubt eine qualitativ höchstwertige Vollendung. Dieses steinähnliche Objekt ist haptisch eine Freude. Sein Verschluss wird nur durch einen starken Magneten gehalten.

L'élégante simplicité de la bouteille du parfum **Avant Garde** repose sur des techniques de fabrication sophistiquées. Le verre est verni en bleu avec un revêtement métallisé qui lui donne une lumière intérieure, sur lequel est vaporisée une fine couche poudreuse de peinture noire mate. En touche finale, une fine bande verticale est délicatement ôtée au laser dans la peinture noire, tout comme une rayure sur un pantalon de smoking, pour révéler le « jus » à travers une fenêtre bleu vif. C'est la seule technique qui autorise une telle précision et une telle qualité dans la finition. L'objet fini ressemble à une pierre, et est un véritable plaisir à prendre en main. Le bouchon tient sur la bouteille par la simple action d'un puissant aimant.

EAU DE TOILETTE

Art Direction: Sébastien Servaire, Candido de Barros
Technical Development: Erwann Pivert
Photography: Diptyque
Company: R'Pure Studio
Country: France
Category: Perfumes

SILVER PENTAWARD 2012

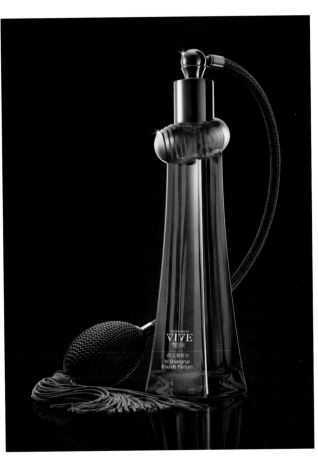

SHANGHAI VIVE

Design: Jahwa creative team
Company: Shanghai Jahwa United Co., Ltd.
Country: China
Category: Perfumes

BRONZE PENTAWARD 2011

JEAN-PAUL GAULTIER MADAME

Design: Patrick Veillet
Company: Patrick Veillet
Country: France
Category: Perfumes

SILVER PENTAWARD 2011

JEAN-PAUL GAULTIER KOKORICO

Design: Hélène Causse, Francesco Moretti
Company: Interbrand
Country: France
Category: Perfumes

SILVER PENTAWARD 2012

**JEAN-PAUL GAULTIER
SILVER MY SKIN**

Creative Direction: Sébastien Servaire
Art Direction: Justine Dauchez
Company: R'Pure Studio
Country: France
Category: Perfumes

BRONZE PENTAWARD 2012

CALVIN KLEIN
BEAUTY

Design: Wilhelm Liden
Company: Liden Design
Country: United Arab Emirates
Category: Perfumes

BRONZE PENTAWARD 2011

VAN CLEEF & ARPELS
MIDNIGHT IN PARIS

Creative Direction: Joël Desgrippes
Art Direction 3D: Eric Douane
Design Direction: Sylvie Verdier
Beauty & Luxury Consultation: Marine Guillou-Doré
Company: Brandimage – Desgrippes & Laga
Country: France
Category: Perfumes

SILVER PENTAWARD 2011

SWAROVSKI
AURA

Design: Gwenaïl Nicolas (Curiosity Inc., Japan)
Company: Jackel France
Country: France
Category: Perfumes

BRONZE PENTAWARD 2011

ESCADA
ESPECIALLY ESCADA

Design: Denis Boudard
Photography: Studio Eric Jacquet
Company: QSLD Paris
Country: France
Category: Perfumes

BRONZE PENTAWARD 2012

To commemorate the 40th anniversary of Cosme Decorte the **AQMW** Skincare Series was given some very special packaging. An elegant pattern of flowers in full bloom, interwoven with buds and overlaying a vibrant garden planted with an evergreen tree that stays in leaf all year round, was the motif chosen to represent skin regeneration and wellbeing. Transferring the design to the container in the form of a relief involved considerable technical difficulty, with two-dimensional patterns being pasted evenly over the surface using high-end three-dimensional modelling and advanced moulding techniques.

Anlässlich des 40. Geburtstags von Cosme Decorte wurde die Hautpflegeserie **AQMW** auf ganz besondere Weise verpackt. Ein elegantes Muster voller blühender Blumen, mit Knospen verschlungen und einen lebendigen Garten überlagernd, worin ein immergrüner Baum das ganze Jahr über seine Blätter trägt — dieses erwählte Motiv sollte die Regeneration der Haut und Wohlgefühl darstellen. Die Übertragung des Designs auf den Behälter in Form eines Reliefs stellte eine beträchtliche technische Herausforderung dar, wobei das zweidimensionale Muster anhand von dreidimensionaler Highend-Modellierung und fortschrittlicher Formungstechniken gleichmäßig auf die Oberfläche aufgebracht wurde.

Pour célébrer le 40ᵉ anniversaire de Cosme Decorte, la gamme **AQMW** Skincare Series méritait de nouveaux flacons très spéciaux. Un élégant motif de fleurs épanouies entrelacées avec des bourgeons superposé à un beau jardin orné d'un arbre qui ne perd jamais ses feuilles a été choisi pour représenter la régénération de la peau et le bien-être. Pour transférer ce motif sur le flacon sous forme de relief il a fallu surmonter des difficultés techniques considérables : les traits bidimensionnels ont été appliqués uniformément sur la surface à l'aide d'un procédé de modelage tridimensionnel dernier cri et de techniques de moulage complexes.

COSME DECORTE
AQMW SKINCARE SERIES

Art Direction: Marcel Wanders
Creative Direction: Tatsuo Kannami
Design: Gabriele Chiave, Kazuhiro Niikura
Company: Kosé Corporation
Country: Japan
Category: Cosmetics

GOLD PENTAWARD 2011

POLA WHITISSIMO

Creative Direction: Takeshi Usui
Art Direction: Chiharu Suzuki
Design: Taishi Ono, Haruyo Eto
Company: Pola Chemical Industries, Inc.
Country: Japan
Category: Cosmetics
SILVER PENTAWARD 2011

ORCHIDÉE IMPÉRIALE
GUERLAIN
PARIS
ORCHIDÉE IMPÉRIALE
CONCENTRÉ DE LONGÉVITÉ
LONGEVITY CONCENTRATE

The result of 10 years of research using **Guerlain**'s orchidarium, this exclusive anti-ageing serum is based on concentrated extracts from orchids. To celebrate this work, a special symbolic casing was conceived: a "capsule-flask", a blue chamber holding the precious ointment as if protecting it from the passage of time. The vial is seamless and appears hermetically sealed, but a ring may be rotated to release a nozzle at one end and a button at the other. The vertical use of this newly-patented concept is unique in cosmetics, and permits the precise dose of cream to be delivered in a manner that feels ritualised and select. The flask rests horizontally in a blue case marked with an orchid symbol.

Das Ergebnis der zehnjährigen Forschung mit dem Orchidarium von **Guerlain** ist dieses exklusive Anti-Aging-Serum, das auf konzentrierten Extrakten von Orchideen basiert. Um diese Arbeit entsprechend zu feiern, entwickelte man ein symbolisches Gehäuse: ein „Kapselflakon", der in seiner blauen Kammer die kostbare Salbe aufnimmt, als bewahre er die Creme vor der verrinnenden Zeit. Die Phiole ist nahtlos und wirkt hermetisch versiegelt, aber durch Drehen eines Rings erscheint am einen Ende ein Röhrchen und am anderen ein Knopf. Die vertikale Verwendung dieses erstmalig patentierten Konzepts ist bei Kosmetika einzigartig und erlaubt die präzise Dosierung der Creme auf eine Weise, die sich sehr ritualisiert und erlesen anfühlt. Die Phiole ruht waagrecht in ihrem blauen, mit einem Orchideen-symbol verzierten Behältnis.

Résultat de 10 ans de recherche dans l'orchidarium de **Guerlain**, ce sérum anti-âge luxueux est basé sur des extraits d'orchidée concentrés. Un flacon symbolique très spécial a été conçu pour fêter cet accomplissement : une « flasque-capsule », une ampoule bleue qui abrite le précieux onguent, comme pour le protéger contre le passage du temps. Elle semble hermétiquement scellée, mais recèle un anneau qui tourne pour laisser apparaître une canule à une extrémité, et un bouton à l'autre. L'utilisation verticale de ce nouveau concept breveté est unique dans le secteur de la cosmétique, et permet de doser la crème précisément en conférant à cette opération une aura de rituel et d'exclusivité. La flasque est couchée dans un coffret bleu marqué d'un symbole d'orchidée.

GUERLAIN
ORCHIDÉE IMPÉRIALE

Art Direction: Sébastien Servaire, Candido de Barros
Photography: Guerlain
Company: R'Pure Studio
Country: France
Category: Cosmetics

GOLD PENTAWARD 2012

ESPRIQUE POINT MAKE-UP

Creative Direction: Chihiro Hayashi
Art Direction: Shigeru Yamasaki
Design: Emiko Saito
Company: Kosé Corporation
Country: Japan
Category: Cosmetics

SILVER PENTAWARD 2011

POLA B.A

Creative Direction: Takeshi Usui
Art Direction: Takashi Matsui
Design: Yushi Watanabe, Kentaro Ito
Company: Pola Chemical Industries, Inc.
Country: Japan
Category: Cosmetics
SILVER PENTAWARD 2012

GUERLAIN
ABEILLE ROYALE

Art Direction: Sébastien Servaire
Design: Candido de Barros
Account Management: Virginie Bourgoin
Illustration: Yael Bibliowicz
Photography: Arnaud Guffon
Company: R'Pure Studio
Country: France
Category: Cosmetics

BRONZE PENTAWARD 2011

HAIR GROWTH TONIC Z

Design: Shohei Yagi
Company: Nippon Menard Cosmetic Co., Ltd.
Country: Japan
Category: Cosmetics

BRONZE PENTAWARD 2011

HAKU
WHITENING BEAUTY LOTION

Design: Yoji Nobuto, Yuka Nagasaki
Company: Shiseido Co., Ltd.
Country: Japan
Category: Cosmetics

SILVER PENTAWARD 2011

HERBORIST

Creative Direction: Jun Xu
Design: XianQing Zhao
Company: Shanghai Jahwa United Co., Ltd.
Country: China
Category: Cosmetics

BRONZE PENTAWARD 2012

CLARINS

Creative Direction: Olivier Desdoigts,
Marie-Laurence Aubin
Company: Desdoigts & Associés
Country: France
Category: Cosmetics

SILVER PENTAWARD 2012

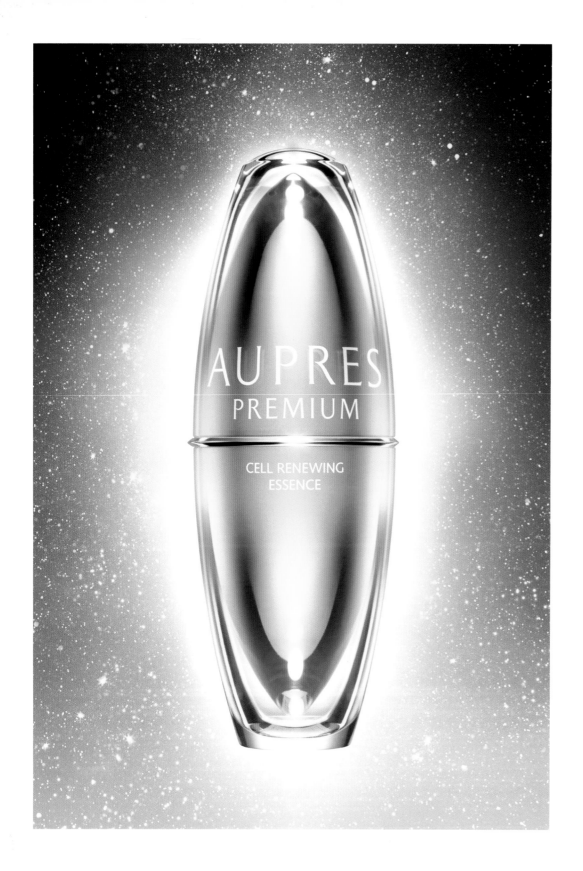

AUPRES PREMIUM

Creative Direction: Noriko Matsubara
Art Direction: Taisuke Kikuchi
Design: Asako Hase, Sachiko Hamada
Company: Shiseido Co., Ltd.
Country: Japan
Category: Cosmetics

BRONZE PENTAWARD 2012

ALLVIT HYEALL CREAM

Design Direction: Won-Hee Lee
Container Design: Hyung-Gil Ham, Ju-Seop Kim
Company: Woongjin Coway Co., Ltd.
Country: South Korea
Category: Cosmetics

BRONZE PENTAWARD 2012

Royal Salute is a super-premium whisky brand, relatively new to customers, which competes primarily with Cognac in its core markets (Asia). It is the pinnacle of luxury whisky and retails at US$ 2,200 a bottle. In order to stand out amongst such top-end spirits, whilst retaining the brand's distinctive visual style, keeping the bottle shape was key before embellishing it with a crest and an ornate crown-like stopper. The porcelain flagon usually associated with the brand was, however, retired in favour of the greater luxury of cut crystal. The new decanter is hand-blown and cut by master craftsmen at Dartington Crystal, each one taking over 40 hours to make, and conveys a sense of nobility and allure which helps set it apart from Cognac.

Royal Salute ist eine Whiskymarke der Superpremium-Klasse und für Kunden relativ neu — sie konkurriert auf ihren (asiatischen) Kernmärkten primär mit Cognac. Sie stellt den Gipfel der luxuriösen Whiskysorten dar und wird pro Flasche für 2.200 US-Dollar angeboten. Damit dieses Produkt neben den anderen Top-End-Spirituosen hervorsticht und gleichzeitig der charakteristische visuelle Stil der Marke gewahrt bleibt, war es essenziell, die Flaschenform zu bewahren, bevor sie mit Wappen und kronenähnlichem Verschluss geschmückt wird. Normaler-weise kennt man die Marke in einer Flasche aus Porzellan, aber um des größeren Luxus willen wurde hier einem Gefäß aus geschliffenem Kristall der Vorzug gegeben. Der neue Dekanter wurde bei den Meisterhandwerkern von Dartington Crystal mundgeblasen und geschliffen. Jede Flasche erfordert über 40 Arbeitsstunden und vermittelt das Gefühl von Adel und Faszination, was sie noch besser vom Cognac abhebt.

Royal Salute est une marque de whisky très haut de gamme, relativement nouvelle pour les clients, qui fait principalement concurrence au cognac sur son cœur de marché (Asie). C'est le summum du whisky de luxe, et son prix de vente atteint 2 200 US $ par bouteille. Pour se faire remarquer aux côtés des spiritueux les plus exclusifs, tout en préservant le style visuel qui caractérise la marque, il était essentiel de conserver la forme de la bouteille avant de l'embellir avec des armoiries et un bouchon très orné en forme de couronne. La bouteille en porcelaine habituellement associée à la marque a cependant été remplacée par du cristal taillé, plus luxueux. La nouvelle carafe est soufflée à la bouche et taillée par les maîtres-artisans de Dartington Crystal. Chaque unité nécessite plus de 40 heures de travail, et transmet un sentiment de noblesse et d'élégance qui aide à démarquer ce produit du cognac.

PERNOD RICARD
ROYAL SALUTE 62 GUN SALUTE

Design Direction: Stuart Humm
Company: Coley Porter Bell
Country: UK
Category: Spirits

GOLD PENTAWARD 2011

COGNAC DE LUZE

Design: Sébastien Schalchli
Brand Positioning: Laurent Berriat
Management: Stéphane Aussel,
Robert Eastham (Cognac De Luze)
Company: Toscara
Country: France
Category: Spirits

SILVER PENTAWARD 2011

REMY MARTIN
CENTAURE DE DIAMANT

Art Direction: Sébastien Servaire
Design: Candido de Barros
Illustration: Yael Bibliowicz
Photography: Arnaud Guffon
Account Management: Virginie Bourgoin
Company: R'Pure Studio
Country: France
Category: Spirits

SILVER PENTAWARD 2011

MAKER'S 46

Design: Ares Marasligiller
Company: LPK
Country: USA
Category: Spirits

BRONZE PENTAWARD 2011

DAVIDOFF
XO

Creative Direction: Sébastien Servaire,
Candido de Barros
Art Direction: Yael Bibliowicz
Company: R'Pure Studio
Country: France
Category: Spirits

SILVER PENTAWARD 2012

GOLD SLEEP

Design: Kuan Fu Wu
Company: Shenzhen Excel Package Co., Ltd.
Country: China
Category: Spirits

BRONZE PENTAWARD 2012

FINE & SPIRITS
FLEUR COGNAC

Design: Linea design team
Company: Linea
Country: France
Category: Spirits

SILVER PENTAWARD 2012

ID
THE BLACK ONYX EDITION

Creative Direction: Claire Parker
Design Direction: Zayne Dagher, Denise Faraco
Design: Reins Vellinga
Company: Design Bridge
Country: UK
Category: Spirits

BRONZE PENTAWARD 2011

BACARDI SUPERIOR RUM
150TH ANNIVERSARY
CELEBRATION DECANTER

Creative Direction: Jon Hamer
Design: Justine Morgan
Project Management: Ellie Jackson
Company: Twelve
Country: UK
Category: Spirits

BRONZE PENTAWARD 2012

WELSH WHISKY
FIVE VODKA

Creative Direction/Design: Glenn Tutssel
Design: Phil Dall
Copy Text: Ian Crammond
Company: The Brand Union
Country: UK
Category: Spirits

BRONZE PENTAWARD 2011

22 MARQUIS

Design: Linea design team
Company: Linea
Country: France
Category: Spirits

BRONZE PENTAWARD 2012

BLINK
BRUT SPARKLING WINE

Creative Direction: Yiannis Charalambopoulos, Alexis Nikou, Vagelis Liakos
Photography: Kostas Pappas
Company: Beetroot Design Group
Country: Greece
Category: Fine wines, champagne

GOLD PENTAWARD 2011

RONGZI

Design: Kuan Fu Wu
Company: Shenzhen Excel Package Co., Ltd.
Country: China
Category: Fine wines, champagne

SILVER PENTAWARD 2012

**TRUETT HURST
DRY CREEK VALLEY
VML**

Design: Kevin Shaw, Cosimo Surace
Company: Stranger & Stranger
Country: USA
Category: Fine wines, champagne
GOLD PENTAWARD 2012

Biodynamic winemaking may well sound like organic farming but actually has its roots in pagan mythology and alchemy — early winemakers would bury stag heads and bladders filled with petals as part of their manufacturing. Even so, label design for this class of wines is conspicuously dull and undistinguished, which left an opening to introduce some magic into the sector. With certain practices still today that sound like witchcraft, the biodynamic winemaker could be shown on labels as head of a coven, surrounded by her faithful worshippers.

Biodynamischer Weinbau — das hört sich vielleicht nach organischer Landwirtschaft an, aber tatsächlich wurzelt der Weinbau in heidnischer Mythologie und Alchemie: Die ersten Bauern vergruben in ihren Weinbergen Hirschköpfe und mit Blütenblättern gefüllte Blasen. Doch trotz dieses Wissens ist die Etikettengestaltung für diese Klasse Weine oft auffallend langweilig und recht mittelmäßig — eine Lücke, die man durch etwas Magie füllen kann. Auch heute noch gibt es bestimmte Praktiken, die nach Hexerei klingen. So wird der biodynamische Weinbauer auf den Etiketten passenderweise als Herr eines Hexenzirkels gezeigt, umgeben von treuen Anbetern.

La viticulture biodynamique peut sembler avoir beaucoup en commun avec l'agriculture organique, mais elle prend en fait ses racines dans la mythologie païenne et dans l'alchimie. Les premiers viticulteurs enterraient des têtes de cerf et des vessies remplies de fleurs. Pourtant, les étiquettes de ce type de vin brillent par leur manque d'imagination, ce qui laissait une ouverture pour introduire un peu de magie dans le secteur. Les viticulteurs biodynamiques d'aujourd'hui ont encore certaines pratiques qui ressemblent à la sorcellerie, c'est pourquoi l'étiquette les représente sous les traits de sorciers entourés de fervents adorateurs.

R.I.P.

Design/Art Direction: Luis Piano
Copy: Magdalena Oyanedel
Company: Piano & Piano
Country: Chile
Category: Fine wines, champagne

SILVER PENTAWARD 2012

SIETE PECADOS
AVARICIA, IRA, GULA, PEREZA, SOBERBIA, LUJURIA, ENVIDIA

Design: Francisco Valverde
Company: Sidecar
Country: Spain
Category: Fine wines, champagne

SILVER PENTAWARD 2011

MHCS
MOËT & CHANDON ICE IMPÉRIAL

Design: Place du Marché (now Makheia Group)
Company: Sleever International
Country: France
Category: Fine wines, champagne

SILVER PENTAWARD 2011

ANATHIMA

Creative Direction: Gregory Tsaknakis
Company: Mousegraphics
Country: Greece
Category: Fine wines, champagne

SILVER PENTAWARD 2011

SAINTS HILLS

Design Direction: Mary Lewis
Design: Mary Lewis, Sarah Roberts, Nile Hope
Illustration: Graham Everden
Client: Ernest, Ivana Tolj, Saints Hills
Company: Lewis Moberly
Country: UK
Category: Fine wines, champagne

BRONZE PENTAWARD 2011

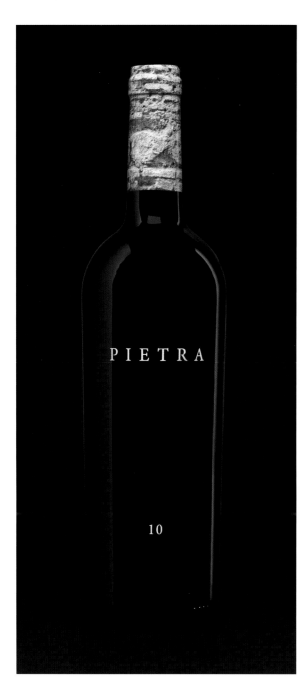

MENHIR SALENTO PIETRA

Design: Eduardo del Fraile
Company: Eduardo del Fraile
Country: Spain
Category: Fine wines, champagne

BRONZE PENTAWARD 2012

CENTURY 2008 SUNTORY

Creative Direction: Shizuko Ushijima
Art Direction: Tsuneki Maeda
Design: Tsuneki Maeda, Natsue Isozaki
Company: Suntory
Country: Japan
Category: Fine wines, champagne

BRONZE PENTAWARD 2011

BLUEBERRY

Design: Kuan Fu Wu
Company: Shenzhen Excel Package Co., Ltd.
Country: China
Category: Fine wines, champagne

BRONZE PENTAWARD 2012

GREY GOOSE VODKA BY CHOPARD

Executive Creative Direction: Pierre Abel
Creative Direction: Vincent Fichet
Design: Marc Usmati
Company: FutureBrand
Country: France
Category: Casks, cases, gift boxes, ice buckets

SILVER PENTAWARD 2011

CÎROC
ICE BUCKET

Design/Creative Direction: Denis Boudard
Photography: Studio Eric Jacquet
Company: QSLD Paris
Country: France
Category: Casks, cases, gift boxes, ice buckets

GOLD PENTAWARD 2011

CÎROC
HALO

Design: Denis Boudard
Photography: Studio Eric Jacquet
Company: QSLD Paris
Country: France
Category: Casks, cases, gift boxes, ice buckets

BRONZE PENTAWARD 2012

The Mr Clicquot champagne-bottle stopper is one amongst a number of accessories created for the animation and events marking the invention of Veuve Clicquot. The global animation concept that goes by the name of **Mr Clicquot** is an entire universe with an offbeat narrative inspired by the dandy's stylish image and which perfectly expresses the brand's positioning. The creative intention was to imagine an essential but non-conformist accessory that would result in a new "chic" attitude: by fitting the bottle with a stopper shaped like an umbrella-handle, it could be carried on the arm, hung on a bar, in a tree, from the ceiling! Point-of-sale options were also totally renewed by virtue of this original idea.

Der Champagnerflaschenverschluss Mr Clicquot gehört zu einer Reihe von Accessoires, die für die Events zu Ehren der Erfindung von Veuve Clicquot geschaffen wurden. Das globale Animationskonzept firmiert unter dem Namen **Mr Clicquot**. Es bildet ein ganzes Universum mit einer ausgefallenen Geschichte, die vom stilvollen Image des Dandys inspiriert ist, und drückt hervorragend die Positionierung der Marke aus. Die kreative Intention war ein wesentliches, aber nicht-konformistisches Accessoire, das auf neuartige Weise „chic" sein sollte: Die Flasche mit ihrem Verschluss in Form eines Schirmgriffs kann am Arm getragen, an eine Theke oder einen Ast oder gar an die Decke gehängt werden! An den jeweiligen Verkaufsstellen entstanden durch diese originelle Idee völlig neue Möglichkeiten.

Le bouchon à champagne Mr Clicquot fait partie d'une gamme d'accessoires créée pour les animations et événements qui célèbrent l'invention de la Veuve Clicquot. Le concept d'animation global, baptisé **Mr Clicquot**, est tout un univers bâti autour d'un fil conducteur excentrique inspiré par l'image élégante du dandy, et exprime parfaitement le positionnement de la marque. L'intention créative était d'imaginer un accessoire essentiel mais anticonformiste qui donnerait naissance à une nouvelle attitude « chic » : un bouchon en forme de poignée de parapluie monté sur la bouteille permet de la porter au bras, de l'accrocher à une barre, un arbre, ou même au plafond ! Cette idée originale a aussi complètement renouvelé les options sur le point de vente.

VEUVE CLICQUOT MR CLICQUOT

Art Direction: Sébastien Servaire, Candido de Barros
Technical Development: Erwann Pivert
Photography: Veuve Clicquot Ponsardine, R'Pure Studio
Company: R'Pure Studio
Country: France
Category: Casks, cases, gift boxes, ice buckets

GOLD PENTAWARD 2012

VEUVE CLICQUOT PONSARDINE

Design: Grapheine
Design: Julien Ceder (Veuve Clicquot)
Project Management: Mathilde Le Scornet
(Veuve Clicquot)
Production: Virojanglor
Company: Virojanglor
Country: France
Category: Casks, cases, gift boxes, ice buckets

SILVER PENTAWARD 2012

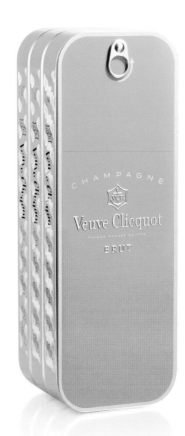

MOËT HENNESSY
VEUVE CLICQUOT CLICQ'UP ICE BUCKET

Design: Mathias Van De Walle
Production: MW Creative Ltd.
Company: MW Creative Ltd.
Country: UK
Category: Casks, cases, gift boxes, ice buckets

SILVER PENTAWARD 2012

SHANGRILA-CHATEAU MARSAN

Design: Wu Kuan Fu
Company: Shenzhen Excel Package Co., Ltd.
Country: China
Category: Casks, cases, gift boxes, ice buckets

SILVER PENTAWARD 2011

JOHNNIE WALKER
PLATINUM LABEL

Design: Denis Boudard
Photography: Studio Eric Jacquet
Company: QSLD Paris
Country: France
Category: Casks, cases, gift boxes, ice buckets

BRONZE PENTAWARD 2012

KRUG CHAMPAGNE FLÂNERIE

Design: Gérald Gladini,
François Takounseun, Gabriel Brouste
Company: Partisan du Sens
Country: France
Category: Casks, cases, gift boxes, ice buckets
BRONZE PENTAWARD 2012

PROAD MOON TEA-SET GIFT BOX

Design: Jennifer Tsai
Company: Proad Identity
Country: Taiwan
Category: Casks, cases, gift boxes, ice buckets
BRONZE PENTAWARD 2011

MARTELL
GIFT BOXES

Creative Direction: Yan Chiabai
Art Direction: Jérémy Vince
Account Direction: Estelle Pillet
Account Management: Delphine Oberto
Company: Raison Pure International
Country: France
Category: Casks, cases, gift boxes, ice buckets

BRONZE PENTAWARD 2011

MOËT & CHANDON

Design: 5.5 designers
Brand Management: Jessy Baretta,
Maxime Chanson (Moët & Chandon)
International Marketing Management:
Marie-Laure Trichard (Moët & Chandon)
Product Development Management:
Fabien Gaudard (Moët & Chandon)
Company: Virojanglor
Country: France
Category: Casks, cases, gift boxes, ice buckets

BRONZE PENTAWARD 2011

The fish's tail is one of the main visual elements used on this frozen seafood packaging series, both for the logo and the structure of the packages themselves. The black background and understated typography were used in conjunction with seafood illustrations to suggest delicatessens and a quality product, whilst the window holes on the designs match the part of the seafood contained within and allow customers to see exactly what they are buying.

Der Fischschwanz ist eines der wichtigen visuellen Elemente, das bei dieser Verpackungsserie für Tiefkühlfisch sowohl für das Logo als auch die Struktur der Packung selbst eingesetzt wird. Zusammen mit dem schwarzen Hintergrund und der zurückhaltenden Typografie wurden Illustrationen von Meeresfrüchten genutzt, um Delikatesse und Qualitätsprodukte zu suggerieren. Die in die Packung gestanzten Öffnungen passen zu dem darin enthaltenen Meerestier, und der Kunde sieht sofort, was er kauft.

La queue de poisson ou de crustacé est l'un des principaux éléments visuels utilisés sur cette série de boîtes de fruits de mer congelés, que ce soit pour le logo ou pour la structure même des boîtes. Le fond noir et la typographie sobre sont complétés par des illustrations de fruits de mer pour suggérer la saveur et la qualité du produit, tandis que les fenêtres découpées sur les dessins correspondent par leur forme au contenu et permettent aux clients de voir ce qu'ils achètent.

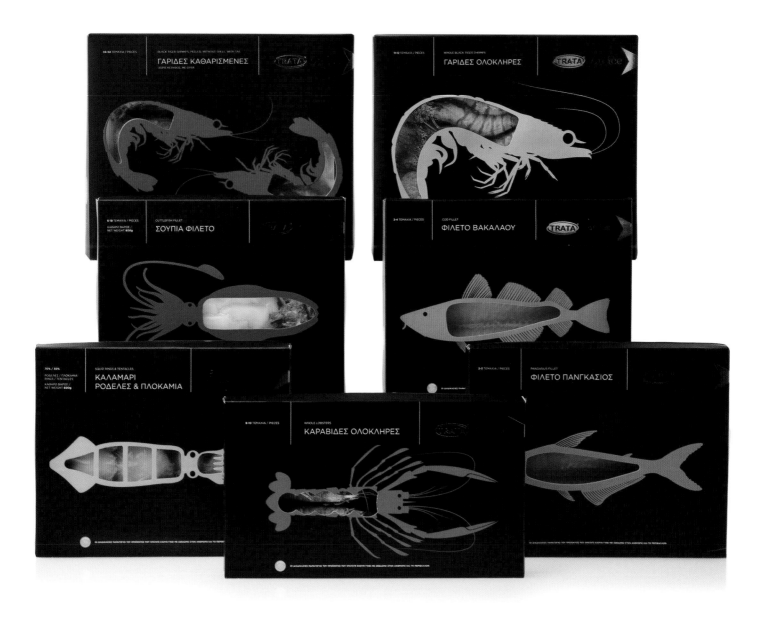

KIMURA SUISAN FUNAZUSHI

Creative Direction: Masahiro Minami
Design: Shuji Hikawa
Company: Masahiro Minami Laboratory
Country: Japan
Category: Gourmet food

SILVER PENTAWARD 2011

TRATA ON ICE BY KONVA

Creative Direction: Yiannis Charalambopoulos,
Alexis Nikou, Vagelis Liakos
Photography: Kostas Pappas
Company: Beetroot Design Group
Country: Greece
Category: Gourmet food

GOLD PENTAWARD 2011

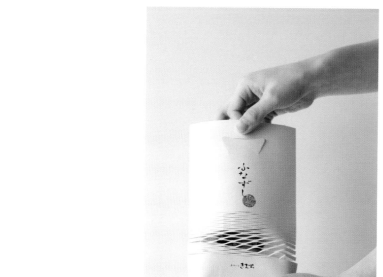

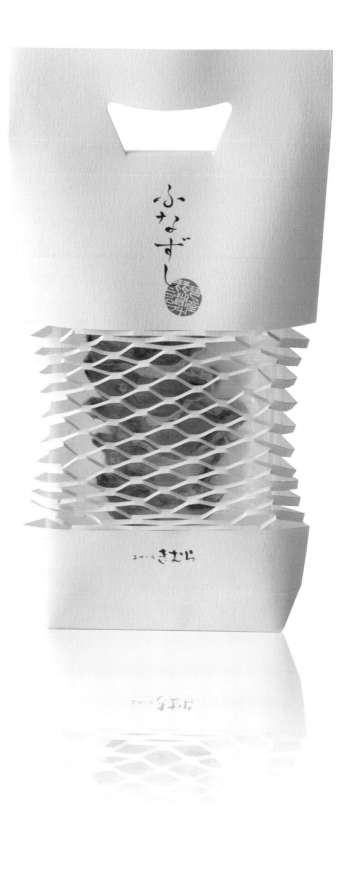

FIVE OLIVE OIL

Design: Dimitris Koliadimas, Dimitris Papazoglou
Company: Designers United
Country: Greece
Category: Gourmet food

GOLD PENTAWARD 2012

ETESIAN GOLD

Creative Direction: Gregory Tsaknakis
Illustration: Ioanna Papaioannou
Company: Mousegraphics
Country: Greece
Category: Gourmet food

SILVER PENTAWARD 2012

PURE ARISTELEON

2012
ETESIAN
GOLD
TRADITIONAL
GRANITE-MILLED
EXTRA VIRGIN
OLIVE OIL

PRODUCT OF GREECE

TRUE PREMIUM

2012
ETESIAN
GOLD
TRADITIONAL
GRANITE-MILLED
EXTRA VIRGIN
OLIVE OIL

PRODUCT OF GREECE

CLASSIC PREMIUM

2012
ETESIAN
GOLD
TRADITIONAL
GRANITE-MILLED
EXTRA VIRGIN
OLIVE OIL

PRODUCT OF GREECE

KAVIARI
EN-K DE CAVIAR

Design: Armand Delsol
Company: Vanille Design
Country: France
Category: Gourmet food

SILVER PENTAWARD 2012

GAIBOM

Design: Jennifer Tsai
Company: Proad Identity
Country: Taiwan
Category: Gourmet food

SILVER PENTAWARD 2011

BONHO

Design: Kristy Wen Ho, Amone Hsieh
Company: Hohoengine Co., Ltd.
Country: Taiwan
Category: Gourmet food

BRONZE PENTAWARD 2011

NEUHAUS
LADY CHEFS

Design: Hugues Tomeo, Gaby Gentenaar
Company: Neuhaus
Country: Belgium
Category: Gourmet food

BRONZE PENTAWARD 2011

9 world renowned Lady chefs create
9 deliciously feminine pralines for Neuhaus

SEÑORIO DE JAÉN

Design: Ekosistema Creative Boutique
Company: Olife S.A.
Country: Spain
Category: Gourmet food

BRONZE PENTAWARD 2011

DE HORTUS HONEY

Design: Marcel Verhaaf
Company: PH Ontwerp
Country: Netherlands
Category: Gourmet food

BRONZE PENTAWARD 2012

BOMBAY SAPPHIRE
250-YEAR ANNIVERSARY BOTTLE

Design: Dominic Burke, Sarah Fagan
Company: Webb deVlam
Country: USA
Category: Limited editions,
limited series, collectors' items

GOLD PENTAWARD 2011
SLEEVER INTERNATIONAL PRIZE

In celebration of 250 years of **Bombay Sapphire**'s secret gin recipe, a limited-edition bottle was designed using traditional glass-blowing skills alongside modern laser-etching and an internal blue optic to create a stunning "bottle within a bottle" effect. The 10 botanicals and Queen Victoria's brandmark were etched so that they appeared to float within the crystal, while the specially designed crystal stopper features a gold crown encrusted with blue gems to represent the royal patronage. Housed in presentation boxes, 350 of these exclusive bottles were made available for Christmas 2010, in London, New York and Madrid, with a further limited distribution worldwide in 2011.

Zur 250-Jahr-Feier der geheimen Rezeptur für **Bombay Sapphire** Gin wurde eine Flasche in einer beschränkten Auflage designt. Neben traditionellem Glasbläserkönnen kamen auch moderne Lasergravur und eine interne blaue Optik zum Einsatz, um für den verblüffenden „Flasche in der Flasche"-Effekt zu sorgen. Die zehn Pflanzen und das Queen-Victoria-Label wurden so eingraviert, dass es wirkt, als würden sie in dem Kristall treiben. Der besonders gestaltete Kristallverschluss zeigt eine goldene, mit blauen Edelsteinen besetzte Krone, um die royale Klientel zu verdeutlichen. Verpackt in speziellen Präsentationskartons, waren 350 dieser exklusiven Flaschen zur Weihnacht des Jahres 2010 in London, New York und Madrid erhältlich und wurden im folgenden Jahr dann auch in begrenzter Auflage weltweit vertrieben.

Une bouteille en édition limitée a été conçue pour célébrer les 250 ans de la recette secrète du gin **Bombay Sapphire**. Elle allie des compétences traditionnelles de soufflage du verre et des techniques modernes de gravure au laser, ainsi qu'une couche interne de verre bleu pour créer un superbe effet de « bouteille dans la bouteille ». Les dix herbes botaniques et l'effigie de la reine Victoria sont gravées de façon à sembler flotter dans le cristal, tandis que le cabochon en cristal conçu tout spécialement est décoré d'une couronne en or incrustée de pierres bleues pour représenter le patronage royal. 350 de ces bouteilles exclusives et leurs coffrets de présentation ont été mis en vente pour Noël 2010 à Londres, New York et Madrid, et une réédition limitée a été lancée dans le monde entier en 2011.

BALLANTINE'S
FORTY YEAR OLD BLEND

Design: Bernard Gormley, Mike Parsonson
Photography: Julian Ward
Company: Nude Brand Creation
Country: UK
Category: Limited editions,
limited series, collectors' items

SILVER PENTAWARD 2012

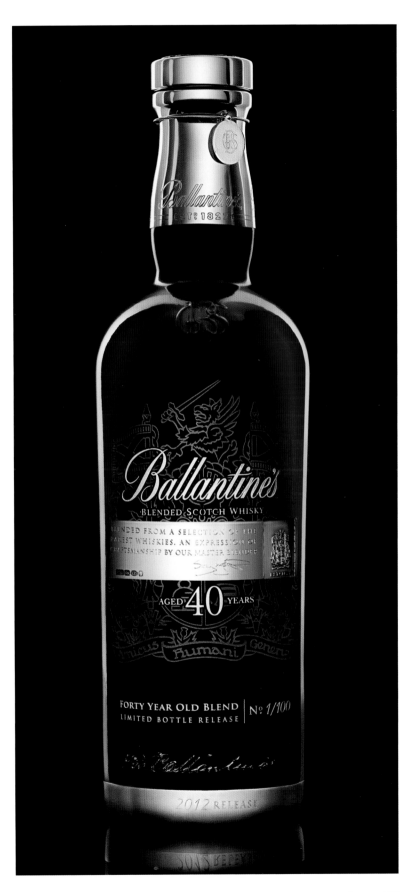

John Walker & Sons Diamond Jubilee is a limited-edition whisky created as a tribute to HM Queen Elizabeth II's 60 years of enlightened leadership. The diamond-shaped decanter stands on six pillars representing each decade of the Queen's reign, and has 60 facets to reflect the diversity and dynamism of the Commonwealth, the radiance of the decanter reflecting Her Majesty as the royal guiding light. The decanter is accompanied by two hand-engraved crystal glasses and a hand-bound booklet chronicling the detailed craftsmanship, all housed within a custom oak cabinet. The bottle was made for presentation to the Queen, with just 60 replica versions produced for sale. Diamond Jubilee profits will go to fund the Queen's charity, QEST, which supports craft education.

Dieser Limited-Edition-Whisky John Walker & Sons Diamond Jubilee erschien zu Ehren des 60. Thronjubiläums Ihrer Majestät Queen Elizabeth II. Die sechs Säulen, auf denen der diamantförmige Dekanter ruht, stehen für die sechs Dekaden der Regentschaft Ihrer Majestät. Mit seinen 60 Facetten verweist der Dekanter auf die Vielfalt und Dynamik des Commonwealth, und seine glanzvolle Ausstrahlung reflektiert die königliche Autorität Ihrer Majestät. Zum Dekanter gehören zwei handgravierte Kristallgläser und ein handgebundenes Büchlein, in dem detailliert das Kunsthandwerk seiner Herstellung beschrieben wird. All dies befindet sich in einem extra angefertigten Eichengehäuse. Die Flasche wurde hergestellt, um vor der Königin präsentiert zu werden. Im Handel sind davon nur 60 Kopien erhältlich. Die durch Diamond Jubilee erzielten Einnahmen gehen an QEST. Diese von der Queen geförderte Wohltätigkeitsorganisation setzt sich für die Ausbildung im Handwerk ein.

John Walker & Sons Diamond Jubilee est un whisky en édition limitée créé en hommage aux 60 ans de règne éclairé de SM la reine Élisabeth II. La carafe en forme de diamant repose sur six piliers qui symbolisent chacune des décennies du règne, et se compose de 60 facettes pour refléter la diversité et le dynamisme du Commonwealth, tandis que son éclat représente la lumière de la reine, guide de la nation. Elle est accompagnée de deux verres en cristal gravés à la main et d'un livret relié à la main qui relate tout le processus de fabrication artisanal, le tout abrité dans un coffret sur mesure en chêne. La bouteille a été fabriquée pour être présentée à la reine, et seulement 60 répliques ont été mises en vente. Les bénéfices de Diamond Jubilee seront reversés à l'organisation caritative de la reine, QEST, qui soutient l'éducation à l'artisanat.

JOHN WALKER & SONS
DIAMOND JUBILEE

Creative Direction: Laurent Hainaut, Lorena Seminario (Raison Pure NYC), Katy Holford (Cumbria Crystal)
Project Lead: Steve Wilson (Invigor8tion)
Crystal Cold Workshop: Yves Parisse (Baccarat)
Silversmith & Workshop Management: John Hunt (Hamilton & Inches)
Cabinet Design: Neil Stevenson
Bookbinding: Lara West
Calligraphy: Sally Magnum
Glass Hand-Engraving: Philip Lawson Johnston
Global Design Direction: Jeremy Lindley (Diageo)
Design: Marco Leone, Alex Boulware (Raison Pure International)
Design Direction: Harry Chong (Raison Pure International)
Production Management: Linda Tseng (Raison Pure International)
Company: Raison Pure International
Country: USA
Category: Limited editions, limited series, collectors' items

GOLD PENTAWARD 2012
SLEEVER INTERNATIONAL PRIZE

**CARCHELO WINES
EXTENSIVE**

Art Direction/Design: Eduardo del Fraile
Company: Eduardo del Fraile
Country: Spain
Category: Limited editions,
limited series, collectors' items

SILVER PENTAWARD 2011

HAKUSHIKA

Design: Keiko Hirano
Company: Communication Design Laboratory
Country: Japan
Category: Limited editions,
limited series, collectors' items

BRONZE PENTAWARD 2011

EGOFACTO
SCENTED CANDLE

General Partnership: Chantale Coussaud
Creative Direction: Françoise Bouchez
Art Direction: Pascal Morlighem, Laetitia Arrighi
Account Planning: Olivier Raymond
Company: Bayadères
Country: France
Category: Limited editions, limited series,
collectors' items

BRONZE PENTAWARD 2011

SUNTORY SINGLE MALT WHISKY YAMAZAKI AGED 50 YEARS

Creative Direction: Tsuneki Maeda
Art Direction: Akiko Furusho
Company: Suntory
Country: Japan
Category: Limited editions, limited series, collectors' items

SILVER PENTAWARD 2012

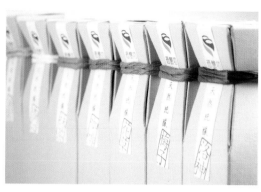

YANGDA BIOTEC
FU NIANG FANG VINEGAR

Design: Wu Chun Chung
Company: Bosin Design
Country: China
Category: Limited editions,
limited series, collectors' items

BRONZE PENTAWARD 2012

As reassuring as a waterfall, this exclusive fragrance is imbued with the subtle yet profound energy of water. Taking its source of inspiration from the vigorous bursting of a spray of water, this image has been translated into a relief on the sides of the bottle. The other parts are coloured a deep blue, offsetting and emphasising the relief itself. Masking and colouring each container by hand has resulted in an aura of craftsmanship in the final product quite unlike any mass-produced item. This fragrance was especially developed as a complimentary offering for **Shiseido**'s shareholders.

So beruhigend wie ein Wasserfall ist dieser exklusive Duft, durchdrungen von der subtilen und doch profunden Energie des Wassers. Das Bild vom kraftvollen Bersten eines Wasserstrahls war Inspiration für das Relief an den Seiten der Flasche. Die anderen Teile sind tiefblau gefärbt. Sie heben sich vom Relief selbst ab und betonen es dadurch umso stärker. Dass jedes Gefäß per Hand abgedeckt und koloriert wurde, verleiht dem Produkt letztendlich die Aura vollendeter Handwerkskunst, die sich deutlich von jedem Gegenstand aus Massenproduktion unterscheidet. Dieser Duft wurde speziell als Geschenk für die Aktionäre von **Shiseido** entwickelt.

Aussi apaisant que le son d'une cascade, ce parfum exclusif est imprégné de l'énergie subtile mais profonde de l'eau. Cette image a été inspirée par un vigoureux jet d'eau, traduit dans le relief sur les côtés de la bouteille. Les autres parties sont colorées en bleu profond pour créer un contraste avec ce relief et le mettre en valeur. Chaque bouteille est masquée et colorée à la main, ce qui donne au produit fini une aura artisanale qui le démarque de tout autre produit de série. Ce parfum a été conçu tout spécialement en tant que cadeau pour les actionnaires de **Shiseido**.

SHISEIDO
EAU DE PARFUM 2011

Design: Yoji Nobuto, Yuka Nagasaki
Company: Shiseido Co., Ltd.
Country: Japan
Category: Limited editions,
limited series, collectors' items
BRONZE PENTAWARD 2012

JOHNNIE WALKER
THE DIRECTORS BLEND

Design Direction: Mary Lewis
Illustration: Sarah Cruz
Screen-Printing: Nigel Nesbitt, The Art of Presentation
Client: Jeremy Lindley (Head of Global Design, Diageo)
Company: Lewis Moberly
Country: UK
Category: Limited editions, limited series, collectors' items

BRONZE PENTAWARD 2011

THE ENDEAVOUR
BANKS RUM

Direction of 3D/Innovation: David Helps
Design: Hayley Barrett
Client Management: Rebecca York
Company: Design Bridge
Country: UK
Category: Limited editions, limited series, collectors' items

BRONZE PENTAWARD 2012

Lolly Tools are a limited-edition series of lollipops in six different flavours shaped like screwdrivers and packaged in a leather tool-bag. By reversing the normal form of the sweet, the screwdriver design changes the way you look at it. In this case the handle isn't the stick, but the edible part itself. In expanding The Deli Garage food label's range to include lollipops the packaging had to follow the brand's distinctive aesthetic based on garage and workshop products.

Lutschwerkzeug ist ein Limited-Edition-Set mit Lutschern in Form von Schraubenziehern in sechs Geschmacksrichtungen. Sie sind in einer ledernen Werkzeugtasche verpackt. Indem die Schraubenzieherform unser übliches Bild von einem Lutscher auf den Kopf stellt, betrachten wir ihn anders. In diesem Fall ergreift man nicht den Stiel, sondern der Griff selbst ist der essbare Teil. Auch die erweiterte Produktpalette der Lebensmittelmarke The Deli Garage hält im Verpackungsdesign ihre charakteristische Ästhetik bei und basiert auf Garagen- und Werkstattprodukten.

Lolly Tools est une série en édition limitée de six sucettes en forme de tournevis, présentée dans un étui à outils en cuir. En modifiant la forme habituelle de ce bonbon, le tournevis change aussi le regard que l'on porte sur lui. Ici, le manche n'est pas le bâtonnet, mais la partie comestible. Pour cet ajout à la gamme de la marque alimentaire The Deli Garage, l'emballage devait suivre l'esthétique caractéristique de la marque, basée sur les objets que l'on trouverait dans un garage ou un atelier.

THE DELI GARAGE
LOLLY TOOLS

Creative Direction: Katrin Oeding
Art Direction: Reginald Wagner
Copy Text: Till Grabsch, Gereon Klug
Graphic Design: Paul Svoboda, Sarah Gossner
Production: Produktionsbuero Romey (Malottky GmbH)
Account Management: Kristina Wulf
Client: T.D.G. Vertriebs GmbH & Co. KG
Marketing Direction: Felix Negwer
Company: Kolle Rebbe/Korefe
Country: Germany
Category: Distributors'/Retailers' own brands

GOLD PENTAWARD 2011

THE DELI GARAGE
CHEESE PENCILS

Creative Direction: Katrin Oeding
Art Direction: Reginald Wagner
Copy Text: Thomas Voelker
Photography: Ulrike Kirmse
Production: Franziska Ziegler
Account Management: Marie Steinhoff
Client: T.D.G. Vertriebs GmbH & Co. KG
Marketing Direction: Felix Negwer
Company: Kolle Rebbe/Korefe
Country: Germany
Category: Distributors'/Retailers' own brands

BRONZE PENTAWARD 2011

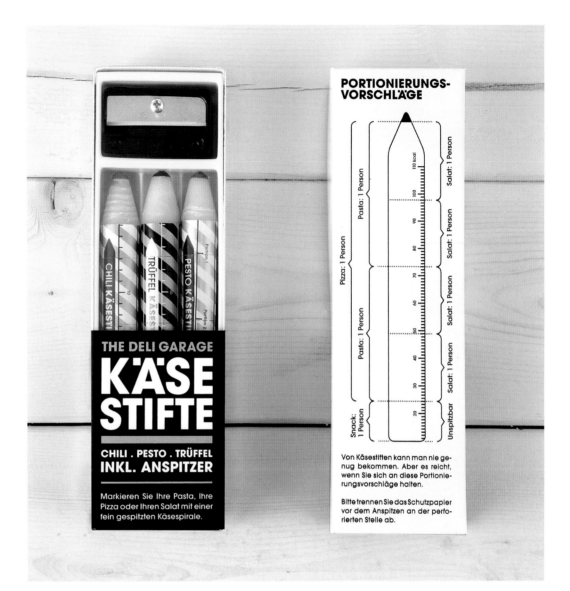

WAITROSE
DUCHY ORIGINALS

Design Direction: Mary Lewis
Design: Mary Lewis, Ann Marshall, Alastair Hamp
Photography: Gerrit Buntrock
Company: Lewis Moberly
Country: UK
Category: Distributors'/Retailers' own brands

SILVER PENTAWARD 2011

ORGANIC

CAMOMILE
INFUSION

WITH A DELICATE FLAVOUR

20 TEA BAGS

ORGANIC

GREEN TEA WITH
JASMINE

A DELICATE AND REFRESHING FLAVOUR

20 TEA BAGS

ORGANIC

NETTLE
INFUSION

GENTLY AROMATIC
WITH A REFRESHING FLAVOUR

20 TEA BAGS

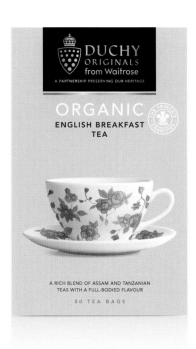

ORGANIC

ENGLISH BREAKFAST
TEA

A RICH BLEND OF ASSAM AND TANZANIAN
TEAS WITH A FULL-BODIED FLAVOUR

50 TEA BAGS

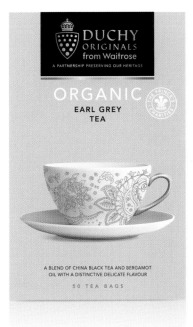

ORGANIC

EARL GREY
TEA

A BLEND OF CHINA BLACK TEA AND BERGAMOT
OIL WITH A DISTINCTIVE DELICATE FLAVOUR

50 TEA BAGS

ORGANIC

ASSAM
TEA

ASSAM TEA WITH A ROBUST AND
FULL-BODIED FLAVOUR

50 TEA BAGS

ORGANIC

DARJEELING
TEA

DARJEELING TEA WITH A DELICATE
AND REFRESHING FLAVOUR

50 TEA BAGS

KAMAASA SYOTEN
BAGS AND WRAPPING PAPER

Creative Direction: Akihiro Nishizawa
Art Direction: Akihiro Nishizawa
Design: Akihiro Nishizawa, Katoh Nami
Company: Eight Branding Design Co., Ltd.
Country: Japan
Category: Distributors'/Retailers' own brands
BRONZE PENTAWARD 2011

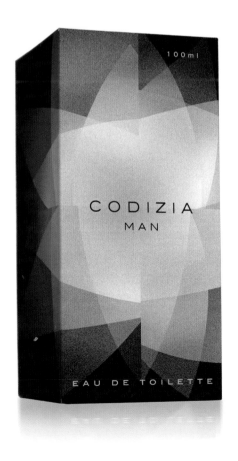

CODIZIA
MAN

Design: Nacho Lavernia, Alberto Cienfuegos
Company: Lavernia & Cienfuegos
Country: Spain
Category: Distributors'/Retailers' own brands
BRONZE PENTAWARD 2011

PAÑPURI

Design: Vorravit Siripark, Pañpuri design team
Company: Puri Co., Ltd.
Country: Thailand
Category: Distributors'/Retailers' own brands

SILVER PENTAWARD 2011

PAÑPURI
FEMME FATALE COLLECTION

Design: Vorravit Siripark, Pañpuri design team
Company: Puri Co., Ltd.
Country: Thailand
Category: Distributors'/Retailers' own brands

BRONZE PENTAWARD 2012

Habit is a company that specialises in drug rehabilitation and cessation products and believes in offering an exclusive and discreet service through its wide range of products. For the treatment of addictions ranging from nicotine to heroin, each product in the redesigned packaging line is housed in an individual black bottle or container to ensure rehabilitation with style. The project is equally a critique of the glamour and glitz associated with drug culture and at the same time a parody of the high-end luxury industry, while hoping still to be able to stand on its own as a product of beauty and design.

Die Firma **Habit** spezialisiert sich auf Hilfsmittel für Drogenentzug und Entwöhnung und setzt durch seine große Produktpalette darauf, eine diskrete und exklusive Dienstleistung zu erbringen. Die Behandlung von Abhängigkeiten reicht von Nikotin bis zu Heroin. Jedes Produkt aus der neu gestalteten Linie wird in einer individuellen schwarzen Flasche oder einem anderen Behälter verpackt, um eine stilvolle Rehabilitation zu gewährleisten. Das Projekt ist ebenso Kritik am Glanz und Glitter, der mit der Drogenkultur verknüpft wird, wie auch Parodie auf die Highend-Luxusindustrie — und außerdem hofft man, für sich allein als Produkt für Schönheit und Design stehen zu können.

Habit est une entreprise spécialisée dans le traitement de la toxicomanie et les produits de sevrage, et veut offrir un service exclusif et discret à travers une vaste gamme de produits. Pour le traitement d'addictions allant de la nicotine à l'héroïne, chaque produit de la ligne remodelée est conditionné dans une bouteille ou un contenant noir individuel pour une réhabilitation tout en style. Ce projet est également une critique du glamour associé à la culture de la drogue, mais aussi une parodie de l'industrie du luxe, et tente dans le même temps d'exister en tant qu'objet de design.

HABIT

Design: Morey Reed Talmor (student)
School: Shenkar School of Engineering and Design
Country: Israel
Category: Packaging concept (luxury)
SILVER PENTAWARD 2012

BLACK BEACH ORGANICS

Design: Sara Jones
Company: Anthem Worldwide
Country: UK
Category: Packaging concept (luxury)
BRONZE PENTAWARD 2012

ZEN PERFUME

Design: Igor Mitin
Company: Good!
Country: Kazakhstan
Category: Packaging concept (luxury)

SILVER PENTAWARD 2012

CALVADOS ELYSIUM

Creative Direction: Arthur Schreiber
Design: Arthur Schreiber
3D: Anastasia Chamkina
Company: StudioIN
Country: Russia
Category: Packaging concept (luxury)

BRONZE PENTAWARD 2012

Best of the category
Household maintenance
Home improvement & decoration
Electronic
Non-electronic
Automobile products
Distributors'/Retailers' own brands

other markets

Pet products
Entertainment
Miscellaneous
Tobacco products
B2B products
Packaging concept
Ecological concept

Essay by

DANIEL DITTMAR

Director of Brand Design at Bic USA Inc.
Pentawards Jury Member 2011–2012

"Creativity is an engaging and strategic opportunity. Let's create something together!"

This is my mantra for daily design practice; as such it keeps me humble in knowing that I'm not the center of the creative process, but rather, a helping guide working in partnership with an array of influencers. I take responsibility to see that we have optimized our design leadership function.

It is an amazing opportunity and responsibility to be a designer and a catalyst for change in our unique world. Think about this; we begin each day on the assumption that somewhere in the course of our exposure and relational connections, we will have a profound impact on something! Personally, I believe that I make a difference by venturing deeper into new thought processes and delivering fresh approaches to design solutions, unique packaging prototypes, and breakthrough visual identity systems. And then, right at my high point, I run straight into a real corporate world, which confronts me with a different vision mindset, budget restrictions, pessimism, limited integration, and with untrained decision-makers who dare to challenge my holistic approach to engaging creativity. How can this be?!

The beauty of the world today, and the discipline of design thinking, is knowing that you can make a difference by being open to all ways of thought, and embracing your place within a sphere of constant change. I like how Donald Miller expresses the notion of how we are placed in God's story. His book, *A Million Miles in a Thousand Years*, states that we should enjoy our place in the story, but still create within it in big meaningful ways, and as grateful participants. Wow, what a chance this is, to forge ahead with remarkable accountability and to produce remarkable things at whatever capacity! And if you're not doing this, then choose to stay living in a meaningless dimension.

I believe that designers are powerful and insightful beings, who are specially programmed to deliver strategic products and meaningful experiences for real people. We are seeing this take shape in a world that has evolved into a relational 360-degree communication exposé. And in this newly shaped world, designers are leaping forward to impact new methods that transform meaningful connections with social platforms, products, brand development, and communication positioning.

I can't say that I approach design for the "Other Markets" category any differently than I would approach any other brand identity assignment. I'm currently working for a global brand (BIC) that delivers great brand value and builds on emotional brand influence within the distinctive product categories that it serves. I believe that the BIC brand has far-reaching capacity and will continue to leverage the visual and emotional opportunities beyond its current range of product offerings. This is a strategic opportunity for a brand that can extend its core values to other categories because of its consumer appeal. Around the world, BIC is embraced as a "born local" brand, and continues to grow its international presence and appeal. This "born local" advantage will help shape the BIC brand of the future as well as invigorate its people charged with finding new product pathways.

I think consumers expect brands to meet their needs in unique ways, that is, to make them feel good about themselves, and to be part of their lives through trust and effectiveness. If I'm a brand, I want a lasting relationship with those I'm interacting with. This means delivering on a real purpose to be the best that I can be while sharing my unique offering in partnership with them to meet their needs. It's all about engaging the strategic opportunity and knowing that something "BIG" can be created working together.

„Kreativität ist eine verpflichtende und strategische Gelegenheit. Lasst uns kreativ gemeinsam etwas schaffen!"

Das ist das Mantra meiner alltäglichen Designpraxis. Es hält mich bescheiden, denn ich weiß, ich bin nicht das Zentrum des kreativen Prozesses, sondern sehe mich vielmehr als hilfreichen Leiter, der mit einem ganzen Spektrum von Einflüssen in Partnerschaft arbeitet. Ich übernehme Verantwortung, dafür zu sorgen, unsere marktführende Funktion beim Design zu optimieren.

Es ist eine unglaubliche Chance und Verantwortung, als Designer auch Katalysator für die Veränderungen unserer einzigartigen Welt zu sein. Betrachten Sie es einmal so: Jeden Tag beginnen wir mit der Annahme, dass wir irgendwann im Laufe unserer Auseinandersetzung mit der Welt und ihren Vernetzungen wesentlich auf etwas einwirken können! Ich persönlich bin der Überzeugung, etwas bewirken zu können, indem ich neue Gedankenprozesse tiefer erforsche und frische und neuartige Ansätze für Designlösungen, für einzigartige Verpackungsprototypen und bahnbrechende visuelle Identitätssysteme liefere. Und auf meinem Zenit pralle ich dann direkt auf reale Unternehmenswelten, die mich mit völlig anderen Visionen und Einstellungen konfrontieren, mit Budgetbeschränkungen, Pessimismus, beschränkter Integration und ungeschulten Entscheidungsträgern, die es wagen, meine holistische Einstellung zum Thema engagierte Kreativität zu hinterfragen. Wie kann das sein?!

Das Schöne an der Welt von heute und der Selbstdisziplin des Denkens als Designer ist das Wissen, dass man etwas bewegen kann, indem man allen Denkarten gegenüber offen ist und innerhalb einer Sphäre konstanter Veränderung seinen eigenen Platz akzeptiert. Mir gefällt, wie Donald Miller es als Konzept ausdrückt, dass wir alle unseren Platz in Gottes Geschichte einnehmen. In seinem Buch *Eine Million Meilen in Tausend Jahren* stellt er fest, dass wir unseren Platz in der Geschichte Gottes genießen, aber darin auf eine große und bedeutungsvolle Art und als dankbare Teilnehmer weiterhin kreativ sein sollten. Toll! Was für eine Chance, in bemerkenswerter Verantwortung voranzuschreiten und bemerkenswerte Dinge zu produzieren — in welchem Umfang auch immer! Und wenn man es nicht tut, entscheidet man sich dafür, mit dem Leben in bedeutungslosen Dimensionen fortzufahren.

Ich glaube fest daran, dass Designer mächtige und einfühlsame Wesen sind — speziell dazu programmiert, strategische Produkte und bedeutungsvolle Erfahrungen für echte Menschen abzuliefern. Wir sehen gerade, wie das in einer Welt Formen annimmt, die sich zu einem beziehungsreichen 360-Grad-Kommunikationsentwurf entwickelt hat. Und in dieser neu gestalteten Welt setzen Designer zum Sprung nach vorne an, um neue Methoden zu prägen, die mit sozialen Plattformen und Produkten, der Entwicklung von Marken und der Positionierung von Kommunikation bedeutungsvolle Verbindungen transformieren.

Ich kann nicht sagen, dass ich das Design in der Kategorie „Andere Märkte" irgendwie anders angehe als bei meinen sonstigen Aufträgen für die Markenidentität. Ich arbeite momentan für die globale Marke BIC, die großartige Markenwerte liefert und innerhalb ihrer klar abgegrenzten Produktkategorien auf eine emotionale Beeinflussung setzt. Meiner Überzeugung nach sind die Kapazitäten der Marke BIC besonders weitreichend, und sie wird auch künftig über ihre aktuelle Produktpalette hinaus weitere visuelle und emotionale Möglichkeiten nutzen. Mit dieser Strategie und ihrer Resonanz bei Verbrauchern kann die Marke ihre Kernwerte auch auf andere Kategorien ausdehnen. Überall auf der Welt wird BIC als „lokal entstandene" Marke begrüßt, und ihre internationale Präsenz und Ausstrahlung wächst zunehmend. Dieser Vorteil einer „lokal entstandenen" Marke hilft, die Marke BIC für die Zukunft zu formen und ihre verantwortlichen Personen darin zu bestärken, neue Produktpfade zu finden.

Meines Erachtens erwarten die Konsumenten von Marken, dass diese ihre Anforderungen und Bedürfnisse in neuartiger und unverwechselbarer Weise erfüllen. Von der Marke hängt es also ab, wie wohl sich Konsumenten mit ihr fühlen, ob sie durch Vertrauen und Effizienz zu einem Teil ihres Lebens wird. Wenn ich eine Marke wäre, würde ich eine langfristige Beziehung zu jenen aufbauen wollen, mit denen ich zu tun habe. Das bedeutet letztlich, mit wahren Absichten das Beste zu liefern, während ich gleichzeitig mein einmaliges Angebot der Partnerschaft aufrechterhalte, um die Bedürfnisse anderer zu erfüllen. Es geht nur darum, sich für die strategische Chance zu engagieren in dem Wissen, in gemeinsamer Zusammenarbeit wirklich etwas „Großes" schaffen zu können.

Essay by

DANIEL DITTMAR

« La créativité est une opportunité fascinante et stratégique. Créons quelque chose ensemble ! »

C'est mon mantra pour la pratique quotidienne du design ; il m'oblige à rester humble en me rappelant que je ne suis pas au centre du processus créatif, mais que je ne suis qu'un guide qui travaille en partenariat avec de nombreux prescripteurs. Je prends la responsabilité de veiller à ce que nous optimisions notre fonction de leader dans le design.

C'est une opportunité magnifique et une grande responsabilité que d'être un designer et un catalyseur du changement dans notre monde. Imaginez un peu : nous commençons chaque jour en présupposant que quelque part au cours de notre exposition au monde et de nos connexions relationnelles, nous aurons un impact profond sur quelque chose ! Personnellement, je pense que je change les choses en m'aventurant plus loin dans les nouveaux processus de pensée et en inventant de nouvelles façons d'approcher les solutions de design, des prototypes originaux, et des systèmes d'identité visuelle révolutionnaires. Et puis, juste quand j'atteins mon maximum, je me heurte aux réalités de l'entreprise, qui me mettent en face d'une vision différente, de restrictions de budget, du pessimisme, d'une intégration limitée, et de décisionnaires ignorants qui osent remettre en question mon approche holistique du processus créatif. Comment cela est-il possible ?!

La beauté du monde actuel, et la discipline de la pensée dans le design, est de savoir que vous pouvez changer les choses en étant ouvert à toutes les façons de penser, et en assumant votre place dans une sphère de changement constant. J'aime beaucoup la façon dont Donald Miller explique notre place dans l'histoire de Dieu. Son livre, *A Million Miles in a Thousand Years*, affirme que nous devrions savourer notre place dans l'histoire, mais aussi nous servir de ce cadre pour créer de grandes choses, en tant que participants reconnaissants. Quelle formidable chance, de pouvoir aller de l'avant avec une responsabilité remarquable et produire des choses remarquables quelle que soit notre capacité ! Et si vous ne le faites pas, alors vous choisissez de vivre dans une dimension dénuée de sens.

Je pense que les designers sont des êtres puissants et perspicaces, qui sont tout spécialement programmés pour concevoir des produits stratégiques et des expériences pleines de sens à l'intention des gens de la vraie vie. Nous voyons cela prendre forme dans un monde qui est devenu une présentation de communication à 360 degrés. Et dans ce nouveau monde, les designers font de grands bonds en avant pour arriver à de nouvelles méthodes qui transforment les connexions significatives avec les plateformes sociales, les produits, le développement de marque et le positionnement de la communication.

Je ne peux pas dire que j'aborde le design pour la catégorie « Autres marchés » différemment de n'importe quelle autre mission d'identité de marque. Je travaille actuellement pour une marque internationale (BIC) qui sait créer de la valeur et tirer parti de son influence émotionnelle dans les différentes catégories de produits où elle est active. Je pense que la marque BIC a d'énormes capacités et continuera de valoriser les opportunités visuelles et émotionnelles au-delà de sa gamme de produits actuelle. C'est une opportunité stratégique pour une marque qui peut étendre ses valeurs fondamentales à d'autres catégories grâce à l'attrait qu'elle exerce sur les consommateurs. Dans le monde entier, BIC est considérée comme une marque « locale », et continue de faire croître sa présence internationale et son pouvoir de séduction. Cet avantage du « local » contribuera à façonner la marque BIC du futur ainsi qu'à stimuler ses employés chargés de trouver de nouvelles voies pour ses produits.

Je pense que les consommateurs veulent que les marques satisfassent leurs besoins avec originalité, qu'elles les aident à se sentir bien dans leur peau, et qu'elles trouvent une place dans leur vie en se montrant dignes de confiance et efficaces. Si je suis une marque, je veux une relation de longue durée avec les gens. Cela implique d'atteindre un but bien réel, celui d'être la meilleure marque que je puisse être tout en partageant mon offre unique en partenariat avec eux pour satisfaire leurs besoins. Il s'agit avant tout de saisir l'opportunité stratégique et de savoir que l'on peut créer quelque chose de « grand » ensemble.

For a range of laundry care packaging for UK-based supermarket **Morrisons** the design had to cover a variety of products and packaging formats from powders to liquids. This meant clarifying and simplifying on-pack information to make the benefits of the various product types (Bio, Non Bio, 2 in 1 and Colours) the key message to shoppers. A simple, strong design scheme that mimics fabric care labels on clothing ties the whole range together and still allows the basic differences between product type and format to be clearly identified. Secondary information, such as number of washes and washing temperatures, is indicated by icons in the style of washing instructions found on clothing labels.

Für ein Waschmittelsortiment des britischen Supermarkts **Morrisons** sollte das Design verschiedene Produkte und Packungsformate von Pulvern bis zu Flüssigkeiten abdecken. Klarheit und Einfachheit auf der Verpackung waren nötig, um dem Kunden die zentrale Botschaft zu vermitteln, nämlich die Vorteile der verschiedenen Produkttypen (Bio, Non Bio, 2 in 1 und Colours). Das einfache, starke Designschema ahmt die Pflegeetiketten an Kleidungsstücken nach. Das verbindet das ganze Sortiment miteinander und erlaubt dennoch, die grundlegenden Unterschiede zwischen den Produkttypen klar zu identifizieren. Die sekundären Informationen, etwa über die Zahl der möglichen Waschvorgänge oder Waschtemperaturen, werden durch Symbole im Stil der Waschanleitung auf Kleidungsetiketten vermittelt.

Pour une gamme de produits de lessive des supermarchés britanniques **Morrisons**, le concept devait couvrir toute une série de produits et de formats différents, poudres ou liquides. Il fallait donc clarifier et simplifier les informations imprimées sur les emballages pour mettre les avantages des différents types de produit (bio, non bio, 2 en 1 et couleurs) au cœur du message adressé aux clients. Un graphisme simple et fort qui imite les étiquettes d'instruction de lavage des vêtements unifie toute la gamme, mais permet d'identifier clairement les différences de base entre les types de produit et les formats. Les informations secondaires telles que le nombre de lessives et les températures de lavage sont indiquées par des icônes qui imitent aussi les étiquettes des vêtements.

MORRISONS
LAUNDRY CARE

Design: Lysa Millergill
Creative Direction: Glenn W. Taylor
Account Design Direction: John Benson
Photography: Paul Kaczmar
Company: Stocks Taylor Benson
Country: UK
Category: Best of the category other markets

PLATINUM PENTAWARD 2011

Rubber boots are an underestimated product in many respects — everyone is aware of their primary function, protection from water, but as high-quality specialised footwear for fishing the better brand should make its advantages clear. Instead of using a bland box with the manufacturer's logo, a packaging design was therefore developed depicting the boot immersed in water and surrounded by potentially harmful aquatic creatures. The packaging is also intended to serve as a mini-stand and to promote the product in stores, distinguishing it dramatically from the competition since most such boots are almost identical in appearance and are typically located on the lower shelves in a dense group, making it difficult for consumers to decide on any particular brand.

Gummistiefel sind in mancherlei Hinsicht unterschätzte Gegenstände: Alle kennen ihre primäre Funktion, vor Wasser zu schützen. Aber wenn eine Marke für qualitativ hochwertiges Spezialschuhwerk zum Angeln besonders gut ist, sollte sie ihre Vorteile deutlich herausstellen. Anstatt nur das Logo des Herstellers auf einem langweiligen Karton zu zeigen, wurde darum ein Verpackungsdesign entwickelt, das den Stiefel in Wasser getaucht zeigt, umgeben von potenziell gefährlichen Wasserbewohnern. Der Packkarton fungiert wie eine Minibühne und bewirbt so das Produkt im Laden. Damit unterscheidet er sich dramatisch von der Konkurrenz, bei der alle Stiefel praktisch gleich aussehen und massenweise meist die unteren Regalreihen füllen. So können die Verbraucher sich kaum für eine bestimmte Marke entscheiden.

Les bottes en caoutchouc sont un produit sous-estimé à bien des égards. Tout le monde connaît leur fonction principale, protéger contre l'eau, mais les marques haut de gamme devraient mieux communiquer sur leurs avantages en tant que chaussures spécialisées pour la pêche. Au lieu d'utiliser une boîte sans imagination ornée du logo du fabricant, l'emballage montre donc un pied immergé dans l'eau et encerclé de créatures aquatiques potentiellement dangereuses. Il est également pensé pour servir de petit présentoir qui met le produit en valeur dans les magasins, en le démarquant spectaculairement de la concurrence puisque la majorité des bottes de ce genre sont habituellement toutes regroupées pêle-mêle sur les étagères du bas, ce qui n'aide pas les consommateurs à se décider pour une marque particulière.

FISHERMAN
RUBBER BOOTS

Design: Igor Mitin, Berik Yergaliyev, Darina
Baimukhanova, Rustam Gareyev, Farhat Omirbaev,
Andrey Serdyuk
Company: Good!
Country: Kazakhstan
Category: Best of the category other markets

PLATINUM PENTAWARD 2012

Hampi natural tableware is a range of disposable plates and bowls made sustainably from fallen palm leaves. At first they were sold directly to caterers but to sell them as a lifestyle choice to consumers repackaging became necessary, whether they were to be sold in department stores or in supermarkets. The design depicts the story of this special product by showing the transformation of the leaf into reusable natural plates. The sides and top of the packs show the beautiful patterns the leaves create, whilst the shapes used in the logo were a source of inspiration for the actual boxes.

Das natürliche Geschirr von Hampi ist ein Sortiment aus Einmaltellern und -schalen, umweltverträglich hergestellt aus abgefallenen Palmenblättern. Zuerst wurde das Produkt direkt an Gastronomen geliefert, aber um das Geschirr als Lifestyle-Artikel auch dem Endverbraucher verkaufen zu können, wurde eine neue Verpackung notwendig, sei es für Kaufhäuser oder Supermärkte. Das Design schildert die Herstellungsgeschichte dieses besonderen Produkts, indem es darstellt, wie sich das Blatt in wiederverwendbares natürliches Geschirr verwandelt. Seiten und Deckel des Kartons zeigen die schönen Muster der Blätter, während die Formen im Logo als Inspirationsquelle für die eigentlichen Kartons dienen.

La vaisselle naturelle Hampi est une gamme d'assiettes et de bols jetables issus de la production durable, fabriqués à partir de feuilles de palme tombées à terre. Au début elle était vendue directement aux traiteurs, mais pour la vendre aux consommateurs en grand magasin ou en supermarché il a fallu revoir l'emballage en la positionnant comme un choix de style de vie. La boîte illustre l'histoire de ce produit très spécial en montrant la feuille qui se transforme en assiettes naturelles réutilisables. Les côtés et le haut des paquets montrent les superbes motifs créés par les feuilles, tandis que les formes utilisées dans le logo ont été une source d'inspiration pour la forme des boîtes.

HAMPI PRODUCTS
NATURAL TABLEWARE

Creative Direction: Marcel Verhaaf
Project Coordination/Artwork: Jeroen Meijer
Managing Direction: Robert Kuiper
Client Services Direction: Sabine Louët Feisser
Photography: Nishikie fotografie
Company: Brandnew
Country: Netherlands
Category: Home improvement & decoration

GOLD PENTAWARD 2011

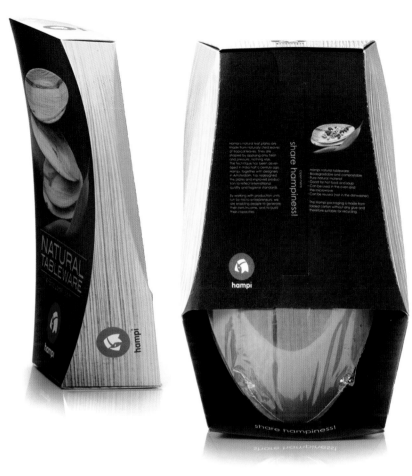

NATURAL
TABLEWARE
4x Extra Large | 32cm

hampi

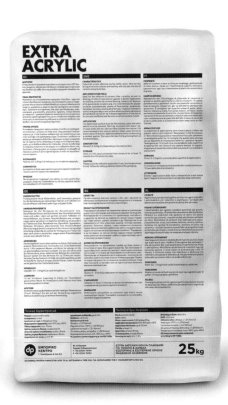

COL & EXTRA ACRYLIC

Design: Dimitris Koliadimas,
Dimitris Papazoglou
Company: Designers United
Country: Greece
Category: Home improvement & decoration

BRONZE PENTAWARD 2012

BRÜKEN

Creative Direction: Gregory Tsaknakis
Design: Aris Pasouris
Company: Mousegraphics
Country: Greece
Category: Home improvement & decoration

SILVER PENTAWARD 2011

ESCO
NEW LIGHT

Design: Oleg Beriev, Julia Filatova, Vera Razdobarina
Company: Mildberry Brand Building Solutions
Country: Russia
Category: Household maintenance

SILVER PENTAWARD 2012

ÊTRE VERT

Design: Caracas creative team
Company: Caracas
Country: France
Category: Home improvement & decoration

BRONZE PENTAWARD 2011

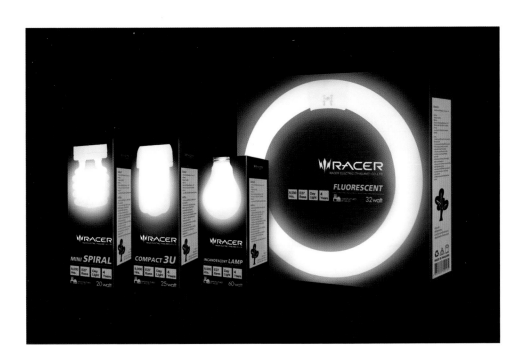

RACER ELECTRIC

Creative Direction: Somchana Kangwarnjit
Design: Nantawat Rodchau, Sawat Charoensansuk,
Patipat Kannarong
Company: Prompt Design
Country: Thailand
Category: Household maintenance

GOLD PENTAWARD 2012

RECYCLING FOR EVER

Design: Fabrice Peltier
Company: P'référence
Country: France
Category: Home improvement & decoration
BRONZE PENTAWARD 2011

DUALSAW

Creative Direction: Paul van den Berg
Design Direction: Bill Kerr
Strategy Direction: Georgia Thunes
Account Direction: Elainne Roberton
Company: CB'a Brand Engine
Country: USA
Category: Home improvement & decoration

BRONZE PENTAWARD 2011

KIMTECH AVIATION WIPES

Creative Direction: Jure Leko
Design: Paul Heidenreich
Company: Grain Creative Pty Ltd.
Country: Australia
Category: Household maintenance

SILVER PENTAWARD 2012

GLADE EXPRESSIONS

Design Research: William Gordon,
Jon Mandel (SC Johnson), Smart design team
Company: SC Johnson
Country: USA
Category: Household maintenance

BRONZE PENTAWARD 2012

RADIANT

Design Direction: Glen Crawforth
Design: Kim Oataway
Copy: Harley Augustine
Account Management: Lyndal Kearney
Production Management: Phil Curlis-Gibson
Company: Elmwood
Country: UK
Category: Household maintenance

BRONZE PENTAWARD 2012

INTRATUIN
POTTING SOIL

Creative Direction: Paul Roeters
Design: Max Kortsmit
Company: Studio Kluif
Country: Netherlands
Category: Home improvement & decoration

GOLD PENTAWARD 2012

TUINAARDE

Voor ophogen en egaliseren
van de tuin en border

- Geschikt voor het ophogen en egaliseren van tuin en border
- Niet geschikt voor het planten van gewassen in tuin, potten of bakken

25 L

TUINTURF

Verbetert de bodemstructuur

- Goed te gebruiken bij o.a. heide en coniferen
- Geschikt voor verbetering van zand- en kleigrond

40 L

MEST KORRELS   *Gedroogde*

Voor siertuin en gazon,
ook geschikt voor groenten en fruit

- Makkelijk strooibaar, stuift niet
- Verbetert de bodemstructuur

25 L

HYDRO KORRELS

Voor drainage in potten en hydrocultuur

- ...ert de waterhuishouding
- ... ...chikt als decoratie

40 L

CACAO DOPPEN

Decoratieve bodembedekker

- Voor gebruik in borders
- Voorkomt uitdroging van de grond, slakken- en onkruidwerend

50 L

KOKOS

Duurzame decoratieve bodembedekker

- Voor het aanleggen van paden, speelplaatsen en border
- Voorkomt uidroging van de grond, onkruidwerend

50 L

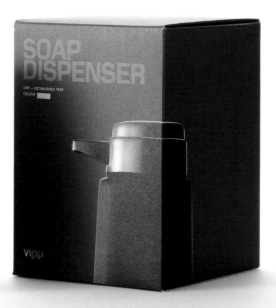

VIPP BATH RANGE

Design: Vipp, Box House
Company: Vipp
Country: Denmark
Category: Home improvement & decoration

SILVER PENTAWARD 2011

For everyday household use, this smart reimagining of the water-filtering jug does away with the usual second reservoir, which drains slowly and typically needs to be filled several times, to deliver pure water in an instant. Holding more than its appearance would suggest (64oz/2l), the slim design also frees up space as the jug fits neatly into refrigerator doors. The **bobble** jug is free of BPA, phthalates and PVC and uses an activated carbon filter, which is super-effective at reducing the taint of chlorine commonly detected in tap-water. The filter is available in 6 vivid colours, visible through the packaging window, whilst the box's cut-out aligns with the jug's handle to make for easy carrying.

Bei dieser pfiffigen Neuerfindung eines Wasserfilters für den Alltagsgebrauch im Haushalt wurde das zweite Reservoir abgeschafft. Früher musste es umständlich mehrmals befüllt werden und leerte sich nur langsam. Mittels neuem Filter erhält man sofort reines Wasser. Durch das schlanke Design nimmt die Karaffe mehr Wasser auf, als es den Anschein hat (bis zu 2 Liter), sie spart auch Platz, weil sie nun gut in die Kühlschranktür passt. Die Kanne **bobble** ist frei von BPA, Phthalaten und PVC. Sein Aktivkohlefilter reduziert höchst effizient das Chlor aus dem Haushaltswasser. Der Filter ist in sechs leuchtenden Farben erhältlich, die man durch ein Fenster im Karton sehen kann. Ein Ausschnitt im Karton macht es möglich, die Karaffe an ihrem Griff leicht zu transportieren.

Pour une utilisation quotidienne à la maison, cette réinvention astucieuse de la carafe filtrante abandonne le réservoir secondaire typique qui laisse passer l'eau lentement et qu'il faut remplir plusieurs fois, pour servir de l'eau pure en un instant. Elle contient plus qu'elle n'en a l'air (2 l), et sa ligne élancée économise l'espace et lui permet de tenir dans les portes des réfrigérateurs. La carafe **bobble** ne contient ni BPA, ni phtalates ni PVC, et emploie un filtre au charbon actif, extrêmement efficace pour réduire les traces de chlore que l'on détecte souvent dans l'eau du robinet. Le filtre est disponible en 6 couleurs vives, visibles à travers la fenêtre de l'emballage, tandis que les découpes de la boîte s'alignent sur la poignée de la carafe pour faciliter le transport.

BOBBLE JUG

Creative Direction: Stephanie Smiedt (Move Collective)
Associated Creative Direction: Katie Eaton (Safari Sundays)
Art Direction: Craig Hench (Safari Sundays)
Design: Karim Rashid (Karim Rashid Inc.)
Account Direction: Jen Vest (Safari Sundays)
Company: Move Collective
Country: USA
Category: Home improvement & decoration

SILVER PENTAWARD 2012

THE KIDS COOKING COMPANY

Design Direction: Mary Lewis
Design: Silja Holm, Poppy Stedman
Company: Lewis Moberly
Country: UK
Category: Home improvement & decoration

SILVER PENTAWARD 2012

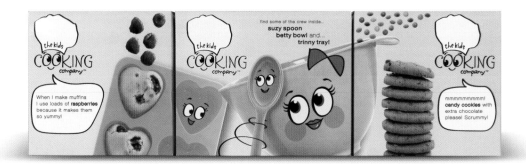

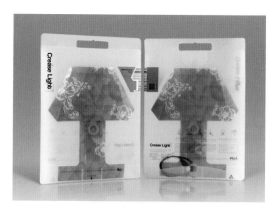

CREASE LIGHT

Design: Pega – Design & Engineering
Company: Pegatron Corporation
Country: Taiwan
Category: Home improvement & decoration

BRONZE PENTAWARD 2012

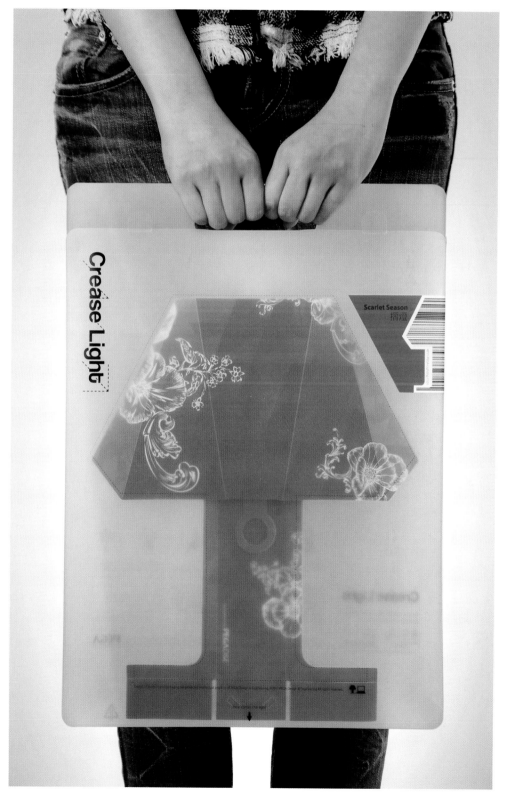

PETS AT HOME VENTURE BRAND

Creative Direction: Glenn W. Taylor
Graphic Design: Lysa Millergill
Company: Stocks Taylor Benson
Country: UK
Category: Distributors'/
Retailers' own brands

GOLD PENTAWARD 2012

ALBERT HEIJN CATFOOD

Design: Vincent Limburg
Company: Brandnew
Country: Netherlands
Category: Distributors'/
Retailers' own brands

SILVER PENTAWARD 2012

BARONESSE

Creative Direction/Design: Bjørn Rybakken
Design: Emelie Spjuth
Account Management: Bente Hauge
Managing Direction: Linda Frid (Fargerike Norway)
Brand Management: Kristian Sørli (Fargerike Norway)
Company: Tangram Design
Country: Norway
Category: Distributors'/Retailers' own brands
BRONZE PENTAWARD 2012

HEMA
PAINTS

Design: Richard Mooij
Company: PROUDdesign
Country: Netherlands
Category: Distributors'/
Retailers' own brands
SILVER PENTAWARD 2012

PLANTRONICS
GLOBAL PACKAGING REDESIGN

Creative Direction: David Turner, Bruce Duckworth
Design Direction: Sarah Moffat
Design: Brian Steele
Production: Craig Snelgrove
Company: Turner Duckworth, London & San Francisco
Country: USA
Category: Electronic

GOLD PENTAWARD 2011

Plantronics has long been a pioneer in communication technology but in recent years competitors in the Bluetooth category have taken a lead with more successful packaging. To redress this a new positioning was developed based on simple, smarter communication and represented by the SoundWorld icon, a melding of perfect sound quality, symbolised by the sound-wave, and details from the world around us, such as a park scene, a commuter's journey or a music venue. Each SoundWorld thus relates to the target consumer for a particular product line, further differentiated by finish and colour in a clear, modern design. The packaging further permits 360-degree product visibility, and can cater for increased security and multiple component combinations for a global packaging system.

Plantronics ist schon lange ein Pionier der Kommunikationstechnologie, doch in den vergangenen Jahren ergriffen die Mitbewerber der Kategorie Bluetooth mit ihren erfolgreicheren Verpackungen die Führung. Um dem abzuhelfen, positionierte man sich neu, basierend auf einer einfachen, cleveren Kommunikation und repräsentiert durch das SoundWorld-Symbol. Hier verschmilzt die perfekte Klangqualität — die Schallwelle symbolisiert sie — mit Details aus der Welt um uns herum, z. B. Szenen aus einem Park, dem Arbeitsweg eines Pendlers oder einer Musikveranstaltung. Jedes SoundWorld-Produkt bezieht sich auf den Zielkonsumenten für eine bestimmte Produktlinie, die dann durch Ausführung und Farbe in einem klaren, modernen Design weiter differenziert wird. Die Verpackung erlaubt überdies eine Rundumsichtbarkeit des Produkts und sorgt für verbesserte Sicherheit und mehrere Kombinationsmöglichkeiten der Komponenten dieses globalen Verpackungssystems.

Plantronics a longtemps été un pionnier des technologies de la communication, mais ces dernières années ses concurrents ont pris la tête dans la catégorie du Bluetooth grâce à des emballages plus réussis. Pour redresser la situation, un nouveau positionnement a été mis au point, basé sur une communication plus intelligente et représenté par le symbole SoundWorld, qui allie l'idée de qualité sonore parfaite, symbolisée par l'onde sonore, et des détails du monde qui nous entoure, comme un parc, le trajet quotidien pour aller au travail, ou une salle de concert. Chaque SoundWorld établit donc une connexion personnelle avec le consommateur cible de chaque gamme de produits, qui est de plus différenciée par la finition et la couleur dans un graphisme clair et moderne. L'emballage permet en outre d'observer le produit sous tous les angles, et est compatible avec les mesures de sécurité les plus strictes et les combinaisons de composants multiples pour un système d'emballage global.

LG ELECTRONICS
MACHJET PRINTER INK CARTRIDGE

Design: Munhwa Kim, Youngmi Yoon, Byungjin Oh
Company: LG Electronics Inc., Corporate Design Center
Country: South Korea
Category: Electronic

SILVER PENTAWARD 2011

LG ELECTRONICS
LOLLIPOP T CELLPHONE

Design: Byungjin Oh, Youngseok Seo, Yongkeun Kim,
Hansol Choi, Anke Weckmann
Company: LG Electronics Inc., Corporate Design Center
Country: South Korea
Category: Electronic

BRONZE PENTAWARD 2011

P AROUND

Design: Somchana Kangwarnjit, Chidchanok
Laohawattanakul, Mathurada Bejrananda
Company: Prompt Design
Country: Thailand
Category: Non-electronic
(paper, writing materials, stationery etc.)

BRONZE PENTAWARD 2011

C'LITE

Design: Séverine Platteau,
Annemieke Dupont
Company: Crea
Country: Belgium
Category: Automobile products

BRONZE PENTAWARD 2011

PSA PEUGEOT CITROËN STORE PACKAGING

Design: Pulp creative team
Company: Pulp
Country: France
Category: Automobile products

SILVER PENTAWARD 2011

KMC PINK LADY

Creative Direction: David Pan
Management Direction: Zoe Huang
Design: David Lin, Yihuey Lin, May Weng
Company: Gidea Group
Country: Taiwan
Category: Automobile products

GOLD PENTAWARD 2011

MICHELIN
MOUNTAIN BIKE

Creative Direction: Sébastien Canu
Art Direction: Lorenzo Santangelo
Graphic Design: Florent Soissons
Package Engineering: Christian Gaillard
Account Management: Aurore Nolf
Company: Japa
Country: France
Category: Automobile products

SILVER PENTAWARD 2012

KATZ MENU

Design: Tom Desmet, Kristof Devos
Company: Magenta
Country: Belgium
Category: Pet products

GOLD PENTAWARD 2011

PETCUREAN
PET NUTRITION
GO!

Creative Direction:
Matthew Clark, Roy White
Design: Matthew Clark
Copy: Pete Pallet, Jaimie Turkington,
Matthew Clark
Illustration: Liz Wurzinger (pet icons)
Photography: GO! Packaging
Pets: David Ellingsen
Production: Peel Plastics
Company: Subplot Design
Country: Canada
Category: Pet products

GOLD PENTAWARD 2012

NEST4NATURE

Creative Direction: Juris Dzenis
Graphic Design: Ğirts Rozenbergs
Company: Octagon Branding
Country: Latvia
Category: Pet products

SILVER PENTAWARD 2012

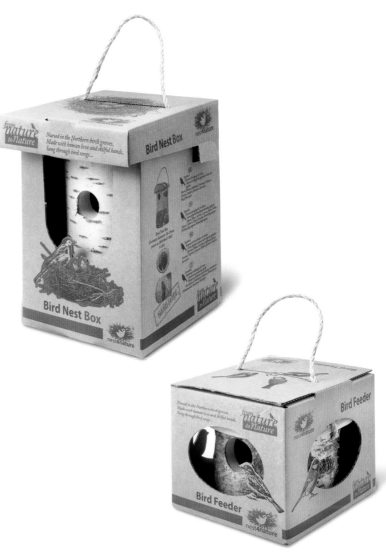

PINO MININO
CAT LITTER ECOPACK

Design: David Freyre, Carolina Alzate,
Francisco Hernandez, Andres Gallo
Company: ImasD
Country: Colombia
Category: Pet products

SILVER PENTAWARD 2012

PETCUREAN PET NUTRITION NOW FRESH

Creative Direction: Matthew Clark, Roy White
Design: Matthew Clark, Ross Chandler
Copy: Pete Pallet, Jaimie Turkington, Matthew Clark
Illustration: istock & Matthew Clark
(NOW signage), Liz Wurzinger (pet icons)
Production: Peel Plastics
Company: Subplot Design
Country: Canada
Category: Pet products

BRONZE PENTAWARD 2012

NORTHERN BISCUIT

Account Direction: Lawrence Dadds
Design: Jeff Boulton
Company: Davis
Country: Canada
Category: Pet products

BRONZE PENTAWARD 2012

The original **Rampant Rabbit** from Ann Summers was the first vibrator to offer simultaneous stimulation to vagina and clitoris. However, its success led to a flood of imitations and this meant there was an urgent need to re-launch the range and re-claim ownership of these classic sex toys, thereby making them all the more desirable. The revamp took in everything from structure to pack copy, with the initial R of the logo being turned upside-down to make it look like a rabbit's head. The styling of the letter recalls the neon signs of sex shops, while the "vibration lines" around it repeat the movement of the vibrator itself, in its newly styled premium box.

Der originale **Rampant Rabbit** von Ann Summers war der erste Vibrator, der gleichzeitig Vagina und Klitoris stimuliert. Durch seinen Erfolg diente er einer Flut von Nachahmern als Vorbild. Somit gab es großen Bedarf, dieses Produkt wieder auf den Markt zu bringen und die Eigentümerschaft an diesem klassischen Sex Toy erneut zu betonen. Gleichzeitig wird es so noch begehrenswerter. Bei der grundlegenden Überarbeitung der Gesamtgestaltung nahm man sich von der Struktur bis zu den Packungstexten alles im Einzelnen vor. Der Anfangsbuchstabe R wurde als Logo umgedreht, um wie ein Hasenkopf auszusehen. An der neu gestalteten Premiumbox spielt das Styling des Schriftzuges auf Sexshop-Neonschilder an, während die „Vibrationslinien" drumherum die Bewegungen des Vibrators aufgreifen.

Le **Rampant Rabbit** original d'Ann Summers a été le premier vibromasseur qui a proposé la stimulation simultanée du vagin et du clitoris. Mais son succès a mené à un déluge d'imitations, et il était urgent de relancer la gamme et de réaffirmer l'autorité de la marque sur ces sex toys classiques, en les rendant encore plus désirables. Tout a été revu, depuis la structure jusqu'au texte de l'emballage, et le R du logo a été renversé pour le faire ressembler à une tête de lapin. Son graphisme évoque les néons des sex shops, tandis que les vibrations suggérées autour de lui reprennent le mouvement du vibromasseur, à l'abri dans sa nouvelle boîte de luxe.

ANN SUMMERS
RAMPANT RABBIT

Creative Direction: Adam Ellis
Design: Martyn Hayes, Digby Gall
Copy: Laura Forman
Account Direction: Caroline Dilloway
Company: Elmwood
Country: UK
Category: Entertainment

GOLD PENTAWARD 2012

VERDES INNOVATIONS
V-CUBE 2

Art Direction/Design: Andreas Kioroglou
Company: Matadog Design
Country: Greece
Category: Entertainment

SILVER PENTAWARD 2011

2010 US OPEN TENNIS
TICKET INVITE

Creative Direction: Stan Church
Design: Chung-Tao Tu, Stan Church
Company: Wallace Church, Inc.
Country: USA
Category: Entertainment

BRONZE PENTAWARD 2011

STIGA
PURE

Design: Jörgen Lindström (product and package)
Company: Stiga Sports
Country: Sweden
Category: Entertainment

SILVER PENTAWARD 2012

LIVRARIA CULTURA

Creative Direction: Gustavo Piqueira
Design: Gustavo Piqueira,
Samia Jacintho, Luiz Sanches
Design Assistance: Ana Lobo
Company: Casa Rex
Country: Brazil
Category: Entertainment

BRONZE PENTAWARD 2012

CARAN D'ACHE FANCOLOR

Design: Keith Kesselring,
Steve Pierrehumbert, Annick Baehler
Company: ARD Design Switzerland
Country: Switzerland
Category: Entertainment

BRONZE PENTAWARD 2011

LOU REED AND METALLICA
LULU

Creative Direction: Sarah Moffat,
David Turner, Bruce Duckworth
Design: David Turner
Photography: Stan Musilek, Anton Corbijn
Company: Turner Duckworth,
London & San Francisco
Country: UK
Category: Entertainment

SILVER PENTAWARD 2012

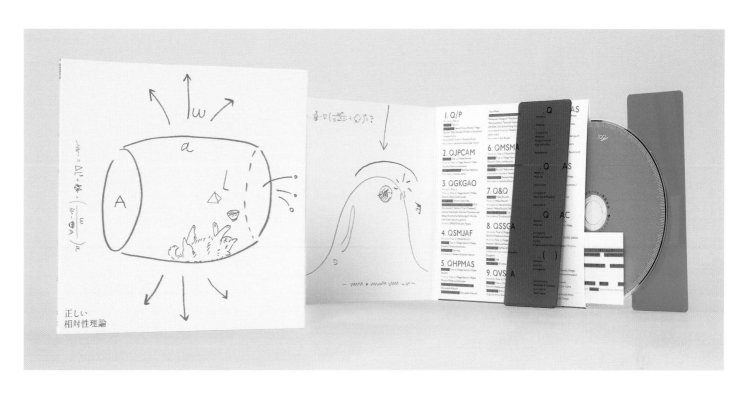

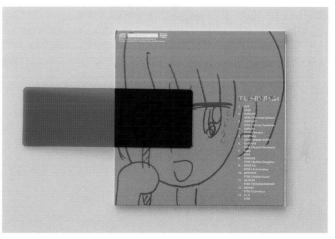

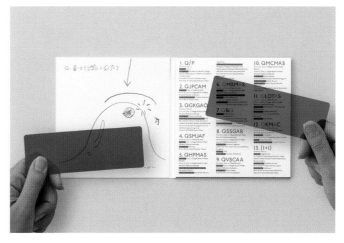

TADASHII SOUTAISEIRIRON

Art Direction/Design: Hirokazu Kobayashi,
Haruna Yamada
Illustration: Etsuko Yakushimaru
Company: Spread Ltd.
Country: Japan
Category: Entertainment

BRONZE PENTAWARD 2012

When tankards or bags are sold in aid of the Foundation for the Preservation of **Staufen**'s Historic Old Town they are packaged in white cardboard boxes, each one marked by a crack that follows the cardboard's corrugations. This symbolises the cracks in the buildings of the old town caused by underground rivers and so makes the purpose of the foundation tangible with an image recognisable to all. The box has become an expressive and eye-catching packaging design for the charitable cause, especially when stacked up in displays where they together create a wall criss-crossed by many continuous cracks.

Die Stiftung zur Erhaltung der historischen Altstadt von **Staufen** bietet Bierkrüge und Taschen zum Verkauf an. Diese werden dann in weiße Kartons verpackt, alle mit einem charakteristischen Riss gekennzeichnet, der der Riffelung des Kartons folgt. Er symbolisiert die durch unterirdische Flüsse verursachten Risse in den Gebäuden der Altstadt und verdeutlicht mit diesem für alle wiedererkennbaren Bild greifbar den Zweck der Stiftung. Die Schachteln wurden zum ausdrucksstarken und auffälligen Verpackungsdesign für diesen gemeinnützigen Zweck, vor allem wenn sie im Verkaufsraum aufeinandergestapelt werden und so eine Wand bilden, die kreuz und quer von vielen fortlaufenden Rissen durchzogen wird.

Les pichets et sacs vendus pour récolter des fonds au profit de la Fondation pour la préservation de la vieille ville historique de **Staufen** sont emballés dans des boîtes en carton blanc, qui présentent une crevasse suivant les ondulations du carton. Elle symbolise les crevasses des édifices de la vieille ville, causées par les rivières souterraines, et donne ainsi une image concrète et identifiable de l'objectif de la fondation. La boîte est devenue un emballage expressif et accrocheur pour cette cause charitable. Lorsque plusieurs unités sont empilées sur les présentoirs, elles créent un mur quadrillé par les crevasses.

STAUFEN FOUNDATION

Creative Direction: Joseph Poelzelbauer
Art Direction/Design: Jean Mierecke
Design: Marcel Ermes, Reinhard Groh
Company: identis GmbH
Country: Germany
Category: Miscellaneous

GOLD PENTAWARD 2011

QR CODE
Scan it with your
mobile phone and enter
the world of unlimited!

RONHILL
UNLIMITED

Creative Direction: Davor Bruketa, Nikola Žinić
Art Direction: Miran Tomicic (senior), Neven Crljenak
Design: Tanja Pruzek Simpovic
Account Executive: Ivana Drvar
DTP: Radovan Radicevic
Company: Bruketa&Žinić OM
Country: Croatia
Category: Miscellaneous

BRONZE PENTAWARD 2011

BIC
FLICK MY BIC

Executive Creative Direction: Sam J. Ciulla
Design Direction: Shelley Scheer, Julie Wineski
Design: Krzysztof Tenenberg
Company: Ciulla Assoc.
Country: USA
Category: Tobacco products

SILVER PENTAWARD 2011

BIC LIGHTERS
HISPANIC THEME

Design: Bic USA Inc. Brand Design,
Joe Ray (E.B. Lane)
Creative Direction: Joe Ray (Estudio Ray)
Company: Bic USA Inc.
Country: USA
Category: Tobacco products
BRONZE PENTAWARD 2012

CAMEL

Creative Direction: Claire Parker
Design: Julian Roerhs
Design Direction: Jordy Huisman, Matt Thompson
Company: Design Bridge
Country: UK
Category: Tobacco products
SILVER PENTAWARD 2011

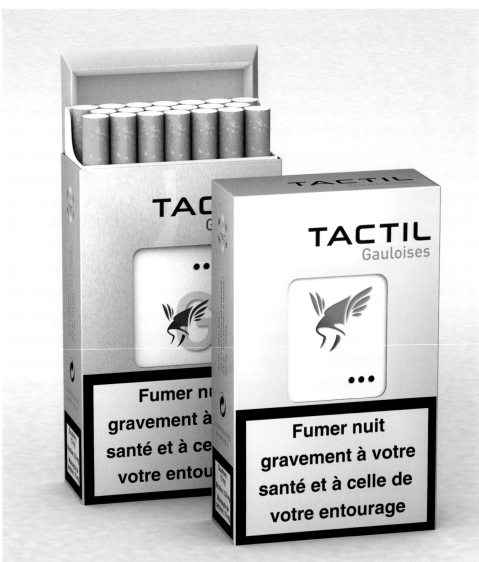

GAULOISES
TACTIL

Design: Louis Comolet,
Guillaume Toutain, Madeline Berger
Company: CLTG
Country: France
Category: Tobacco products

GOLD PENTAWARD 2012

LAMBERT & BUTLER

Design: Dragon Rouge design team
Company: Dragon Rouge
Country: Germany
Category: Tobacco products

BRONZE PENTAWARD 2012

DOUBLE HAPPINESS

Design: Pan Hu
Company: Tsinghua Ses Communication
Country: China
Category: Tobacco products

SILVER PENTAWARD 2012

HENGTA-JINMEN

Design: Pan Hu
Company: Tsinghua Ses Communication
Country: China
Category: Tobacco products

SILVER PENTAWARD 2012

O-I VORTEX BOTTLE

Design: O-I research and development team,
O-I product innovation team
Company: O-I North America Glass
Country: USA
Category: B2B products

GOLD PENTAWARD 2011

The innovative **O-I Vortex** bottle uses special design technology to create internally embossed grooves inside the bottle's neck for a distinctive look intended to intrigue consumers at point-of-purchase. This new form of glass packaging was pioneered for the standard 12-ounce, long-neck beer bottle and relied on the successful development of an internal design of intertwining spirals substantial enough to be seen on the outside of the bottle and able to be replicated at a high rate of production. The exterior was left smooth for ease of label application. The bottle was first seen by the public in 2010 when it was taken up by Miller Lite.

Die innovative Flasche **O-I Vortex** schafft anhand einer speziellen Designtechnologie eingeprägte Rillen im Inneren des Flaschenhalses. Der so entstehende auffällige Look soll den Konsumenten vor dem Regal faszinieren. Diese neue Form der Glasverpackung galt bei der 0,3-Standard-Langhalsbierflasche als Pionierstück. Hier setzte man auf die erfolgreiche Entwicklung eines inneren Designs von miteinander verschlungenen Spiralen – deutlich genug, um von außen sichtbar zu sein, und auch bei hoher Produktionsrate leicht replizierbar. Um das Etikett einfach aufbringen zu können, ließ man das Äußere der Flasche glatt. Die Flasche erschien zum ersten Mal 2010 in der Öffentlichkeit, als sie von Miller Lite vorgestellt wurde.

Le tourbillon en relief dans le col de la bouteille **O-I Vortex** a été créé à l'aide d'une technologie spéciale, et lui confère un aspect caractéristique qui vise à intriguer les consommateurs sur le lieu de vente. Ce nouveau genre de conditionnement en verre a été testé pour la bouteille de bière standard de 12 ounces (35 cl) à long col. Son succès dépendait de la mise au point d'un motif interne de spirales entrelacées suffisamment marqué pour être visible de l'extérieur, et pouvant se prêter à une cadence de production élevée. L'extérieur est lisse pour faciliter l'application des étiquettes. Le public a pu voir la bouteille pour la première fois en 2010, lorsque Miller Lite a décidé de l'utiliser.

SATINO
DARE TO BE BLACK

Design: VanBerlo Communications team
Company: VanBerlo Communications
Country: Netherlands
Category: B2B products

SILVER PENTAWARD 2011

DOGGIE DAZZLE
DOG GROOMING

Design: Mathilde Solanet (student)
School: CAD (College of Advertising & Design)
Country: Belgium
Category: Packaging concept (other markets)

GOLD PENTAWARD 2012
BIC STUDENT PRIZE

Svanströms is one of Sweden's oldest suppliers of office products and services, and in the course of launching a new identity recently they decided on a temporary design campaign that highlighted the fast deliveries for which they are known. The concept for this entailed changing the packaging style for their office supplies for a different format and presenting it in a new and exciting way that people immediately associate with speed. This reimagined identity focuses first and foremost on communicating faster deliveries.

Svanströms gehört zu Schwedens ältesten Lieferanten von Büroprodukten. Als man kürzlich eine neue Identität launchen wollte, entschied man sich für eine kurzzeitige Designkampagne, die die bekanntlich kurzen Lieferzeiten in den Vordergrund stellt. Bei diesem Konzept wurde der Verpackungsstil für die Büroprodukte in einem anderen Format überarbeitet, und außerdem sollten sie neu und spannend präsentiert werden, damit sie sofort mit dem flotten Tempo in Bezug gesetzt wird. Die umgebildete Identität konzentriert sich in erster Linie darauf zu kommunizieren, wie schnell die Auslieferung erfolgt.

Svanströms est l'un des plus anciens spécialistes de fournitures de bureau et de services aux entreprises en Suède.. Pour le lancement de sa nouvelle identité, la société a décidé de faire une campagne de design temporaire qui soulignait la rapidité de livraison pour laquelle elle est connue. Le concept impliquait de changer le style des emballages des fournitures de bureau, afin de créer une nouvelle présentation engageante que l'on associe immédiatement avec la rapidité. Cette identité réinventée est centrée avant tout sur l'idée de la rapidité des livraisons.

SVANSTRÖMS OFFICE SUPPLY

Design: Amal Hassan (student)
School: Broby Grafiska – College of Cross Media
Country: Sweden
Category: Packaging concept (other markets)

SILVER PENTAWARD 2012

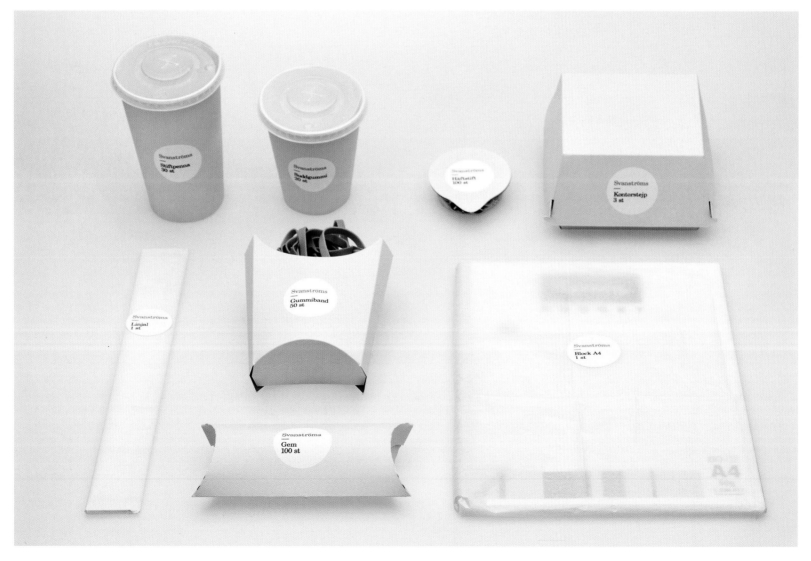

MAGIC WIPES

Creative Direction: Kirill Konstantinov
Concept: Julia Turusheva
Design: Evgeny Morgalev
Company: Kian Branding Agency
Country: Russia
Category: Packaging concept (other markets)

SILVER PENTAWARD 2012

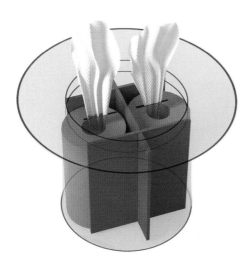

Magic Wipes is a brand of paper napkins designed to be fun for children. Tissues that are sold in transparent plastic bags don't offer much scope for design, but the packaging for these wipes transforms our expectations in a simple way. Something very ordinary is turned into something amazing by the magician's top hat, and children can do tricks by pulling out a rabbit with white wipe ears. The packaging is made from recycled cardboard and has two rolls inside; when they are used up, the hat bottom can be easily removed and new rolls put in.

Magic Wipes ist eine Papierserviette, deren äußere Gestaltung Kindern Spaß machen soll. Wenn Papiertücher in transparenten Plastikhüllen verkauft werden, bietet das nur geringe Möglichkeiten fürs Design, aber die Verpackung dieser Serviette transformiert auf einfache Weise unsere Erwartungen. Etwas ganz Alltägliches verwandelt sich durch den Zauberzylinder in eine erstaunliche Sache. Die Kinder entdecken sich selbst als Zauberer, indem sie an weißen Serviettenohren ein Kaninchen hervorziehen. Die Verpackung besteht aus recyceltem Karton und enthält zwei Rollen Papier. Sind diese leer, öffnet man den Zylinderboden und tauscht sie aus.

Magic Wipes est une marque de lingettes en papier conçues pour les enfants. Les mouchoirs vendus dans des sachets en plastique transparent ne se prêtent guère à un design original, mais l'emballage de ces lingettes déjoue nos attentes en toute simplicité. Le chapeau claque du magicien transforme un produit très ordinaire en jouet étonnant, et les enfants peuvent faire des tours en attrapant les oreilles de lapin que forment les lingettes. L'emballage est fabriqué en carton recyclé et contient deux rouleaux. Lorsqu'ils sont vides, il suffit d'ouvrir le fond du chapeau pour les remplacer.

AIR CORK

Design: Peter Johnson, Martin Short
Company: Swerve Inc.
Country: USA
Category: Packaging concept
(other markets)

BRONZE PENTAWARD 2012

JOBEUR
NAIL BOXES

Design: Pier-Philippe Rioux (student)
School: École de design (UQAM)
Country: Canada
Category: Ecological concept
(other markets)

SILVER PENTAWARD 2012

DETERGENT CLEANJET

Design: Pavla Chuykina, Anna Moiseenko,
Lyubov Maslennikova, Natalia Kuchumova (students)
School: British Higher School of Art and Design
Country: Russia
Category: Packaging concept (other markets)

BRONZE PENTAWARD 2012

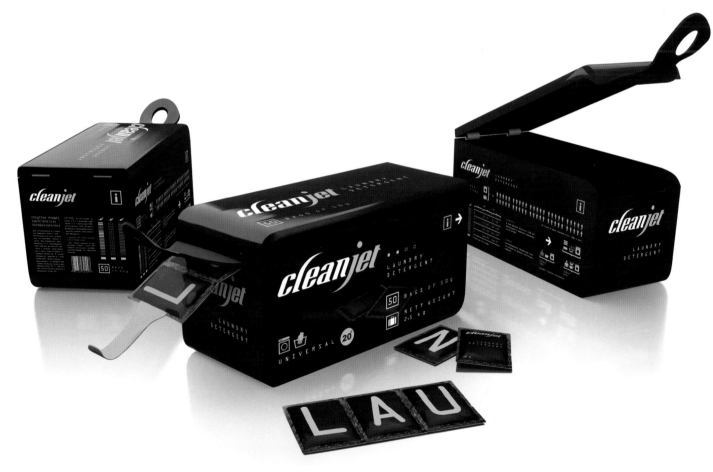

BOOLBOOL PACK

Design: Igor Palichev, Ramil Sharipov,
Dima Zeibert, Larisa Mamleeva
Company: DarkDesignGroup
Country: Russia
Category: Packaging concept (other markets)

BRONZE PENTAWARD 2012

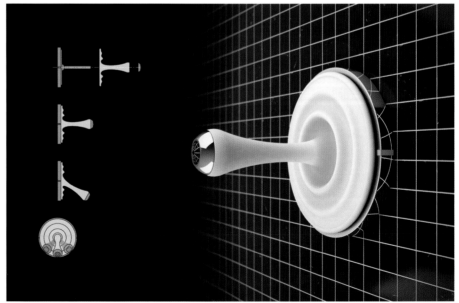

CHINESE BRUSH
DUAL-USE PACKAGING

Design: Li Xu, Qin Zou
Company: QL Design Studio
Country: China
Category: Ecological concept (other markets)

BRONZE PENTAWARD 2012

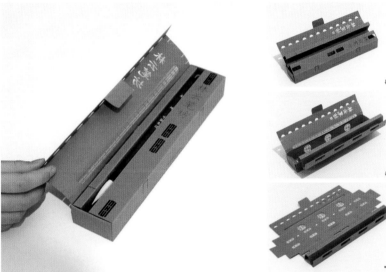

PENTAWARDS JURY

GÉRARD CARON
France, Chairman of the International Jury
+ Regarded as the founder of marketing design in France and Europe. + Set up Carré Noir in 1973 (today a member of the Publicis group). + Co-founder and former president of PDA (Pan-European Brand Design Association). + Author of many publications, organiser of conferences and seminars. + Designed the most complete website for design www.admirabledesign.com. + Has created no fewer than 1,200 brand identities and 13,000 package designs.

MICHAEL AIDAN
France, Danone Waters
+ Graduated in marketing from ESCP, Paris, in 1988. + Brand Manager at P&G and YSL international perfumes division. + Account & Marketing Director at Cato Gobe & Associates, New York. + Marketing Manager from 1993 to 2006, responsible for major brands at Pepsico (Lays, Pepsi-Cola, Tropicana). + VP Marketing at Danone Waters. + Lecturer in master's degree classes at ESCP-EAP and HE.

MARK COWAN
Australia, Founder, Managing Director of Cowan
+ Started his career in the Safeway Head Office in Melbourne as a grocery buyer and special projects marketer. + This led to Mark becoming a keen judge of packaging communication and accurately predicting success rates of new launches. + In 1987, Mark launched Cowan, a consumer brand communications company. + Cowan is now the largest consumer brand design agency in Australia. + Offices in Melbourne, Sydney, London, Auckland, Shanghai, Beijing and Ho Chi Minh City. + Clients include blue chip FMCG brands such as Coca-Cola, Arnotts, Yoplait, Heinz, Nestlé and Uncle Toby.

DAN DITTMAR
USA, Director of Brand Design, BIC USA Inc.
+ BS Graphic Design, University of Maryland. + MS Organizational Leadership, Quinnipiac University. + Previous experience leading brand design & packaging identity for the Campbell Soup Company across multiple product categories. + Currently leading brand & packaging identity for all BIC branded categories (BIC Stationery, BIC Lighter & BIC Shaver portfolio segments). + Previous Presenter at Design Management Institute International Conference. + 2011 Presenter at Destination Design Management Conference.

BRUCE DUCKWORTH
UK, Founding partner of Turner Duckworth, London & San Francisco
+ Bruce established Turner Duckworth in 1992 with David Turner, specialising in brand identity and packaging. + Based in London, Bruce is jointly responsible with David Turner for the creative output of both studios for clients as varied as the Coca-Cola Company, Homebase, Shaklee, Johnson & Johnson and Metallica. + Over 200 international design awards including: Cannes Festival Inaugural Design Lions Grand Prix 2008, D&AD Silver Award, DBA Design Effectiveness Award, Clio Awards, Design Week Awards, LIAA, Pentawards, FAB Awards Agency of the Year 2008, Creativity Awards, EPICA, Graphis. + Judging stints: ADC New York's 87th Annual Design jury, D&AD Awards, Design Week Awards, LIAA Royal Society of Arts Student Design Awards, Pentawards 2009/2010. + Lectures/Speeches: numerous lectures at art colleges and universities/British Council, Design Council, International Institute of Research, The Design Show.

RAF DE GEYTER
Belgium, Design Manager, P&G
+ Master's in Industrial Design, Artesis Hogeschool Antwerp. + Master's in Marketing Management, Vlerick Leuven Gent Management School, Ghent.
+ Joined Procter & Gamble in 1998, gaining 12 years of experience in leading package and product design for brands such as Ariel, Lenor, Dreft, Tide, Swiffer and Mr. Clean. Currently responsible for upstream design innovation programmes in fabric care.

ANDRÉ HINDERSSON
Sweden, Creative Director and Co-founding Partner of Silver in Stockholm
+ His design work embraces brand and company identities, services and packaging design for a wide range of clients ranging from iconic global brands such as Oriflame and H&M to local heavy-metal record labels. + He lives in Stockholm but has had a second home in London since his student years at CSM. + A specialist in cosmetic packaging for years, André always aims to bring out the personality of the product, often adding a humorous twist. + Holds an MA in Communication Design from Central Saint Martins college (CSM) in London and a BA from Grafiska Institutet at Stockholm University. + He is also an accredited ISIA ski instructor.

BRIAN HOUCK
USA, Director, Creative Services, The Dial Corporation, A Henkel Company, USA
+ Bachelor of Fine Arts, Northern Arizona University. +Previous experience includes advertising for diverse companies in the Southwest and event design and staging for clients such as Norelco and Delta Airlines. + Has led the package design for Dial brands for 21 years including Dial Soap, Right Guard Antiperspirant, Purex Detergents, Renuzit Air Fresheners and Soft Scrub Cleansers. + Winner of numerous industry awards in package design and printing.

YOSHIO KATO

Japan, Creative Director and Senior Specialist, Design Department of Suntory Business Expert Ltd.
+ Graduated from Nagoya City Industrial Arts High School (Design Course) in 1972 and from Aichi Prefectural University of Fine Arts and Music (Major in Design) in 1979. + Joined Suntory Ltd. Design Department in 1979. + 1997 Creative Director and General Manager, Suntory's Ltd. Design Department. + 2011 Senior Specialist and Creative Director, Suntory Ltd. Design Department. + External positions: 1997, Vice Chairman of the Board, Japan Package Design Association; member of Japan Graphic Designers Association; Director on Board, DAS Designers Association Publications.

KYU-WOO KU

South Korea, Managing Director of the Aekyung Design Centre, Seoul
+ Graduated from Dankook University in 1983. + Joined Aekyung Industrial Co., Ltd. Design Department in 1991. + External positions: President of Korea Package Design Association; Vice-president of Korea Design Management Association; Design Organization Member of the Asian Games Organizing Committee for 2014.

ADRIAN PIERINI

Argentina, Founder and General Creative Director of Pierini Partners
+ Graduated, with honours, as a graphic designer in 1992. + Pierini Partners develops branding and packaging designs for companies in Argentina, Brazil, Mexico, China, Japan, Colombia, Paraguay and the UK. + Started his professional career in some of the most prestigious design studios in Argentina, the USA and Mexico. + Teaches courses on such subjects as "Design and Brand Image", "Packaging Design", and "Introduction to Strategic Design" in a private university in Argentina, and gives a number of seminars on design in universities and institutions in Argentina, Bolivia, Chile, Colombia, Ecuador, Mexico, Paraguay and Peru. + He has written various articles for specialised media and "Designers Go!" on applied methodology oriented to students and young professionals (Comm Tools Editorial, 2006).

CHRIS PLEWES

Canada, Vice-president and Creative Director at Davis Design
+ Graduated from the Graphic Lyceum, Amsterdam. + Started his career at Design Bridge in 1994. + Founded in 1986, Design Bridge is active in 50 countries worldwide through their three offices in London, Amsterdam and Singapore. + Has won several awards: Winner of Norwegian Design Award, 2nd place Mobius Award, Nomination Dutch Design Award, Diamond Pentaward (best of show), Bronze Pentaward, 1st place Mobius Award.

CHRISTOPHE PRADERE

France, Managing Director of BETC Design Paris
+ Master's in design at Domus Academy in Milan. + Euro RSCG Design: responsible for the retail and corporate design divisions of clients such as Auchan, Leclerc, Intermarché, Air France and Peugeot and also luxury brands such as Lancôme, L'artisan, Parfumeur and Christofle. + Founded BETC Design in 2001. + His focus is on global design and design management approaches in the creative industry markets for customers such as Orange, Air France, Alstom Peugeot, Louis Vuitton, Rémy Martin, Louis XIII, Chivas, Jean-Paul Gaultier, L'Oréal and Piper Heidsieck. + He develops his brand experience through a holistic approach combining social sciences, marketing and global creative strategy. + Lectures: Parsons School for Design; IMF; ESSEC; École Nationale Supérieure des Arts Décoratifs; SKEMA Business School.

JONATHAN SANDS

UK, Chairman of Elmwood
+ Jonathan Sands led a management buyout of Elmwood in 1989, aged 27, and his ambition and drive hasn't dwindled since. + With offices in Asia, North America and Europe, Elmwood is an ideas-based business and Jonathan in particular always has the courage of his convictions. + His vision is for Elmwood to be the most effective brand design consultancy in the world. + Elmwood's clients include ASDA, BBC, Durex, The COI, Glasgow 2014, McCain, Royal Mail, Nestlé and Nike.

GRAHAM SHEARSBY

UK, Group Creative Director of Design Bridge
+ Born in East London, Graham entered the creative world, unusually, straight from school back in 1979. + Joining the John Blackburn Partnership as a studio junior, he received the accolade of a D&AD Yellow Pencil for Typography for Cockburn's Ports in 1985. + Joining Allied International Designers in 1986, he met his future partners in what would become the fledgling Design Bridge later that year. + The company has grown from a handful of people to over 200 across the offices and won a wealth of international awards. + Committed to design education, Graham is a member of the D&AD Education Council and a representative of the Design Advisory Panel for Creative and Cultural Skills.

YUAN ZONGLEI

China, Chief Designer at Jahwa Group, Shanghai
+ Born in Shanghai in 1961. + Syndic of the Shanghai packaging consortium. + Bachelor of Fine Arts, Shanghai Institute of Technology. + Started his career at Jahwa in 1992. + In charge of various design projects, essentially for packaging design, display design and interior design. + Winner of numerous industry awards in packaging design.

INDEX

INDEX

ACKNOWLEDEMENTS

The publication of this second volume, which brings together so many examples of quality packaging design, would not have been possible without the participation of the numerous product designers and advertisers from around the world who took part in the 2011 and 2012 Pentawards. We would like to take this opportunity to thank them and congratulate them on the standard of their designs.

Thanks to Benedikt Taschen for placing his trust in us again, and also to Julius Wiedemann, who was able to discover the potential of the Pentawards. Without him this book would not exist. Thanks also to our jury of leading professionals from across the globe for their inestimable contribution, and to the jury chair, Gérard Caron, for his rigorous management and impartiality.

We would also like to thank Daniel Siciliano Bretas and his team for the graphic design and technical support they provided in the day-to-day work, from the start of the project through to the launch of the book. They not only managed to highlight the creativity and appeal of the designs presented, but also their practical value.

And finally, thanks to you, the reader, and to all those who find themselves inspired by this book and who will not hesitate to take part in the next Pentawards.

JEAN JACQUES AND BRIGITTE EVRARD
Founders of the Pentawards
www.pentawards.org

DANKSAGUNGEN

REMERCIEMENTS

Die Publikation dieses zweiten Bandes, der viele Beispiele qualitativ hochwertiger Verpackungsgestaltung versammelt, wäre nicht möglich gewesen ohne die Mitarbeit der zahlreichen Produktdesigner und Werbetreibenden aus aller Welt, die an den Pentawards der Jahre 2011 und 2012 teilnahmen. Wir möchten diese Gelegenheit nutzen, um uns bei Ihnen allen bedanken und Ihnen für das Niveau Ihrer Designs zu gratulieren.

Unser Dank gilt Benedikt Taschen, der uns wieder sein Vertrauen schenkte, und auch Julius Wiedemann, der das Potenzial der Pentawards zu entdecken vermochte. Ohne ihn würde dieses Buch nicht existieren. Wir danken auch unserer Jury, in der führende Profis aus den verschiedensten Ländern sitzen, für ihre unschätzbare Mitarbeit, und deren Vorsitzenden Gérard Caron für sein konsequentes Management und seine Unvoreingenommenheit.

Ein ganz herzlicher Dank geht an Daniel Siciliano Brêtas und sein Team für das Grafikdesign und die technische Unterstützung, die tagein, tagaus seit dem Start des Projekts bis zur Publikation dieses Buches geleistet wurde. Ihnen ist es gelungen, nicht nur die Kreativität und den Reiz der präsentierten Designs hervorzuheben, sondern auch deren praktischen Wert.

Und schließlich danken wir Ihnen, den Leserinnen und Lesern, und allen, die sich von diesem Buch inspirieren lassen und nicht zögern, an den nächsten Pentawards teilzunehmen.

JEAN JACQUES UND BRIGITTE EVRARD
Begründer von Pentawards
www.pentawards.org

L'édition de ce second livre qui réunit autant d'emballages de qualité n'aurait pas été possible sans la participation des nombreux packaging designers et annonceurs du monde entier aux Pentawards 2011 et 2012. Nous tenons à les remercier ici et à les féliciter pour la qualité de leurs créations.

Merci à Benedikt Taschen, pour sa confiance renouvelée, et aussi à Julius Wiedemann, qui a su détecter le potentiel des Pentawards, sans lui ce livre n'existerait pas. Merci également à notre jury composé de grands professionnels des 4 coins du monde, pour leur contribution inestimable, et à Gérard Caron, président du jury, pour sa gestion rigoureuse et son impartialité.

Merci à Daniel Siciliano Bretas et son équipe, qui nous ont apporté leur soutien graphique et technique au jour le jour, du début du projet au lancement du livre. Ils ont su mettre en valeur la créativité, le glamour, mais aussi l'efficacité des packagings présentés.

Et enfin, merci à vous qui parcourez ce livre et à tous ceux et celles qui en seront inspirés, et qui sans doute, participeront aux prochains Pentawards.

JEAN JACQUES ET BRIGITTE EVRARD
Fondateurs des Pentawards
www.pentawards.org

IMPRINT

© 2012 TASCHEN GmbH
Hohenzollernring 53, D-50672 Köln
www.taschen.com

To stay informed about upcoming TASCHEN titles, please
request our magazine at www.taschen.com/magazine or
write to TASCHEN, Hohenzollernring 53, D-50672 Cologne,
Germany, contact@taschen.com, Fax: +49 221 254919.
We will be happy to send you a free copy of our magazine
which is filled with information about all of our books.

Editor
Julius Wiedemann
Editorial Coordination
Daniel Siciliano Bretas
Editorial Assistant
Nora Dohrmann

Design
Sense/Net, Andy Disl and Birgit Eichwede, Cologne
Layout
Birgit Eichwede and Daniel Siciliano Bretas
Production
Stefan Klatte

English Revision
Chris Allen
French Translation
Aurélie Daniel for Delivering iBooks & Design, Barcelona
German Translation
Jürgen Dubau

Printed in Germany
ISBN 978–3–8365–2968–6